CAREER DEVELOPMENT

BY DESIGN

CAREER DEVELOPMENT

BY DESIGN

Sharon L. Hanna

PRENTICE HALL
Upper Saddle River, New Jersey 07458

Library of Congress Cataloging-in-Publication Data

Hanna, Sharon L.,
　　Career development by design / Sharon Hanna.
　　　　p.　　cm.
　　Includes bibliographical references and index.
　　ISBN 0-13-527383-8 (alk. paper)
　　1. Career development.　I. Title.
　H5381.H135　1998
　650.14--dc21

96-53631
CIP

Acquisitions Editor: *Todd Rossell*
Managing Editor: *Mary Carnis*
Director of Manufacturing and Production: *Bruce Johnson*
Production Editor: *Denise Brown*
Manufacturing Buyer: *Ed O'Dougherty*
Marketing Manager: *Frank Mortimer, Jr.*
Interior Design: *Kevin Kall*
Creative Director: *Marianne Frasco*
Cover Design: *Bruce Kenselaar*
Cover Art: *Susan J. Brasch*
Compositor: *Naomi Sysak*

©1998 by Prentice-Hall, Inc.
A Viacom Company
Upper Saddle River, New Jersey 07458

Printed in the United States of America

10　9　8　7　6　5　4　3　2　1

ISBN 0-13-527383-8

Prentice-Hall International (UK) Limited, *London*
Prentice-Hall of Australia Pty. Limited, *Sydney*
Prentice-Hall Canada Inc., *Toronto*
Prentice-Hall Hispanoamericana, S.A., *Mexico*
Prentice-Hall of India Private Limited, *New Delhi*
Prentice-Hall of Japan, Inc., *Tokyo*
Simon & Schuster Asia Pte. Ltd., *Singapore*
Editora Prentice-Hall do Brasil, Ltda., *Rio de Janeiro*

DEDICATION

To Bob Dinkel, my husband and best friend,
who has contributed so much of his time, effort, and support
to my career while being successful in his own;

To Lisa and Lyn Patterson, my daughters,
who have begun their own successful career paths
and of whom I'm justifiably proud;

To Trish Reimer who is the ideal employee
and a wonderful person;

and

To past, present, and future students
from whom I've learned and grown and will continue
to do so.

Contents

CHAPTER THREE

Getting What You Want   59

CHAPTER FOUR

You in Writing   95

CHAPTER FIVE

You in Person 135

CHAPTER SIX

Your Career Path 169

CHAPTER SEVEN

Relationships in the Work Environment 205

CHAPTER EIGHT
Challenges in the Work Place 231

Preface

Why do people work? The first answer that often comes to mind is money. Yet, is that all there is to it? If so, thousands of educators, including myself, would have pursued other careers.

As you design your career, you are wise to ponder the question of why you want to work and consider the reasons you have chosen a particular path. If your career involves what you consider to be meaningful work, the rewards are innumerable.

- To gain a significant purpose in life
- To use talents and abilities
- To broaden knowledge
- To enlarge one's social sphere
- To become more interesting *and* interested
- To experience enjoyment and have fun
- To increase self-esteem
- To develop better physical and mental health
- To make a meaningful contribution

The list goes on and on. To avoid or shortchange this vital part of life would be a major mistake, and to work only for money invites dissatisfaction and disappointment.

Think of the most personally rewarding reasons for pursuing a career. Then, consider what would be the most satisfying career for you—just the first of several important decisions. After a selection, the active design of your career takes center stage. Satisfaction is possible, yet not probable, without deliberate planning and action. This book leads you through an entire career life.

Beginning with the *self*, you will gain insight and understanding. Learning to interact positively with others, including ways to improve interpersonal skills, follows. The actual career design includes research and choices, then culminates with a successful job search. The final chapters invite you to examine the entire career path, learn about positive work relationships, and become aware of possible challenges.

As you either have or will discover, one point is clear. No one way is 100 percent best for everyone's career development. This book contains several opinions, ideas, research findings, and recommendations. Even though general consensus exists, much is debatable, and critical thinking can lead you to choose what will work best for you.

This book can be a most useful companion as you design your own career path. I agree with Larry Hubka, Ph.D., dean of Business and Mass Media at Southeast Community College, who says,

"There is an old adage in the business world that says, 'You never have a second chance to make a good first impression.' Unfortunately, colleges have not done a very good job preparing students to apply in writing and to interview for career positions. I believe all college-level curricula should address these critical areas."

By reading the book and completing the activities in KEY STEPS, along with taking any available courses, you will have an advantage that will set you apart from the competition. I would like to know how the process goes for you. Ways to contact me are at the end of this section. I invite comments, suggestions, and questions from you—the reader!

Is a career that important? My response is an enthusiastic "Yes"! Even though being a wife and mother have both been greatly rewarding, my life would not be fulfilled without the rewards of an extremely satisfying career. My hope is that through this book you will catch my enthusiasm and then learn and apply the material to ensure your own career success. Above all, enjoy the process and the rewards of career development by your own design!

Sharon L. Hanna
Southeast Community College
8800 O Street
Lincoln, NE 68520
402-437-2472
Fax: 402-423-4103
e-mail: slhanna@sccm.cc.ne.us

Acknowledgments

Praise is good for both the receiver and the giver. One of the most gratifying parts of completing a book is to thank those who were so helpful.

My husband and best friend Bob took over even more tasks, offered encouragement and support, and was always "there" for me. Our shared marriage, so full of love and affirmation, allows us both to live very satisfying professional and personal lives. I'm deeply grateful to him.

My family and friends may have felt neglected as I worked on this project. Their understanding and support is appreciated.

Lyn and Lisa Patterson, my daughters, were willing to share their experiences in this book. They also came to my rescue and provided special help. They are tremendous individuals.

Trish Reimer, our office manager and "life" assistant, who in her positive way brightens each day, made numerous contributions to this project.

Susan Dunn, reference specialist at Southeast Community College, cheerfully assisted in research and was willing to share some of her career story in this book.

Karen and Jerry Baxter, Jon Bresnahan, and Heather MacPhee willingly provided needed help.

Ben Thomas, cartoon artist, and Susan Brasch, cover artist, were very cooperative. I admire their talents.

In sharing their experiences and advice, employers throughout the country and the faculty, staff, and students at Southeast Community College contributed immeasurably to the credibility and practicality of the book.

Even though reading what reviewers say isn't always a pleasant task, their suggestions were most constructive, and several were incorporated into the book. I appreciate the time and expertise of: Rita Delude, New Hampshire Community Technical College; Rosann Rookey, Middle Georgia College; Nellie Boyd, Norfolk State University; Lane Johnson, N. Harris College; and Charissa Dunn, Bartlesville Wesleyan College.

The tremendous group of people at Prentice Hall were always available and helpful in a positive and professional manner. They include: Todd Rossell, senior editor; Jennifer Collins, editor's assistant; Mary Carnis, managing editor; Denise Brown, production editor; Kathy Wanamaker, marketing coordinator; and Elizabeth Sugg, senior editor, who was my first contact and, in such an encouraging way, initiated this project. Laura Mann, Prentice Hall sales representative, was also very helpful and offered advice to the readers of the book.

As these acknowledgments come to an end, my recommendation is that you generously recognize the contributions of people as you pursue a career. Acknowledge their well-meant advice, praise, constructive criticism, help, and services. Those who are appreciative are invariably appreciated and are more likely to enjoy a successful professional life.

To everyone who helped in the design of this career development book, my deepest appreciation.

Sharon L. Hanna

CHAPTER ONE

Beginning with the Self

Picture yourself happily involved in a career. You love your job and, most of the time, are eager to go to work. Does this sound impossible? Close your eyes and visualize an ideal job. This dream can become a reality with successful career design and development. Unfortunately, four out of five workers dislike some major aspect of their jobs (Diamond and Golin, 1991).

How does one design a fulfilling career? The beginning is the self. According to Professor Linda A. Hill, Ph.D., of Harvard Business School, effective career managers are prepared to learn about themselves, are willing to make necessary changes, and can cope with associated stress and emotions. Self-knowledge is consistently found to be a key characteristic in success (1994). Self-discovery is an evolving process; we are ever-changing so our quest is never completed. A starting point is the self-appraisal in KEY STEPS (page 266).

YOUR DEVELOPMENTAL AREAS

A useful framework of self-understanding explores four developmental areas of self: physical, mental, emotional, and social. Together, these comprise a whole self.

PHYSICAL SELF

Appearance and condition of the body make up the physical self. Characteristics such as race, age, bone structure, and certain physical disabilities are outside our control. Yet, we can determine several aspects of appearance and health.

> *HOW WOULD YOU DESCRIBE YOUR PHYSICAL SELF?*

In their self-descriptions, especially related to appearance, individuals tend to overemphasize perceived flaws and be overly critical. "I'm too fat," "I'm too thin," "I have such thin hair," "I have such thick hair," "I'm too short," "I'm too tall" are commonly heard. We might wonder if anyone is satisfied!

The best possible appearance is a worthy goal. Few careers demand the highest standards of attractiveness; yet, most employers are impressed with individuals who are clean and neat and who make an effort to present their best appearance. "I like an inviting smile and a professional appearance," says Sue Collins, director of a day-care center. Unfortunately, attractiveness and gender biases are still present as revealed in a study of 112 managers. Less attractive female applicants were routinely at a disadvantage (Marlowe, Schneider, and Nelson, 1996). As long as attractiveness continues to be a measure of worth, the best one can do is maximize appearance as much as possible. Specific suggestions related to interviewing appearance are covered in Chapter 5.

Making positive changes is exciting and will benefit you both personally and professionally. Think of any changes you can begin to make now that will improve your physical appearance and move you toward **wellness**, which is a high degree of physical and mental well-being.

Increasing the level of physical activity has amazing benefits, and it's well within your reach. You can easily incorporate activity into your regular day. "Instead of parking in the closest spot, I find one that requires me to walk at least a block each way," reported a young man. When you have a "break" in your day, use it to walk, or do what one woman does. "Instead of just listening to music at home, I dance, and when nobody is watching, I can really move!" The body was meant to move, and when it does, both health and appearance are enhanced.

Health is obviously a significant factor in career success. Even though we often think of health only as the absence of illness, a more realistic picture places it on a continuum.

Very ill $\longrightarrow$ Ill $\longrightarrow$ Feeling OK $\longrightarrow$ Well $\longrightarrow$ Very healthy

> *PLACE A MARK ON THE CONTINUUM THAT DESCRIBES YOUR OWN GENERAL STATE AND THEN INDICATE HOW HEALTHY YOU'D LIKE TO BE.*

If you have experienced or are now at the level of total wellness, you know there is a great difference between it and just feeling OK. Feeling energetic, vigorous, rarely tired, alert, and at peace with yourself will reap major rewards as you design your career. One interviewer remarked, "The fact that she radiated good health was a major asset."

Achieving wellness includes physical and mental activity, healthy nutrition, adequate rest, effective stress-coping strategies, and the elimination of destructive health habits such as excessive use of alcohol or other drugs. A particularly deadly habit that can directly affect your career is cigarette smoking. According to *The Economist* (1992), about 250 million people living in developed nations will die because of smoking, and they will die an average of 23 years sooner than people who do not smoke. Because smokers are more apt to be sick and have serious diseases, are absent an average of 5.5 more days, and take more disability leave each year (*Time*, 1994), many employers either hesitate or refuse to hire them. Said one, "If I detect the smell of smoke on an applicant, I don't even consider him or her. It's a real turn-off." Because the research on passive or secondary smoke reflects increased health risks for non-smokers, many companies are smoke-free and encourage or require smokers to quit. Think of all aspects of your physical self and elect to do all you can to achieve the best you can be!

Mental Self

Especially applicable to the career field are your learning abilities, thought-processing patterns, problem-solving skills, beliefs, and attitudes that are

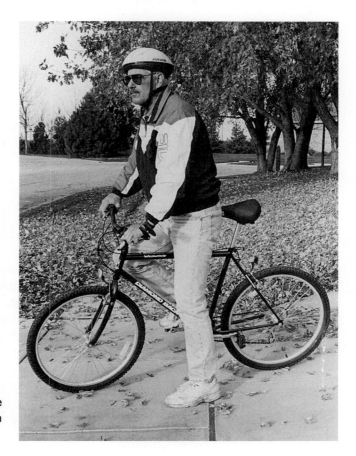

▲ Engaging in an enjoyable activity enhances physical health and psychological well-being.

included in this part of the self. Cognitive (thought) development continues throughout one's life and is integral to career development.

How mentally capable are you? **Intelligence** may be thought of as mental ability and is usually assessed on tests of language, mathematical, and reasoning abilities. The concept of multiple intelligences (Gardner, 1983) broadens the scope and includes a variety of competencies useful in the employment field, such as interpersonal skills. You may have a high *IQ*, which is a score on certain tests given in the educational system; however, this probably won't matter as much as your eagerness to learn and your ability to solve problems.

How well you have performed academically will be of definite interest to many employers. Lisa Patterson, CPA and senior manager at Ernst and Young LLP in Los Angeles, reports that a high GPA is mandatory in many fields, including accounting. A study supported her idea by showing that academic record had a stronger effect on hiring decisions than other factors (Foschi, Sigerson, and Lembesis, 1995).

Academic achievement is usually the result of a high degree of motivation. Those who truly want to do well frequently do. Employers tend to believe that if you were motivated to achieve educational success, you will behave similarly on the job. A common interview question has to do with what motivates you. Hopefully, you have developed a high level of self-motivation.

> *ARE YOU CURIOUS? NAME AT LEAST FOUR SUBJECTS OF CURIOSITY.*

Curiosity about a number of subjects can make you a well-rounded person who is both interested and interesting. Being curious or confused and then asking meaningful questions sets the stage for learning. Asking questions on the job is expected. "At some point I know an employee won't know what's going on, and I want questions," said Leonard Murphy, partner in an accounting firm. Bob Dinkel, a business owner, remarked, "I don't mind mistakes now and then. What is frustrating is when the person doesn't ask a question that could have avoided the error."

> *ARE YOU WILLING TO ASK QUESTIONS? IF NOT, WHAT IS THE REASON?*

If you're hesitant about asking questions, begin to look upon them as ways to learn and then overcome your reluctance.

How much have you ever thought about thinking? Where did you learn to think? Most of us take our thinking abilities for granted, and few people have been taught specifically how to think. **Thinking**, the ability to activate and then pursue mental activity in any number of situations, is necessary in any job. Certain occupations demand creative thinking, the ability to generate new ideas; others require critical thinking, an aptitude for probing deeper and examining the logic of differing points.

Alertness, flexibility, and a keen desire to exercise your brain are critical elements in career development. They also affect life satisfaction. As Carolyn, an older student who had just returned to college, said, "My mind has been resting on a shelf for too long. Now I'm applying my brain power, and it's an exhilarating feeling!"

Undoubtedly, a most invaluable aspect of the mental self is your **attitude**, a broad approach to life which has profound influence. Even if the word has possibly been overused, its impact is too powerful to ignore. Creating and keeping a positive attitude toward your work, your employer, and life in general will enhance your chance for career success. Inability to do this closes many doors of opportunity (Chapman, 1993).

A positive attitude is not equivalent to a "Pollyanna" way of looking at life. That is, you can still have a positive attitude and realize that life is not absolutely wonderful all of the time. Being positive means that you look on the brighter side of events, that you are more "up" than "down," and that you usually feel responsible and in control of yourself. You are a person who emphasizes solutions, not just problems. Positive people are generally energetic, motivated, and alert, with a marvelous zest for life. The opposite is true of those with a negative attitude who are typically perceived as gloomy, lazy, griping, fault-finding, blaming, and impossible to be around. Even though misery may love company, company doesn't love misery (Myers, 1992).

Employers want people with positive attitudes because they personally contribute a great deal and also serve as invaluable role models. "I feel energized being around her" and "It's hard to stay 'down' around him" are typical reactions. A person with a negative attitude can infect other employees. "Working around him is like carrying a heavy pack around all day" was how one employee was described.

> *"Even if a person doesn't have all the necessary skills and knowledge, a positive attitude can make a big difference. It's **crucial**."*
>
> Jody Horwitz, Director of Human Resources
> Turner Broadcasting System, Inc.
> Los Angeles, California

Also important is your belief about the future, which can be described as either optimistic or pessimistic. Research supports the value of optimism in all aspects of life including career. Optimists in a study were generally happier and enjoyed greater successes than pessimists (Myers, 1992). Attitude is definitely noticed by employers and those whom you service. Bob Resz, a college dean, asserts, "What distinguishes the good teachers from the mediocre ones is not method, style, or personality; it's attitude. From such teachers, students intuitively receive the message: You are important, and it's important to me that you learn."

How can attitude be improved? A powerful ally is the mental self which creates much of our reality. Thoughts and subsequent actions construct what is "real" in life. The next time you find yourself thinking dreary thoughts, choose uplifting ones instead. Besides changing thoughts, what else can people do?

Can you teach attitude? Sheryl Piening, instructor of management and human relations courses at a community college, believes that it's certainly possible to teach attitude-altering tools. "After identifying positive and negative behaviors, nearly 50 percent of my students see that they have some attitude work to do," Sheryl says. Eliminating behaviors associated with a negative attitude and developing positive ones can change mental outlook. Other suggestions follow.

- Read books such as *Learned Optimism: How to Change Your Mind and Your Life* (Seligman, 1990) and *Person to Person: Positive Relationships Don't Just Happen* (Hanna, 1995).

- Associate with positive people and model their behaviors.

- Take courses related to personal development and understanding. Your experience may be akin to a student who exclaimed, "After only two interpersonal relations classes, I have a better attitude about life!"

> *Assess your attitude. Name personal behaviors that demonstrate either positiveness or negativity, or both. Think of ways to change your behavior so that you project even more positiveness. What else can you do to develop or maintain a positive attitude?*

If asked about attitude in a job interview, hopefully, you can honestly describe yours as positive and optimistic. A potential employer may not ask; however, attitude has a way of revealing itself in your verbal and nonverbal communication.

What you believe about yourself has a tremendous impact. **Self-fulfilling prophecies** are beliefs that are acted out and, thus, confirmed. For example, Craig believed he was persuasive. He convinced his supervisor to try an idea that could save money for the company. This success confirmed his original belief, and he continued to use these "selling" skills. If he had believed he couldn't persuade others, what do you think the likely result would have been? Examine your self-fulfilling prophecies. Keep the ones that are useful and change those that are not.

Thoughts also influence your emotions. Have you ever felt mildly depressed? What were you thinking at that time? It is likely that your thoughts were either causing or at least contributing to the feeling. Jennifer interviewed for a job she really wanted and was told that someone else was selected. She immediately thought, "Either I didn't interview well, or they just didn't like me. This is probably the way my job search is going to go." As a result of her thoughts, she feels dejected and hopeless. She could use an effective technique called **cognitive restructuring**, or thought changing. "Just because I wasn't selected doesn't necessarily mean I didn't interview well or that they didn't like me. I'll think of this as a learning experience and keep looking." Obviously, her feelings of dejection and hopelessness would disappear.

> *Think of a recent less-than-positive thought, then change it to a positive one. How could your feeling have been different?*

EMOTIONAL SELF

Human beings are emotional, and our feelings both enrich and disturb our lives. Emotions such as happiness, sadness, anxiety, pride, anger, and excitement bring texture and color to human existence. Life without emotion would indeed be drab.

Complex is often the way the emotional self is described. Many people find it difficult to get in touch with their feelings, and they may not know what can occur in the presence of emotion. Three components are possible when emotion is experienced. One is physiological arousal or response. Our nervous system, various glands, and organs within the body are active during an emotional state. Have you ever blushed in an embarrassing situation? The redness of your face was caused by what was going on inside your body. What physiological arousal is likely when you're frustrated or angry?

A second component of emotion is awareness—the realization of the feeling. When you are happy, you may not be aware of physiological arousal; yet, you just know you are experiencing happiness. Emotion's third component is expression—observable verbal or nonverbal behaviors. Expression of emotion can help or hinder people in their careers. For example, facial expressions can reveal what you're feeling. If you look friendly, interested, and enthusiastic, you are much more likely to get and keep a job. Conversely, going through an entire interview with a "poker face" will probably lead to rejection.

> *Check your own emotional expression. What do you actually do when you are happy or sad? Angry or afraid?*

Expressing your feelings can lead to emotional well-being and enhanced relationships. Emotional suppression, not showing feelings, isn't healthy; yet, too often, stoicism is equated with self-control. People who keep their feelings to themselves are often described as "strong." Instead, a healthier belief is that expressing feelings appropriately and constructively requires strength. Emotional control could be defined as deciding whether, when, and how to express. Andrew, a person not used to expressing his feelings, heard a rumor at work that he had been passed over for promotion. He seethed all morning, then stormed into his supervisor's office and announced loudly that he was quitting, and walked out. He stopped to pick up his mail and found a memo congratulating him on his promotion. His display of emotion was not only inappropriate; it was disastrous! A well-adjusted person can choose to express or not to show a feeling and, in a situation, can select from any number of responses.

People who do not have appropriate outlets for emotions such as frustration, anger, and disappointment may have emotional outbursts that destroy career opportunities and relationships. Assertiveness, discussed later in this chapter, can provide a satisfying outlet for most emotions. Additionally, there are ways to release emotion privately that provide relief. When you become annoyed or upset, try any of the following.

- ⊙ deep breathing
- ⊙ taking a brisk walk or engaging in any physical activity
- ⊙ hitting a soft (stuffed) object (privately)!
- ⊙ writing your thoughts and feelings
- ⊙ crushing pieces of paper, then throwing them into the wastebasket (this might clean your work space at the same time)

A favorite is what I call a "primal sigh." It includes taking a deep breath and then making a sighing sound while exhaling. This is preferable to a primal scream, which is not recommended in the work place!

Changing what you feel is possible by altering your thoughts, behaviors, or both. Control theory (Glasser, 1984) emphasizes the importance of what we do. Have you ever whistled or hummed cheerily and then recognized a slight mood elevation? If so, you were using basic control theory.

> WHAT ARE YOU FEELING RIGHT NOW? CHANGE THE EMOTION. FIRST, ALTER YOUR THOUGHTS. THEN, DO SOMETHING THAT IS DIFFERENT FROM YOUR PRESENT ACTIVITY OR BEHAVIOR.

The emotional self is receiving much attention. A best-selling book explains and highly recommends the development of **emotional intelligence** (Goleman, 1995). Characteristics include self-awareness, impulse control, self-motivation, persistence, zeal, empathy, and social deftness. Benefits include being attuned to the feelings of those we deal with, being able to handle disagreements, and having the ability to get into flow states while doing our work. Low levels of emotional intelligence are damaging to a company. Thus, someone who possesses high levels of emotional intelligence is an invaluable commodity in the job market. According to personnel executives, IQ gets you hired, but EQ (an emotional score) gets you promoted (Gibbs, 1995). Doesn't it make sense to do all you can to increase your level of emotional intelligence?

Besides increasing your likelihood for success in the career area, being able to maintain a generally happy or elevated mood can make you healthier. A study showed that antibody response of the immune system was lower on days with high negative moods and higher when the feelings were positive (Stone et al., 1987). The more we learn about our emotional self, the more we can use our feelings to enhance our lives. Everyone can benefit from the full and free experience and expression of our true feelings.

SOCIAL SELF

Who you are in relation to others and how you interact are vital to your well-being and will significantly affect career development. Teamwork is required in today's work world so the ability to get along with others is essential.

You and other individuals create what can be called a social climate. Its influence is either positive or negative. Conflicts occur; yet, congenial people who genuinely like others can manage disagreements effectively. Ways to do so are discussed in Chapter 7.

A social self with an appropriate sense of humor, a cooperative attitude, sensitivity, and fairness is a plus. How well do you get along with people? This is a common interview question. The importance of the social self was underscored by young professionals who were asked, "What do you know now after being in the work world for a few years that you wished you would have known in the beginning?" How to develop camaraderie or fellowship with clients and co-workers was identified as most important by Lee Lamirault, benefits coordinator at Metro-Goldwyn-Mayer in Santa Monica, California. "If you can't communicate, you're nowhere," he said. Mary Dixon concurred that it's necessary to know how to make a client or customer happy and how to provide positive service.

> *"Interpersonal skills are needed as much as technical expertise. Coursework in this vital area would be extremely beneficial."*
>
> Mary Dixon, Administrative Assistant
> Ernst and Young LLP
> Los Angeles, California

Agreeing with the young professionals is Donald O. Clifton, CEO of the Gallup Organization, who says:

> *A Gallup survey indicated how the quality of human relationships in the work place impacts workers' satisfaction, retention of employees, and how well employees do their work. I believe the human relations skills people bring to the work place are the most important skills they bring.*

Personality, the cornerstone of the social self, is covered in this chapter while Chapter 2 discusses interactive skills. Polishing the social self lays the groundwork for career success.

THE WHOLE SELF

Fortunately, we aren't like Humpty Dumpty who couldn't be put back together again! The four developmental areas comprise a whole, and examining the integrated self is fascinating.

> *CAN YOU REMEMBER A TIME WHEN YOU DIDN'T FEEL WELL PHYSICALLY? WHAT WERE YOU LIKE MENTALLY, EMOTIONALLY, AND SOCIALLY?*

Having problems in one area of self usually diminishes one or more of the other three. The good news is that a positive spillover effect occurs. So, when one area is improved, generally, the others are, too. Sara, who was depressed and shy, showed little promise of career success. Then she lost weight and had her hair cut and styled. As a result of physical improvements, she felt happier and became more sociable. The powerful connections among the four areas are exciting and have been the focus of numerous research studies (Cousins, 1991).

Striving for a healthy integrated self is a worthy goal. Additionally, seeking equilibrium deserves attention. Some people devote a great deal of time and energy to their mental self yet exclude their social development and are strangers to their feelings. Others have vigorous social lives to the detriment of their physical and mental well-being. Check yourself periodically and aim for a healthy balance. You don't want to learn the hard way that you are an integrated being!

PERSONALITY: THE UNIQUE YOU

Begin to describe yourself. If you are like many people, you begin with physical descriptors and may have difficulty going further. **Personality** is the "unique you," a distinctive pattern of behaving, thinking, and feeling. A combination of characteristics is possessed only by you and is how you are known to others. Personality gives an individual a separate identity. Have you ever heard someone say, "He has no personality"? While the person may be extremely reserved or dull, there is still a personality!

Personality awareness and understanding can be challenging; yet, as you design your career, knowing who you are and why you behave as you do are instrumental. Consider these cases.

- Jason is miserable at work. He enjoys being around people, yet his job demands that he analyze data in a back office.

- Elizabeth is frustrated because her supervisor often interrupts what she is doing and tells her to work on something else. She wants to complete one task before beginning another one. Also, her job duties are often changed, which annoys her.

- Mary perceives her employer as one who makes illogical decisions and who lets his emotions direct his interactions. Bryan's impression of the same employer is that he is caring and sensitive.

- Kathy and Jeff have become impatient with their supervisor because she has not made a major decision about their positions at work. Additionally, they consider her to be unorganized.

An understanding of personality types would help these people. Carl Jung (1923; 1968), a pioneer in psychological types, believed that behavioral differences are based on the ways people approach life. Based on his typology with some of their own refinements, Isabel Myers and her mother, Katharine C. Briggs, developed the Myers-Briggs Type Indicator (MBTI). Its applications in education, business, the artistic world, and in decision making have been extensive and well received, according to a review of research (Murray, 1990).

Intended to be used for people who are "well," the indicator focuses on positive aspects and preferences for thinking, feeling, and acting. You can use it to make wise decisions about all aspects of life including career choices. An added benefit is that it increases understanding of different behaviors (Myers, 1980b), which can help us cope with people and their differences constructively.

PERSONALITY TYPES

The MBTI uses four categories with opposite preferences in each and indicates a person's partiality for one or the other. It also reveals the strength of each preference. The four pairs of preferences are summarized in Table 1–1.

The meanings of the MBTI preference words are somewhat different from a dictionary definition and popular usage. Frequently misunderstood are extraversion and introversion; and, unfortunately, the confusion has led to the assumption that it's better to be more extraverted. Words used as synonyms for extraverted such as friendly and open are not accurate replacement words. Likewise, introverted may be associated with shyness and aloofness; yet, neither is an accurate definition for introversion.

What is meant by extraversion and introversion? Think in terms of life energy or force. What charges your battery? If your preference is **extraversion (E)**, energy is derived from external sources, including other people, and you probably project energy outward. Extraverted and outgoing mean having an outward orientation and preferring to operate in the outer world of people and things. If there were such a word as "ingoing," it would describe an introverted preference. **Introversion (I)** means an inward orientation and having an interest in the inner world of concepts and ideas. The source of life energy is within and comes from solitary experiences. Those with an introverted preference re-energize themselves and don't rely on external stimuli. In fact, interaction drains their energy, and they need to spend time alone recharging themselves.

People who prefer extraversion will usually behave in a friendly manner and appear open. Those who are more introverted usually do not actively seek out others and may appear to be in their own world; yet, this doesn't mean they

T A B L E   1 – 1 ▲ **PREFERENCES: MYERS-BRIGGS TYPE INDICATOR**

Extraversion–Introversion (E or I)
External or internal orientation to the world and source of life energy
   NOTE: The spelling extraversion is used in this book; extroversion is equally
   correct.

Sensing–Intuition (S or N)
Ways of taking in and processing information

Thinking–Feeling (T or F)
Use of thought or feelings in decision making

Judgment–Perception (J or P)
Modes of dealing with and living in the outer world

aren't capable of friendliness nor that they are shy or snobbish. They are often skilled with people; however, they prefer smaller numbers of people, fewer interactions, and an opportunity to get to know people well. Interestingly, **shyness**, defined as timidity in a social situation, can be experienced by both preferences.

Instead of absolute preferences, we have degrees of both, usually with a partiality toward one. For example, you may enjoy interacting and desire regular social activities, which indicates a stronger extraverted preference, and also enjoy and actually seek solitude and quiet activities because of some introversion.

The other three pairs of preferences are as follows.

If your preference is **sensing (S)**, you tend to be realistic, practical, observant, and good at remembering and working with a great number of facts (Myers, 1980a). If you prefer **intuition (N)**, you value imagination and inspirations, have new ideas, and can solve problems (Myers, 1980a). In their perceptions of reality, sensors (S) are concrete and attuned to details while intuitives (N) are visionary and ablaze with possibilities and ideas. When working on a task, sensors (S) prefer a systematic step-by-step procedure and don't seem to be bothered by repetition. Intuitives (N) often devise their own methods, will work on several steps or projects at once, and prefer variety. Those with an intuitive preference get restless with "sameness" (Hirsch and Kummerow, 1989).

▲ Can you pick out examples of extraversion and introversion? Even around familiar people, personality differences influence social behavior and enjoyment at business social functions.

> *WHAT TYPE OF JOB SITUATIONS WOULD SATISFY A SENSOR (S)? WHAT ABOUT AN INTUITIVE (N)?*

◎   If your preference is **thinking** (T), you use logic and decide impersonally. The other way to decide is through **feeling** (F). You consider anything that matters or is important to you or to other people and decide in a personal way (Myers, 1980a). The difference is between "head" and "heart" decisions. One who has a clear thinking preference views emotions as more of a problem than as part of a solution (Keating, 1984). This person can be oblivious to other people's feelings, while the opposite (a strong feeling person) can "bend over backward" to avoid hurting anyone. Either can be problematic. Both preferences can care a great deal about people and believe that their decisions are based on the "right" motives. Caring from a "T" is more apt to be sympathy and from the "F" empathy (Jeffries, 1991). The two preferences can clash or complement each other; clashing is probably more common. In the career world those with a thinking preference have an easier time making the tough decisions. The "feelers" agonize over choices, especially those pertaining to sensitive areas. Ideally, you can use both preferences appropriately.

> *IMAGINE YOU ARE A COMPANY EXECUTIVE WHO HAS TO DECIDE WHICH EMPLOYEE TO TERMINATE. THE CHOICE IS BETWEEN TWO FEMALES WHO HAVE EQUAL LEVELS OF WORK PERFORMANCE. THE ONLY DIFFERENCES ARE THAT JANET IS A SINGLE PARENT WITH TWO CHILDREN WHILE STEPHANIE IS SINGLE WITH NO CHILDREN AND HAS BEEN WITH THE COMPANY SIX MONTHS LONGER. IF YOU HAVE A THINKING PREFERENCE, YOU WILL PROBABLY DECIDE ALMOST IMMEDIATELY THAT JANET WILL BE FIRED. OBJECTIVELY, SENIORITY MAKES THE DIFFERENCE. IF YOUR PREFERENCE IS FEELING, YOU WILL WANT TO RETAIN JANET BECAUSE YOU "FEEL" FOR HER, OR YOU WILL TRY TO COME UP WITH A WAY TO KEEP BOTH EMPLOYED.*

◎   **Judgment (J)** means that you prefer living in a planned, decided, orderly way, wanting to regulate life and maintain control over events (Myers, 1980a). Planning and preparation are typical behaviors. Judgers (J) seek closure and prefer to reach a decision or judgment quickly. If you like living in a flexible, spontaneous way, wanting to understand and adapt to life (Myers, 1980a), your preference is **perception (P)**. You often "go with the flow" and like to keep your options open. Key words are organization for the judging preference and adaptability for perceivers (Jeffries, 1991). Paul, a strong judger (J), said, "I like the idea of someone throwing me a surprise party, but I want to be prepared for it." He added, "I live by my planner. I take it everywhere, even parties." In contrast to Paul, a perceiver (P) probably wouldn't have a planner or would be like Kari who admitted, "I did buy a calendar diary but don't bother to use it!" In the work place, people of these two extremes can have difficulty getting along. The judger (J) would probably view the perceiver (P) as disorganized or flighty, while the perceptive one could become frustrated with what appears to be an overly organized and inflexible co-worker.

> *THINK OF JUDGING BEHAVIORS THAT CONTRIBUTE TO CAREER SUCCESS. HOW CAN THE ATTITUDES AND ACTIONS OF A PERCEIVER ALSO BE OF VALUE?*

Think about which of the preferences in each of the four categories sounds like you. The combination of the four choices becomes what is called **psychological type**, which provides a broader concept of who you are. Remember that if your preferences are extraversion, intuitive, feeling, and perceiving (ENFP), it doesn't mean you don't have and can't use the opposite preferences as well. Your four preferences interact with each other in a unique way, and each type has a blend of useful behaviors as well as potential pitfalls. Knowledge of type can be especially helpful in determining a satisfying career field, in finding a job that fits you, and in helping you capitalize on your strong points!

You may be able to take the Myers-Briggs Type Inventory in a class or workshop, or a college library or counseling service may have a version of the inventory. If you don't mind paying for it, the MBTI is also offered online. The book *Please Understand Me* (Keirsey and Bates, 1984) includes a questionnaire that yields scores in the four categories. Remember that with any measurement, the results may vary for a number of reasons. Taking the test more than once and being honest in answering the questions will give you a more reliable profile. The indicator identifies a preferred trait and is not intended to exclude other possibilities. For example, you may have a strong preference for using your right hand; yet, you can also use your left.

Especially applicable to the career world are the books *Do What You Are* (Tieger and Barron-Tieger, 1995) and *Type Talk at Work* (Kroeger and Thuesen, 1992). The former helps in making a career choice and then reveals strengths and weaknesses at work related to type. By reading either, you not only learn about yourself but, as important, gain insight into the personalities of others. In the past, a co-worker was annoying to me because he focused on one thing at a time and forced me to wait for his attention until he was completely done with the present task. With an intuition preference, I tend to involve myself with more than one activity at a time (which can be a disadvantage). After learning that he, as a strong sensor, needed to concentrate on one task, which is just another way of doing things and certainly "right" for him, the annoyance decreased considerably.

Personality typing indicates people's strengths. If the two preferences are close, you probably are comfortable using either one. This indicator is not intended to pigeonhole people nor arm them with excuses for behaviors. In certain situations, using the lesser preference is advisable. For example, if someone says, "I can't help that I'm disorganized. My preference is perceiving

(P)," a good response would be, "You also have a judging (J) preference into which you can shift."

Review the four job scenarios at the beginning of this section. Can you see how each person's personality preferences were creating hardships for them? Jason is extraverted, and his job severely limits his contact with people. Elizabeth, with a strong sensing preference, doesn't function well when she isn't able to complete one task before moving to another, and she prefers routine to variety. It is obvious that Mary is more of a thinker while Bryan, with a feeling preference, feels an affinity with their employer. Two employees with a judging preference, Kathy and Jeff, resent the behaviors of a perceiver. Discover how aware you are of personality preferences by completing KEY STEPS (page 271).

Another personality theory (Holland, 1985) categorizes people into clusters, which can then be matched to career fields. The types are realistic, investigative, artistic, social, enterprising, and conventional. If possible, use this measure along with other indicators and compare the results.

> *JUST FROM THE NAMES OF THE CLUSTERS USED BY HOLLAND (1985), SUGGEST SOME CAREER FIELDS FOR EACH.*

All aspects of personality aren't apparent on inventories. Self-knowledge includes appraising all personality traits that can help you design a successful career. Several of these are identified in this and other chapters. Whatever your personality is, you can build on the strengths and alter the weaker aspects.

YOUR PICTURE OF SELF: SELF-CONCEPT

Each of us has a mental representation of ourselves. This **self-concept** can include (1) present descriptors drawn from the four developmental areas of self; (2) **ideal self,** or the image of what you would like to be; and (3) **self-esteem,** the value placed on the self.

Your current self-description and your ideal self may be similar or quite different. Because of unrealistic standards, you may have an impossible ideal. If so, that image is more hurtful than helpful. Mark described himself as overweight, short, eager to learn, impulsive, shy, and generally unhappy. His ideal self, he is quick to describe, is muscular, tall, eager to learn, patient, friendly, and always happy. Which of his ideal descriptors could be useful? Which are just potentially damaging? Knowing what you can and cannot change and formulating a possible ideal self are helpful.

> *DESCRIBE YOUR IDEAL SELF. IS THIS A POSSIBLE SELF?*

Also beneficial is to realize that achieving your ideal self isn't a requirement for high self-esteem or happiness. Instead, as you come closer to your ideal, set your goals even higher. Employers tend to doubt anyone who thinks he or she has reached the highest pinnacle of selfhood. "When I ask applicants about their weaknesses, I'd better get a response. Nobody is perfect," said one business owner. A healthy attitude is to recognize that striving to better oneself is a lifelong process.

Comparing your present descriptors and ideal self helps assess your level of self-worth. Self-esteem can be thought of as a point on a scale ranging from very low to very high; it goes beyond acceptance of self and is a genuine regard for who one is. Some might mistake self-esteem for vanity, conceit, an egotistic existence, and selfishness. Actually, those who fit these descriptors do not have a healthy love for themselves. Self-inflation is usually a cover-up for self-doubt. Genuine love for the self includes self-respect and dignity; it encourages healthy attitudes and behaviors toward others.

Self-esteem affects all aspects of life. Throughout one's career, high self-esteem is a powerful ally. Job seekers with healthy self-worth achieve higher interview ratings and receive more job offers than those with low self-esteem. Because employees' work reflects the degree of their own self-esteem, employers seek applicants who value themselves. On the job an individual with high self-esteem can accept and profit from advice and constructive criticism. He or she is more motivated, willing to take reasonable risks, and more likely to demonstrate competence. Pride in productivity comes from pride in self.

As one advances, regard for the self continues to pay off. Managers with high self-esteem have less trouble giving up control and delegating responsibility, can tolerate frustration better, and are capable of treating their employees with respect. The willingness to learn new skills and continue to improve stems from feeling good about self.

Psychological well-being, a necessity in the work place, is related to level of self-esteem. Experts on self-esteem believe that the judgment we place on ourselves, because it touches the very center of our existence, is the most significant judgment in life (Branden, 1983). Whatever you can do to build and strengthen self-esteem is highly recommended. Some ideas are provided later in this chapter.

YOUR PERSONAL CAPABILITY: SELF-EFFICACY

Closely aligned with self-esteem is a sense of capability or competence, which is called **self-efficacy**. Imagine an employee being assigned the task of producing a mailing list. The belief that "I can do this" indicates self-efficacy, and it's easy to see how this is essential to career success. You may remember that story of the little engine who succeeded by saying, "I think I can, I think I can." People with self-efficacy think they can.

> *THINKING OF YOUR OWN SELF-EFFICACY, WHAT SKILLS OR TASKS COME TO MIND?*

Self-efficacy pertains to a particular event or task, and it isn't necessary to feel competent about everything. However, in areas related to your career, confidence goes a long way.

"Staff members who perceive themselves as capable can work on their own with little supervision; they are highly valued."

Nancy Brown, R.N., Program Manager
Nebraska Department of Health
Lincoln, Nebraska

Potential employers may not use the word *self-efficacy*; however, expect to be assessed on whether or not they think you have a feeling of self-competence. Some caution is in order. As a job applicant or an employee, it is unrealistic to possess total self-efficacy. An honest "I don't know how to do that, and I'm willing to learn" in an interview or making reasonable requests for assistance on the job are mature behaviors.

Self-efficacy is related to self-esteem; as one increases, so does the other. Creating an ever-expanding upward spiral of self-esteem and self-efficacy is a powerful tool in self-enhancement (Canfield and Siccone, 1993). Throughout your career path, being aware of the tasks of which you are capable and developing additional competencies are necessary. You can increase self-understanding and compare your self-concept with how others see you by using the KEY STEPS activity (beginning on page 267).

Making Positive Personality Changes

Necessary for career success is the ability to improve oneself. You can positively alter any of the four developmental areas, develop valuable personality characteristics, build or strengthen self-esteem, and create more self-efficacy.

Pretend you are hiring employees. What characteristics or traits would you want? Check your list against Table 1–2.

Desirable traits valuable in all career fields and useful in almost every job are included in your **transferable assets**. You probably already possess several of

T A B L E   1 – 2 ▲ TRANSFERABLE ASSETS

assertive	creative/innovative
enthusiastic	flexible
responsible	willing to exert effort
dependable	motivated
congenial/friendly	respectful of self and others
able to see alternatives	able to communicate and take criticism
positive	happy most of the time
goal-oriented	stable in mood and temperament
ethical	open-minded
loyal	accepting of diversity
realistic	technically skilled

these assets identified in Table 1–2. Be sure potential employers know that you do. In some cases, the trait may not be evident. For example, not everybody exudes enthusiasm. If you feel excitement for your career choice and a particular job and don't think it shows, you can verbalize it in an interview. Innovation is another valuable characteristic that may not be discernable. Businesses need new ideas about how to stay competitive, so being creative in this rapidly changing world is a definite asset. Executives say they want forward-thinking applicants who can move into a job without needing a lot of direction. If you don't require a great deal of supervision and can handle most tasks on your own, you are definitely marketable. Also use Table 1–2 to identify the assets you lack and then try to develop them.

Recent surveys of employers and program chairpersons at a community college yielded a number of employable characteristics. Along with the obvious need for technical skills, nearly all listed dependability. Several emphasized flexibility in thought and action. "We look for people who are adaptable to change," says Deputy Fire Chief Dean Staberg.

Those who teach career development know what employers seek. "It doesn't matter what you have to offer if you aren't there to offer it. Being there and being on time are essential," is the opinion of Mary Conway, career development instructor. Lois Kemble, instructor of an employment techniques course, says:

> I frequently get calls from employers seeking either part-time or full-time employees. One of the most frequently asked questions is attendance. Second is the applicant's ability to interact with others, and a third is the person's capability of being an independent worker with the capacity to solve problems and to take initiative.

Interpersonal or human relations skills are at the top of the list of qualities desired by employers, according to Sheryl Piening, who teaches management and human relations courses to transportation and building construction students at a community college. "More important than specific job skills, which employers can teach, are a positive attitude and the willingness to take on new tasks," contends Janet Brejda, instructor of academic and career orientation.

Possessing self-discipline and demonstrating a solid work ethic are impressive and generally hard-to-find characteristics, in the opinion of Leonard Murphy, a partner in an accounting firm. He voices the concern of several employers:

> Many people are looking for jobs although they may not be willing to really work. Some people just want to be entertained and get a paycheck at the same time. If they show up and put in eight hours, they think they're being productive. Those who actually do want to work and to produce are greatly appreciated and will be rewarded.

Knowing what employers want gives you an advantage. You'll be even further ahead by developing or strengthening yourself in the specific areas of locus of control, assertiveness, self-esteem, and basic academic skills covered in the rest of this chapter.

DEVELOPING AN INTERNAL LOCUS OF CONTROL

Even though most people think they take responsibility, excuses are plentiful. "I know I was late, but..." or "If she would have left me alone to do my work, I would have finished" or "I was so depressed I just couldn't come to work" are some examples. In a classic study of executives who had experienced high degrees of stressful life events, having what is called an internal locus of control contributed to their psychological hardiness and ability to counteract stress (Kobasa, 1979). An **internal locus of control** is the belief that you are in control of your life as opposed to thinking that external factors are responsible. Honestly assess whether you are more likely to take responsibility for your own behaviors, which include all shortcomings, or to blame someone or something else.

Studies support the value of feeling in control. It has been linked to improved health (Moyers, 1993), empowerment (Spezzano, 1992), emotional calm (Rodin, Schooler, and Schaie, 1990), and happiness (Myers, 1992; Rodin, 1986). Employers want individuals to be responsible in many ways and appreciate those who take responsibility for their actions. "I didn't finish the project on time because I didn't plan well and start on it early enough. I regret that and have learned from my mistake" is refreshing and much preferred to a commonly heard excuse: "The project didn't get finished on time because I'm so busy and just didn't have time." The reality of life is that we all have the same amount of time, and in almost all cases, the project could have been completed. What happened is that there wasn't time left over to do so.

What's the difference between an excuse and a reason? The latter is a statement of fact and indicates self-responsibility. While an excuse can be factual, a "that should get me off the hook" presumption is also included. Excuse making can be detrimental to career success. Not only is making excuses an annoying habit, but those who make excuses also deny themselves the opportunity to learn and grow. Excuses are like antacids that bring temporary relief but do not contribute to long-term success and happiness (Hanna, 1995).

GEECH®   By Jerry Bittle

▲ Geech ©1996 Universal Press Syndicate. Reprinted with permission. All rights reserved.

When you verbally or mentally blame external sources, challenge your thought. Even if you couldn't control the situation, you had a choice as to how to react. When you make a mistake, admit it and resolve to make any needed changes. Chris had a problem with getting to work on time. "I would either blame my faulty alarm clock, the weather, or the traffic, but never myself. When I finally 'woke up,' I realized that I could buy a different alarm clock and could leave for work early enough to take care of both bad weather and heavy traffic. I was responsible for being late, and now I'm in control and can be on time!" Check your locus of control. Then decide that you want to be "in the driver's seat of your life!"

BECOMING ASSERTIVE

Nobody is born assertive so all of us must learn it. **Assertiveness**, defined as the ability to maintain one's legitimate rights and to express thoughts and feelings in non-threatening ways, is valued in today's work world. In contrast to aggressive behavior which is threatening and controlling or nonassertive behavior that is meek and passive, assertiveness is likely to have a positive outcome. Research reveals that interviewers are most likely to employ assertive applicants (Gallois, Callan, and McKenzie, 1992). In this regard, certain personality preferences may have an advantage because assertiveness is related to extraversion in women and the thinking preference on the MBTI for both women and men (Tucker, 1991). However, any personality type can become assertive.

Cognitive restructuring that rids you of fear and anxiety can be especially helpful. You may need to convince yourself that you can be assertive. For example, a thought process may be: Just because I've been aggressive and abrasive in the past doesn't mean I have to continue to be. I can adjust my behavior and become assertive.

If you fear embarrassment or rejection and feel intimidated, a simple technique can be used to sap the strength of the fear-provoking thought (Butler, 1992). When you think, "What if he gets upset when I state my opinion?" change it: "So what if he gets upset when I state my opinion." Another idea is to ask yourself, "What is the worst thing that can happen if I say or do this?" Usually, the worst isn't all that bad, and your fear is relieved.

Thinking is a powerful beginning; however, the key is to employ assertive actions. Assertiveness can be learned from **modeling**, observing and then copying the behaviors of an assertive person. If you have an opportunity to role-play assertiveness, do so. For most people, assertiveness requires changes in both verbal and nonverbal behaviors.

- Verbalize with "I" statements such as "I would like," "I don't want," "I think or believe." This assertive language takes responsibility for your own thoughts and feelings. You will learn about "I" statements in Chapter 2.

- Use a calm and even tone of voice and maintain a moderate rate and volume.

- Make reasonable requests and set reasonable limits, then express these clearly and calmly to others.

⑥   Learn to say "no" to what you don't want and "yes" to what you do. Because saying "no" is difficult for many people, how to do so is covered in Chapter 2.

⑥   Use direct eye contact, appropriate facial expressions, an open body position, confident body stance, and calm and controlled body movements. Avoid threatening gestures such as pointing.

⑥   Be willing to take reasonable risks. Begin with a slight risk and give yourself credit for trying.

> *THINK OF ASSERTIVE BEHAVIORS YOU POSSESS. THEN TAKE THE ASSERTIVENESS INVENTORY IN* **KEY STEPS** *(PAGE 272).*

As with all learned skills, practice will make assertiveness a natural way to act. The path is not necessarily an easy one. As one becomes assertive, others may resent and feel offended by this "new" person, especially if the previous nonassertive behavior served their purposes. "I tried to be assertive with my co-worker, and it led to a confrontation. I'm ready to give up," confessed Jennifer. She would be better off practicing her new assertiveness in situations where success is likely and then approach the co-worker with renewed confidence. Incidentally, it may be necessary to be assertive about your new assertiveness! In other words, express to others that you are making changes and explain what you are trying to do.

> *"In order to succeed, a person has to take chances. I struggle with this, but it's true. There's an old sports analogy: 'You never make a shot you don't take.'"*
>
> Mitch Hall, Divisional Vice President
> Domino's Pizza, Inc.
> Ann Arbor, Michigan

BUILDING AND STRENGTHENING SELF-ESTEEM

An improvement in the self adds to self-esteem. You can also learn specific ways to build and strengthen the value you place on yourself. Eliminating any obstacle comes first. Some people are handicapped by extreme insecurities, major depression, and drug abuse. For some people, just getting through the day is a struggle; thus, they fail in attempts to improve themselves. Professional counseling is usually necessary to elevate them to a level where they can take advantage of self-esteem building. The payoff is invaluable. As expressed by Debra, a young woman, "I found that a decision that you are *for* yourself, not against yourself, is the beginning of an entirely different life."

Basic to self-esteem is living consciously. Your degree of alertness and level of functioning are determined by such choices as how much sleep to get (seven to eight hours is highly recommended) and the use of alcohol and other drugs. Those who walk around "in a fog" are not in a position to build their self-esteem.

An analysis of how your self-esteem developed can be quite helpful. All of us have been criticized or put down even by those who love us. Parents use what resources they possess and almost never intentionally hurt their offspring; yet, they do. Teachers, coaches, and other school personnel can diminish self-esteem because they don't know better ways to direct the lives of others. Sometimes supervisors and co-workers say and do hurtful things because of their own frustrations. Recall any negative comments you have received. Consider the possible reasons. Could it have been because of the person's own feelings of inferiority or lack of self-esteem? Was he or she just being hateful? Did the person have good intentions? Decide what to do with all that has been said and done to you. The past can be a valuable basis for learning and growing; use it in that way and discard any useless self-destructive messages.

Do you concentrate on your strengths? A tendency is to key in on weaknesses and become bogged down. While recognizing drawbacks is beneficial, it's not wise to dwell on them. Focusing on your potential and thinking positively empower the self. A boost to self-esteem can come from the regular use of **affirmations**, which are positive self-thoughts.

WHAT DO YOU LIKE ABOUT YOURSELF? DO YOU LISTEN WELL? DO YOU HAVE A NICE SMILE? ARE YOU CONSIDERATE? LIST YOUR STRONG POINTS.

Demonstrating your strengths is even more rewarding. Whatever you do well, be sure to do it! If you have athletic talent, join a team or simply play for enjoyment. If you're talented in some type of craft, make something as a gift. Accept all compliments and don't put yourself down if your attempts aren't perfect. Getting involved in worthwhile activities is a boost to self-esteem, and these are also extremely valuable assets in your career development. Brent participated in an environmental cleanup project which made him feel good and eventually impressed an interviewer. Giving to others is a gift to yourself.

Making constructive changes improves your present self and ensures a better future. Make an attainable, yet challenging, ideal and improve one developmental area of yourself. The goal-setting information in Chapter 3 will be helpful. Any positive change in yourself means a rise in self-esteem.

Building and maintaining high self-esteem is easier with the help of positive, supportive people. If you find yourself around others who tend to be "downers" about themselves or others, seek other company. Being with people who affirm you and modeling after those with high self-esteem are effective esteem boosters.

NAME AT LEAST TWO FRIENDS AND ACQUAINTANCES WHO ARE POSITIVE AND SUPPORTIVE. THESE ARE PEOPLE TO BE AROUND!

Changing your thoughts, or cognitive restructuring, is a useful self-esteem building technique. Begin by tuning in to your **self-talk**, those thoughts about yourself. Are those thoughts realistic and generally affirming or are they distorted and damaging? If self-talk is unnecessarily negative, reframe or restructure it using these four steps.

1. Identify an untruth, distortion, or belittlement.

2. Determine the truth and the facts.

3. Use this way of restructuring: Just because (*the truth/facts as given in Step 2*) doesn't mean (*the untruth, distortion, or belittlement you were thinking as identified in Step 1*).

4. Give yourself an affirmation.

As an example, pretend you didn't get a job you really wanted. Your immediate thought is: "They must not have liked me. I'll never find a job better than that one." The use of cognitive restructuring follows.

1. They must not have liked me. I'll never find a job better than that one (a belittlement and distortion).

2. I didn't get a job I really wanted (the truth/fact).

3. Just because I didn't get a job I really wanted doesn't mean they didn't like me and that I won't find a job that is better (use of the restructuring formula).

4. I will make an excellent employee, and I'll just keep looking (an affirmation).

Freeing yourself from the distorted thought allows any number of positive ones. You can even think as did Sarah, "It's the company's loss. They missed out on a terrific employee!" Remember that what you think determines much of your life.

Several books include ways of building and strengthening self-esteem (Branden, 1992; Bloomfield, 1985; Hanna, 1995; McKay and Fanning, 1987). Additionally, courses and seminars can help improve your self-concept. We weren't born with self-esteem. Rather than blame others for where we are now, we can overcome the past and build and strengthen self-esteem in the present. A basic question is to ask yourself if you are being as kind and supportive to yourself as you are to a good friend. If you aren't, why not become your own best friend?

Sharpening Your Basic Skills

Companies today are facing a skills gap more pronounced than ever before. Three categories are sorely needed

- basic analytical, communications, and organizational skills (includes reading, writing, and arithmetic)

- technological skills

- leadership skills

More than half the companies surveyed by the National Association of Manufacturers in 1992 reported serious deficiencies among their employees in rudimentary skills while Motorola turns away 90 percent of applicants because of insufficient math and communications abilities (Messmer, 1996).

The SCANS Report, issued by the U.S. Department of Labor in 1991, identified competencies and skills that lead to solid job performance. The competency areas were (1) basic language and mathematics, (2) thinking, and (3) personal qualities such as self-esteem.

Before beginning your career, assess your competencies and take advantage of opportunities to learn or sharpen basic skills. A primary one is writing. Throughout your career, the ability to write correctly and clearly will be a significant asset. On the other hand, individuals have a major handicap if they lack writing, reading, or mathematics skills. If you are deficient in any of these areas, enroll in relevant courses. "Until students have learned to use proper written and spoken language in every facet of their lives, they aren't prepared to enter the work world and be successful," says Larry Hubka, Ph.D., dean of Business and Mass Media, Southeast Community College.

Another beneficial course is public speaking or speech. You may not be expected to make presentations before large audiences; however, most occupations require small group communication. A speech course will also aid in job interview preparation. A definite asset, even though it may not yet be considered basic, is fluency in a second language. Successful coursework typically increases career and job possibilities.

Because computer skills are required in almost every job, taking courses in the basic technology is essential. Sally Beck, a college placement specialist, says, "Not having computer skills today is as much a liability as inability to read and write was a few years ago." Coursework in word processing and spreadsheets will make you even more marketable. You can learn how to use standard office machines either on a job now, from volunteer work, or through coursework. "Learn to use technology that will make you more efficient," is the advice of Lisa Patterson, CPA. Even though equipment varies from one company to another, being familiar with basic operations is a plus.

> OF THE BASIC SKILLS IDENTIFIED SO FAR, WHICH DO YOU POSSESS? IN WHAT AREAS, IF ANY, COULD YOU USE INSTRUCTION?

When young professionals were asked what they now know that they wished they had known while they were preparing for their career, Lyn Patterson, human resources administrator, Turner Broadcasting System, Inc., Los Angeles, advised, "Develop as many basic skills as possible. These are expected of you from the first day and include typing, composing letters and memos using word processing, and operating copy and fax machines."

Another strong recommendation is to cultivate multiple skills. You may not see the connection between office skills and your chosen career field; however, most employers will be impressed with a variety of abilities. Additionally, you could be surprised. Angie, who was hired as a radiologic technologist in a clinic, found herself handling several word processing and billing tasks. She was rewarded verbally and financially for her versatility.

Worthy to note are the new emphasis on sales and the need for selling skills in a variety of fields. "New employees are typically surprised to learn

▲ Computer skills are considered almost as basic as reading and writing in today's job market.

that accountants must be able to sell. Competition is keen for clients, and we make a concentrated effort to bring in new business," says Lisa Patterson, CPA and senior manager for Ernst and Young LLP. Technicians in fields that range from automotive maintenance and repair to graphics design find themselves acting as informal sales representatives for their employer.

Then because the world is changing so rapidly, the ability and willingness to learn and to adapt is essential. For example, the software that you now use could become obsolete and, at a minimum, will be updated on a regular basis. Develop a mental attitude of curiosity and openness and be sure to let a potential employer know that you want to continue to learn throughout your life. The activity in KEY STEPS (page 273) provides enlightenment in the area of skills. If you can convince an employer that you have needed or desired capabilities and are willing to keep updated, you will have an advantage over other applicants.

> *"Most people start in entry level jobs that demand bottom-line competencies. Applicants today are expected to have office skills even if they aren't applying for secretarial positions."*
>
> Lyn Patterson, Human Resources Administrator
> Turner Broadcasting System, Inc.
> Los Angeles, California

EVALUATING YOUR CAREER POTENTIAL

After analyzing yourself in the four developmental areas, assessing your personality, and beginning to make any needed changes, a practical evaluative tool is a balance sheet of assets and liabilities. Use the activity in KEY

STEPS (beginning on page 273) to develop one. Think of **assets** as strengths, skills, and positive experiences that will help you get the job you want. **Liabilities** include drawbacks, weaknesses, skills you lack, and negative experiences that you would rather a potential employer not know. A balance sheet benefits you in several ways.

- You can devote more time and energy to the actual job search because you've compiled all the basic information.
- You'll have a clearer idea of which careers and jobs are best for you.
- Your self-esteem and confidence will be strengthened.
- You'll know what to emphasize (assets) and what may need changing or explaining (liabilities).

What do you think would be considered liabilities to employers? Potential employers will try to uncover any evidence of negative behaviors from your past record. Table 1–3 shows concerns of employers (Cormack, 1992).

If, before you begin your serious job search, you can change any problematic behaviors, "brush up" on skills, and acquire experience, do so. But what if this isn't possible? "I was fired from a job once. I can't change that," was a dour reply from a career seminar participant. You can either avoid revealing a drawback or explain to and convince a potential employer that the negative actions will stay in the past. The key is to plan how to discuss all liabilities. Most of us don't like to be caught "off guard," and during a job interview this is particularly uncomfortable. "Have you ever been fired?" is the question. If you have, which is a better response?

- Uh, no.
- Uh, yes.
- Well, I was, but it wasn't my fault.
- Yes, I have. When I was in my first year of college, I had a job in a restaurant. To be honest, I tried to take too many classes and was overwhelmed. I wasn't as productive at work as I could have been, and after I was late to work two times, the owner said I was no longer needed. Even though it was painful, I learned a great deal from that experience.

T A B L E 1 – 3 ▲ BOTHERSOME EMPLOYEE BEHAVIORS

excuses	theft	falsification
tardiness	poor quality work	loitering
absenteeism	sabotage	vandalism
carelessness	accident proneness	personal conflicts with other employees
quitting	resistance to change	personal conflicts with supervisors
poor service	not following rules	tolerance of negative behavior in others

Knowing how to explain a liability on an application and rehearsing what to say before an interview might even increase your chances. After a practice session in a career development class, the interviewer said, "I would be inclined to hire that young man on the basis of his response about his prison sentence." When the student, who had been quite worried about his blemished record, was told that he might have gotten a job because of the positive way he discussed this liability, he and I both had a good laugh.

A personal balance sheet contains invaluable information. Spend time and thought in developing a complete one, then use it as the foundation for your job search. A successful career path does not begin with your first job. Instead, it begins with *you*. Who you are, how much genuine regard you have for yourself, and what you have to offer in a career field determine the course of your professional life. You can successfully design a career by understanding, improving, and expanding yourself.

KEY POINTS

- Career development begins with self-knowledge.

- Four development areas of the self, physical, mental, emotional, and social, can be explored.

- Making positive physical changes in appearance and health is beneficial to career success.

- Striving to do your best academically, being willing and eager to learn, developing problem-solving skills, and maintaining a positive attitude foster a strong mental self.

- Understanding the emotional self, learning to constructively express emotions, and being able to change what you feel are hallmarks of a mentally healthy individual.

- The ability to interact and relate to others in a positive way is considered essential in all career fields.

- Understanding your own and others' personalities can be extremely helpful. The eight preferences and four types revealed by the Myers-Briggs Type Indicator provide insight.

- The self-concept consists of self-descriptors, ideal self, and self-esteem.

- Self-efficacy, a belief in your capability, is a definite asset in all aspects of a career.

- Employers are seeking certain traits and skills in employees. Knowing what these are will enhance your chances in the job market.

- Developing an internal locus of control helps you direct the course of your life.

- ⊚   Assertiveness is highly desired in today's career world. People are not assertive at birth; it must be learned.

- ⊚   Those who succeed in their careers are successful in developing and strengthening high levels of self-esteem.

- ⊚   Basic skills are necessary in order to get and keep jobs.

- ⊚   Developing a balance sheet of assets and liabilities is an important early step in successful career development.

RECOMMENDED READING

Bloomfield, H. H. with Felder, L. (1985). *Making peace with yourself*. New York: Ballantine Books.

Branden, N. (1992). *The power of self-esteem*. Deerfield Beach, FL: Health Communications.

Carter-Scott, C. (1989). *Negaholism: How to recover from your addiction to negativity and turn your life around*. New York: Villard.

Chapman, E. N. (1993). *Your attitude is showing*. Chicago: Science Research Associates.

Covey, S. (1989). *The 7 habits of highly effective people*. New York: Simon & Schuster.

Goleman, D. (1995). *Emotional intelligence*. New York: Bantam Books.

Hanna, S. L. (1995). *Person to person: Positive relationships don't just happen*. Englewood Cliffs, NJ: Prentice Hall.

Hirsch, S. and Kummerow, J. (1989). *Life types*. New York: Warner Communications.

Jeffers, S. (1996). *Feel the fear and do it anyway*. New York: Fawcett Columbine.

Jeffries, W. C. (1991). *True to type*. Norfolk, VA: Hampton Roads Publishing.

Keirsey, D. and Bates, M. (1984). *Please understand me*. Del Mar, CA: Prometheus Nemesis.

Kroeger, O. and Thuesen, J. M. (1992). *Type talk at work*. New York: Delacorte Press.

McKay, M. and Fanning, P. (1987). *Self-esteem*. Oakland, CA: New Harbinger.

Myers, I. B. (1980). *Gifts differing*. Palo Alto, CA: Consulting Psychologists Press.

Ryan, R. S. and Travis, J. W. (1991). *Wellness: Small changes you can use to make a big difference*. Berkeley, CA: Ten Speed Press.

Seligman, M. E. P. (1990). *Learned optimism: How to change your mind and your life*. New York: Pocket Books.

Tieger, P. D. and Barron-Tieger, B. (1995). *Do what you are*. Boston: Little, Brown.

CHAPTER Two

Interacting Positively with Others

Positive interactions, needed and desired by well-adjusted individuals, are based on a positive relationship with oneself. The previous chapter and other resources can help you develop the best possible self, which then allows you to positively connect with others. Perhaps more than any other characteristic, the ability to interact and relate to others determines the extent of career success. Executives who eventually failed did so most often because of an interpersonal flaw, not a technical inability (Gibbs, 1995). This chapter explores what is needed to develop positive interactions and relationships while Chapter 7 discusses the application of these interpersonal skills at work.

> *"Having strong 'people skills' is a necessity. At work you relate to everyone from the clerks to the president of the company. And if the clients don't like you, you'll soon be out of a job."*
>
> Lisa Patterson, CPA and Senior Manager
> Ernst and Young LLP
> Los Angeles, California

BEING OPEN-MINDED

Interacting and establishing relationships requires an openness to the prospect of meeting and getting to know others, including people who don't look, think, or act as you do. Reserving judgment and learning to appreciate diversity are invaluable.

FIRST IMPRESSIONS

Immediate judgments, known as **first impressions**, are unavoidable. These are almost always based on physical appearance with overt actions also playing a part. Place yourself in an office setting at the beginning of a job interview. The interviewer, an older, sophisticated-looking woman, is reading some notes when you enter. After a minute, she looks up and in a cool tone of voice says, "Good afternoon. I'm Ms. Thomas." Her handshake is overly firm. What would be your impressions? How would these differ if the interviewer greeted you immediately with a bright smile, said, "Hello. I'm Sally Thomas and I'm delighted you are here," and gave you a pleasantly firm handshake?

Allowing a first impression to dictate the course of an interaction or the ensuing relationship is not recommended. For any number of reasons, people are not always what they seem to be. After analyzing an impression, it's best to let time and involvement determine how realistic it was.

ACCEPTANCE AND APPRECIATION

Entire books have been written about prejudice and tolerance. This brief coverage can help you examine some of your attitudes and, hopefully, show you that one of the greatest handicaps to career success is an inability to accept and appreciate differences. It's easy to be prejudiced; yet, the key to success is to eliminate these negative feelings and develop an egalitarian attitude, a belief that all people are equal.

Generalized ideas about groups of people are **stereotypes**. Whenever there is a difference among groups, stereotyping is possible.

> *CHECK TO SEE HOW QUICKLY STEREOTYPES COME TO YOUR MIND. THINK OF A GROUP, THEN ADD ANY STEREOTYPE.*

Even though some stereotypes present a positive picture of a group, the typical ones focus on the negative. In all cases, stereotypes can limit people or place unrealistic expectations upon them. Reducing an individual to a label based on his or her category is misleading and insulting.

The tendency to generalize is especially common when the individual is outside one's own group. One day during a class discussion, an Anglo-American male student volunteered to tell the reason he was prejudiced. "When I was a kid, three black kids came into my yard and beat me up. I hated them for it, and I've hated all black people since then." Obviously, he had suffered from a bad experience and had generalized from it. He was asked to use his imagination and pretend that the three boys had been white. Then he was asked, "Would you now hate all white people because three white boys beat you up?" His quick answer was, "Well, no." Because he was familiar with diversity among his own race of Anglo-Americans, he didn't generalize.

Negative stereotyping usually leads to **prejudice**, an attitude that others are inferior or less than you in some way. What then usually occurs is a feeling of dislike, disgust, or hatred. Prejudice is learned from others and by generalizing from a negative experience. Prejudice is insensitive and illogical; career-wise, being prejudiced is a detriment to success.

Related to prejudice is **discrimination**, which is unfair treatment of people. Because discrimination is usually observable behavior, it can be outlawed. Yet, covert discrimination is still practiced and is often based on prejudice. Discrimination in the work place is discussed in Chapter 8.

Ideally, you do not make decisions based on stereotypes, harbor prejudices, nor discriminate. If your thinking is stereotypic and you have negative feelings about certain people, act in your best interests and challenge these thoughts and feelings. The following questions can help (Hanna, 1995).

- ☉ *Is my thinking reasonable and rational?* If you take pride in your mental abilities, you will want to eliminate inaccurate and unreasonable stereotypic thinking. Refuse to accept the idea that all African-Americans or Anglo-Americans, Catholics or Protestants, old people or young people, and heterosexuals or homosexuals are one way.

- ☉ *Am I being fair?* How would I feel if I were the victim of prejudice? Most human beings are concerned about justice and fairness. Discrimination is unfair, and even the thinking that can lead to it is usually unjust.

- ☉ *Am I basing my impressions on a knowledge of an individual or only on the person as a member of a group?* Negative labeling can keep us from getting to know the "real" person. Moving from a collective impression,

▲ Diversity is the norm in today's work place.

which is a stereotype, to an individual analysis is the key. Being free of prejudice means your positive or negative feelings of a person are not based on preconceived labeling.

⑥   *Can I come up with a good reason to contribute to prejudice in the world?* Individuals and societies suffer from prejudice, and ultimately, everyone is harmed.

In the work world, stereotyping and prejudice create problems. Most employers aren't impressed with fixed, inflexible ways of seeing the world. Those who stereotype and label are perceived not only as negative and lacking in knowledge but also as rigid thinkers. As one employer related: "I realize the applicant was from a rural area where there isn't much diversity, and, perhaps, he hadn't been educated about it, but when he used the term 'colored people,' it was a definite turn-off."

Lack of prejudice does not mean blindness to differences. A person can be aware of diversity in race, ethnicity, sex, age, religion, and even personality preferences; the key is to not let differences stop you from relating. You can learn from diversity and even enjoy it. Sameness can be boring.

All kinds of diversity provide opportunities for expansion of self. The concept of **multiculturalism**—recognition and appreciation of cultural differences—benefits society and its individual members. The ability to view differences as gifts and opportunities is an invaluable personal characteristic.

Using Assertiveness

Healthy relationships of all types thrive on assertiveness, the ability to maintain legitimate rights and express thoughts and feelings in nonthreatening ways. When one person is passive and allows another to dominate, a relationship suffers. Moreover, few people enjoy working with an aggressive individual who wants to dominate and take advantage of others. He or she may prevail; however, the price is high.

A situation can warrant a mild, moderate, or intense degree of assertiveness. Begin with a mild approach—a simple explanation of circumstances and a request for a change. If that doesn't work, you can use a moderate approach which sounds more direct. Only when necessary and after you have weighed the possible consequences would you use the intense level.

Let's look at some possible situations. Another employee named Rod and you share a computer terminal; actually, share is not correct because he uses it much more than you do. It is Friday afternoon, and you want to develop a memo before you leave. The assertive approach would be to say, "Rod, I'd like to talk with you for a few minutes." Then when you have his attention, begin at the mild level: "Over the past few weeks I'm having difficulty completing some work because the computer is not available. I realize you, too, are busy, and I'd like for us to schedule computer time so it's fair for both of us." Remember that your body posture, eye contact, and tone of voice need to reflect confidence, poise, and openness. In most cases, this assertive level would be effective.

A more difficult situation involves a supervisor. Debra has scheduled you to work late several days in succession. You are experiencing a high level of stress and actually feel ill. After requesting an opportune time to discuss the matter, begin by stating the extra efforts you have already made. Express a willingness to be a good team member, then use the mild assertiveness level.

> *I am now at a point where my effectiveness and productivity are low, and I feel ill. I would appreciate it if you could find someone else to handle the extra work right now as that seems to me to be in everybody's best interest.*

Hopefully, your request will be met. However, if it isn't, you can move to the moderate level.

> *I realize that you are in a bind, and I wish there were an easy solution. I think it's only fair that I be given some relief. I prefer not to continue working late right now.*

Before using the intense level, consider the possible outcomes. The worst case scenario would be to lose your job so be sure you are prepared. Generally, a supervisor can handle intense assertiveness.

> *I have given this a great deal of thought and know that I have reached my limit. Even though I want to help and certainly prefer to continue in this job, I am not going to continue to do extra work at this time. I'll be willing to do more again in the future.*

The intense level is risky. Yet, a supervisor who would terminate you because of your assertiveness is not the person for whom you deserve to work. Additionally, people who don't seem to be able to ever say "no" invariably end up with pent-up resentment that is physically and psychologically damaging.

Learning to say "no" is difficult for many people. A basic step is to decide that doing so is acceptable. A cognitive technique can be useful. Ask yourself, "What's the worst thing that will happen if I say 'no'? How does that compare to what happens to me when I say 'yes' and resent it?" Then, continue to think, "What if the person becomes angry with me because I say 'no'? How bad will that be?" Keep telling yourself that you have the right to say "no."

Once you have decided to decline, you can practice how to say it. Of course you can just say the two-letter word nicely; however, most people feel more comfortable with other kinds of statements such as one of the following.

- I have decided not to take on any more right now.
- I would like to say "yes"; however, this time I'm not going to do that.
- I've been doing some time management work and prioritizing, and right now other things come first.
- Thanks for asking; however, I'm not going to participate right now.
- Believe it or not, I'm going to say "no."
- I have a hard time saying "no"; this time I'm going to stick with it.

Saying "no" firmly and politely is assertive behavior. A balance between saying "no" and saying "yes" is reasonable during your career life. See how assertive you are and in what areas you can improve by checking the activity in KEY STEPS (page 272).

How we act, interact, and react with people affects all aspects of life. This chapter and Chapter 7 deal with interactions and relationships that have an impact on career development. Learning and applying positive interpersonal skills will create the successful career you desire.

COMMUNICATION: THE KEY TO INTERACTIONS AND RELATIONSHIPS

Foremost among all relating skills is the ability to communicate. **Communication** is defined as a complex process of mutually exchanging messages between two or more individuals which can enable them to function, learn, share, and grow. Without communication, interaction would not occur, and with positive communication, we can build rewarding relationships.

> *WHEN YOU THINK OF COMMUNICATING, WHAT BEHAVIORS DO YOU INCLUDE? LOOK AROUND YOU. IF YOU ARE IN THE PRESENCE OF ANOTHER PERSON, COMMUNICATION IS TAKING PLACE.*

What exactly transpires as we communicate? Usually, we think of speaking or talking; for some, communication is identified only with talking. "He doesn't communicate," is how a man was described. What was meant is that he rarely talks!

Talking certainly plays a key role in communication; however, equally or even of more import is listening. Nonverbal behaviors, even if nobody is talking or listening, have a critical impact. More than any other factor, communication determines the quality of interactions and relationships. Even though most people are born with the ability to speak and hear, communication skills must be learned.

Research is replete with evidence of the importance of communication. It was found to play a critical role in reducing or moderating the experience of burnout (Miller et al., 1990) and in increasing the level of trust between supervisors and their employees (*Menninger Letter*, 1994). Often in troubled personal relationships, communication is identified as the most problematic factor; conversely, it is credited as the most strengthening factor in successful relationships. Career success is virtually impossible without positive communication skills.

The difference between career success or failure is not the quality of ideas but the quality of our ability to express them (Mackay, 1993). Lack of effective communication skills presents problems. According to Richard Ross, a college dean and former senior vice-president of a savings and loan association, "Difficulties arise because of a lack of understanding between a person delivering services and either a customer or student." Poor communication takes its toll. Inadequate communication was a major source of stress for caregivers and other health-care workers (Riordan and Saltzer, 1992).

"Employers say our students possess needed technical skills. What is often lacking is the ability to communicate in a positive, clear, and effective manner."

Sheryl Piening, Management and Human Relations Instructor
Southeast Community College
Milford, Nebraska

As communication takes place, individuals are continually sending, receiving, interpreting, and reacting. Ideally, the communicators will create and share a common meaning. Unfortunately, experts believe that as much as 70 percent of our communication efforts are probably misinterpreted, misunderstood, rejected, or distorted (Donaldson and Scannell, 1986).

Because communication is so consequential, one might expect it would be formally taught; rarely is this the case. More commonly, we are left to pick it up however we can. If communication skills are left to amateur teachers who learned from other untrained people, is it any wonder that difficulties are plentiful?

CHARACTERISTICS OF A POSITIVE COMMUNICATOR

Several of the same qualities that enhance career potential are beneficial when communicating. A positive attitude and having genuine regard for others come from your own healthy self-esteem and create an environment for positive communication. Honesty in communication means authenticity, an invaluable quality in healthy exchanges. Honest communicators don't mislead or try to manipulate, and they create a climate of trust.

Openness and willingness to share about oneself are essential. A closed person who isn't willing to learn about others or who is reluctant to disclose information is a poor interpersonal communication candidate. Expressiveness of emotion enhances health and well-being, and it also helps people be better communicators. Being interested in others and appropriate self-disclosure are definite assets. A good communicator knows when and how much to share and to ask.

Flexibility is also needed. Rigid individuals aren't enjoyable to be around and are usually frustrating conversationalists. Being close-minded is detrimental to a give-and-take communication process. Opinions can be stated in flexible ways, as will be discussed later.

A sense of humor, while not a necessity, separates good communicators from outstanding ones. Having a sense of humor does not mean telling one joke after another. Instead, you see humor in life, add a witty spark to conversations, don't take yourself too seriously, and appreciate the humor of others. It's important to demonstrate sensitivity and avoid sarcasm.

Finally, being understanding and capable of making reasonable interpretations are needed in order to achieve a shared meaning. Locked-in thinking, the tendency to see things only one way, causes communication problems. Being able to see several alternatives and showing that you want to understand another's point of view contribute to an affirmative atmosphere.

You can check your communication characteristics by completing the activity in KEY STEPS (page 275).

Becoming a Positive Listener

Were you taught to listen or were you just told to listen? For most of us, we were just told; in fact, we were probably told several times! Listening is not a given. Instead, listening is an art that is learned and which can be improved.

Perhaps you actually learned some listening skills; however, for most of us, being able to hear meant that we were expected to know how to listen. Kurt Yost, executive director of a banking association, commented:

> *I spent years in school learning about history, math, and science. In my career I spend most of my time communicating, much of which is listening. How much training did I get in listening? None. If they taught it, I missed it.*

Sadly, most of us missed it because listening usually isn't taught. Of all the language arts learning experiences in our schools, listening is the most neglected.

What is involved in listening? When someone says, "I heard you," is that listening? Actually, hearing, the taking in of auditory sounds, is only a part of **listening**, which is the active process of hearing, interpreting, and then providing feedback.

> *"Listening is the most important communication skill. When you let another person know by your listening that you really want to understand, that is very flattering to him or her."*
>
> Jeanne Baer, President
> Creative Training Solutions
> Lincoln, Nebraska

REMOVING BARRIERS.   Other obstacles, along with a lack of training, can get in the way of positive listening. You can eliminate barriers after you recognize them. The most common ones are lack of interest and preoccupation. If you aren't interested in what someone else is saying, you have choices determined by the circumstances. You may force yourself to listen, you may only pretend to be listening, or you can be honest and tell the person you are not interested. Obviously, if the communication pertains to your job, you are better off listening and trying to develop an interest.

We can be preoccupied for any number of reasons, including thinking about other more pressing or interesting subjects and experiencing certain emotions or high levels of stress. A common source of preoccupation is self-imposed. Someone says, "I can listen to you while I'm doing this." It's possible to do more than one thing at a time; frequently, however, the concentration needed to listen isn't adequate. Not only is it rude to engage in another activity when listening is expected, the chances are that valuable information will be missed or misunderstood. Full attention is required if you are going to do your best listening.

The environment is full of potential barriers. Noise can interfere with conversation. Tim has frustrating conversations with a supervisor who leaves the office door open. "It's hard to concentrate because people are coming and going, the telephone is ringing, and other conversations are taking place." Distraction can also be visual or related to temperature and air flow. Listening situations deserve an environment free from diversions.

An interesting obstacle is our own psychological filter made up of pre-conceived ideas, moods, assumptions, labels, stereotypes, past experiences, degrees of self-esteem, emotions, hopes, and memories. We often let a clogged filter determine our level of listening. As selective listeners, we can hear only half or less of what is being said. For example, if you know the opinions of a co-worker, you are apt to "tune out" him or her. A major problem can occur at work if you assume that you already know what to do and don't listen carefully to directions. Just as a homeowner periodically checks a furnace filter, examining your psychological one is a good idea. You may not be able to entirely eliminate all the "dust," yet being aware and discarding whatever you can will enhance your listening abilities.

Do you know that you can listen at a faster rate than a person can talk? Figures vary; however, the average rate of speech is about 125 to 175 words a minute while the brain thinks at the rate of 500 to 1000 words a minute. Because of this, listeners are likely to mentally finish the speaker's sentence and predict what is coming. During the time difference the mind can wander, which creates a definite barrier.

The listener's intentions can be an obstacle. Without realizing it, people can listen only enough to gain an advantage. They may want to persuade individuals to adopt their ideas or to manipulate others in some way. Instead of truly listening, they are thinking and rehearsing what they will say, and they frequently interrupt in their haste. Some want to use information in harmful ways as in the case of gossip. Certainly we listen for different reasons; however, those interested in becoming positive listeners resist having negative intentions. Eliminating all barriers sets the stage for the best possible listening.

IMPROVING LISTENING BEHAVIORS.   Positive listening is assuredly active, not passive. "Bumps on logs" make terrible listeners! We can improve our listening by focusing on body position and behaviors.

> *DO YOU APPEAR TO BE LISTENING? THINK OF WHAT A GOOD LISTENER DOES.*

The way you position yourself in relation to the speaker makes a major active listening difference. A distance of one and a half to four feet is comfortable for most people. Speaking and listening at a similar eye level sets a positive tone. If one stands while the other sits, the exchange is likely to feel unequal, and the one seated is at a disadvantage. Of utmost importance is to face the speaker. Turning your body away carries a message of disinterest or disgust or both and severely lessens your involvement. Sitting so you are across from the speaker and leaning slightly forward demonstrate attentiveness.

Adopting an open, attentive posture indicates interest, openness, and involvement. Sitting with legs and arms crossed, slouching, and leaning away from the speaker give negative impressions. Instead, a positive listener sits with hands at the sides or on the lap. A slumped posture may be comfortable, yet if you are truly interested, your body usually reflects this by a generally upright posture. It's important to appear relaxed, as well. The next time you are in a classroom or another listening situation, periodically check body position. What impression are you giving?

Maintaining steady eye contact in the American society is expected. Usually, conversations don't start until eye contact is made. Employers often have negative impressions of applicants who don't "look them in the eye." Poor eye contact may be interpreted as a lack of confidence or as a sign of dishonesty. However, direct eye contact may be culturally discouraged; thus, looking down is considered a sign of respect. Often, job candidates from other countries or cultures are surprised to learn that they are expected to look directly at the other person. According to Nancy Brown, R.N., program manager in a state health department, direct eye contact is the most essential nonverbal behavior in getting a job and will make a difference throughout one's career.

How can a person develop steady eye contact? It's helpful to realize that direct eye contact does not mean staring fixedly nor does it even require looking directly into the other person's eyes. If you are within the comfortable distance zone mentioned earlier, you can focus anywhere on the face including the forehead, nose, mouth, or chin. Looking at the speaker's face for about three quarters of the time in glances lasting from one to seven seconds is sufficient. Incidentally, as a speaker, you may look at the listener about half the time and glance away more often. Even though it may sound silly, ask a family member or friend to assess your eye contact and to help you improve, if necessary. Awareness and reminders to yourself will usually lead to better eye contact.

Responsiveness is delivered to a great extent by changes in facial expression. A "poker face" is helpful in a card game, yet is generally useless and often demeaning in the communication process. A positive listener reacts to what is being said by registering appropriate thinking and feeling responses. About 20,000 different facial expressions are possible (Carl, 1980) so it won't be overly difficult to change yours! Maintaining an interested, pleasant look will enhance your standing in all encounters. Joel commented, "I know it's important to smile, but I hate the way my teeth look." He finally decided that getting his teeth fixed was worth the price he had been paying in decreased interactive skills. You can ask a family member or friend to honestly evaluate your facial expressions.

A positive listening behavior is nodding the head. An affirmative nod shows the speaker that you have heard and understood and usually that you also agree. A nod can motivate and energize a speaker so "nodders" are wonderful to have in an exchange. Even a side-to-side nod indicating confusion or disagreement is helpful if the objective is to arrive at a shared meaning. Nodding can be developed and, initially, can seem fake and mechanical, yet, after time, feel natural. It is possible to nod too much as a student on videotape discovered. "I nodded so much during the practice interview, it looked as if my head would fall off," she said as she vowed to decrease her nods by about half. Other body movements such as tilting the head to the side or shrugging the shoulders can also provide helpful feedback.

Touching is not usually thought of as a listening behavior; however, when appropriate, it can be quite effective. Research on touching indicates that the arm is a neutral or nonvulnerable area and usually acceptable. Touch can be a gesture of warmth and concern; it can also be perceived as seductive, impertinent, annoying, or degrading. Examine your reasons for touching and be sure they are positive ones. Professionals can use touch to be supportive and more effective, and in certain settings, it is quite appropriate. Counselors and therapists show concern and support while those in health-related fields are even expected to touch a patient in their job-related duties. A pat on the hand, arm, or shoulder, a squeeze, and even a hug, in proper circumstances, add a dimension to the listening process.

> *OF THE ACTIVE LISTENING BEHAVIORS IDENTIFIED SO FAR, WHICH ONES DO YOU USE?*

Generally, listening is a nonverbal activity, yet verbal responses are signs of a positive listener. These can vary from a simple word such as "oh," to a statement such as, "That's great," or "I had never heard that." Be careful that you don't overuse these as too many interrupt the speaker's flow. "Really," "I

▲ Active listening skills create a positive communication climate.

know," or "I understand" said after each of the speaker's sentences is distracting and annoying. Questions that encourage a speaker to continue or to expand are excellent responses. "What course of action did you take?" "What is the company's policy on that?" "What motivated you to pursue this career?" are examples. If you are a positive listener, your questions do not move the conversation in a different direction. Note the difference in these two exchanges.

1. SPEAKER: I'm upset because she didn't give me the day off.
   LISTENER: Did she just forget?

2. SPEAKER: I'm upset because she didn't give me the day off.
   LISTENER: Well, did you hear that she fired Joe?

When you ask questions that move the conversation in the same direction, you are telling the speaker that what is being said is of interest and you want to hear more. That's affirming!

Verbal responses can include more than short comments or questions. Restating what you thought was said in your own words is **paraphrasing**. Using such lead-ins as "It sounds like," "In other words," "You mean that," "What I hear you saying is," or "Let me make sure I understand what you mean," you don't add to the message; instead, you repeat the meaning as you understand it. For example:

SPEAKER: This job is really getting to me.

LISTENER: It sounds as if your responsibilities are really stressful.

Paraphrasing may seem clumsy, yet with practice, it becomes easier. The benefits are worth the initial discomfort. People like to be understood, and they appreciate your attempt to do so. Paraphrasing can keep anger and other emotions from escalating, can calm a stressful situation, decrease the possibility of misinterpretation, and aid in remembering what was said. In the previous dialogue, the speaker could concur that the responsibilities are stressful, state that there are difficulties with people at work, or describe exactly the reason.

Going a little further than paraphrasing is **clarifying**, which includes restating and questioning in order to get more information. "Do you mean that your responsibilities are overwhelming right now?" or "Do you feel differently now than you did a few months ago?" are examples of clarifying. You can also tell the speaker your interpretation. "It sounds as if you support the seat-belt law," or "I'm getting the impression that you are depressed" can show both interest and concern.

Feedback includes all behaviors that indicate listening. **Verbal feedback**, specifically, is responding with what you, as the listener, think, feel, or sense. The best feedback is offered in an honest, nonthreatening, and supportive way after the speaker is entirely finished. This is the time to let the speaker know how his or her words and actions have affected you, and it can be a "golden opportunity." Janet asked her supervisor if she could leave early for a dentist's appointment. The response was a brusque reply, "If you need to," which seemed to match a facial expression of annoyance. Instead of retreating, Janet clarified by asking, "Are you sure you don't mind?" The supervisor looked surprised and said, "No, why do you ask?" Janet then described the facial expression and tone of voice and was heartened to hear a chuckle and, "I probably looked and sounded annoyed because I was thinking of a meeting I don't want to attend after lunch. I'm glad you said something because I certainly don't want to give the wrong impression."

Assertiveness is helpful when it comes to clarifying and providing honest feedback. Because of the complexity of human behavior, misinterpretations are common. Such variances as tone of voice, volume, facial expression, and body position may be meaningless and still create ill will. Positive listeners are committed to cultivating clarity and shared meaning.

Knowing what not to do when listening deserves attention. Interrupting is common and especially hard to avoid for those who enjoy talking. If you know that you are guilty of jumping in before another is finished talking, make a strong effort to keep still. Certain sounds and actions are also disconcerting. Some of these include: rolling of the eyes, sighing, yawning, pulling back the corners of the mouth, and drumming of a finger on a table or desk. Any behavior that indicates disinterest, insensitivity, or disdain is rude and is to be avoided. How would you rate your listening skills? Take the inventory in KEY STEPS (page 276) and honestly grade yourself.

USING SPECIFIC TYPES OF LISTENING.   Even though all listening is active, specific types of listening are most effective in different situations. Using **receptive listening** means that you resist certain behaviors and remain quiet until the speaker is completely through. As mentioned earlier, interrupting is to be avoided. Even if you don't interrupt, be careful about the following.

◎ *Judging or putting down the speaker.* Keep critical, judgmental, and admonishing reactions to yourself.

◎ *One-upping.* Avoid jumping in with your own comment or story which is more dramatic, more interesting, better, or worse than the speaker's. One especially disturbing lead-in, used far too often, is "That's nothing." What the person has told you is *something* and is to be acknowledged as such.

◎ *Advice-giving and problem-solving.* Even though advice and solutions can be helpful, most of us respond too quickly and don't allow the person to finish. What can happen is that the entire story isn't told, or, in many cases, the speaker is denied a healthy release of emotion.

Empathic listening means awareness of the speaker's emotions to the point that the listener feels similarly. A listener uses nonverbal and verbal responses to show empathy. Saying "I know exactly what you feel" is not recommended. Telling the person that you understand the reason for the feeling or that you have a strong sense of what is being felt is more realistic. In the past empathy was not expected in the work world. Today's supervisors and employees are usually encouraged to demonstrate empathy, and the listening role affords a tremendous opportunity to do so.

More controlling than either receptive or empathic is **directive listening**, which consists of directing the exchange usually by asking questions. A good job interviewer will use directive listening to learn about job candidates. Both the speaker and the listener share the responsibility of information gathering. New employees may use this type of listening to elicit needed information and later to learn new skills and understand policies and procedures.

Different types of questions are used depending upon the circumstances, and experts have ranked them according to desirability (Miller et al., 1988). Least desirable are "why" questions. Reactions of defensiveness and tension are typical when confronted by "Why?" One woman commented, "I hate it when my supervisor comes in and invariably asks me, 'Why are you doing that?' or 'Why are you doing it that way?'" Other ways of asking about reasons are less likely to be negatively received. "How did you decide to do that?" or "What were your reasons for that choice?" are possibilities.

The most desirable type is the open question. Usually beginning with who, what, when, where, or how, it gives the other person several options. "What motivates you?" allows for more information than "Are you motivated by praise?" In a job interview, you are fortunate if open questions are asked as they provide opportunities for elaboration of what you have to offer.

Listening is of great significance in the communication process. If it is one of your strengths, you have an advantage, and it would be wise to let potential employers know of your listening skills. Throughout your career life, listening will be a significant asset.

Developing an Open Style of Verbalizing

Even though you can send a great deal of information without talking, speaking is of primary importance in the communication process. Both what is said and how it is presented deserve attention. During your entire career, others will assess you on both. The most powerful tools in this society are words, according to Harvey Mackay (1993), international speaker, author, and CEO of his own business. He contends that upgrading your communication skills is the surest way to open the door to a job or to jump start a stalled career.

Have you ever thought about the way you deliver your message? **Style** refers to how one verbalizes. Communication styles affect how the speaker comes across and usually elicit a similar type of response. The two general types are closed and open. Note the difference in the following comments.

Closed style: "This company doesn't care about the employees. Nobody is paid enough, and you never get the recognition you deserve. The managers should take a good look at the way they act around the employees before everyone just quits!"

Open style: "I don't think the company shows enough regard for the employees. As far as I'm concerned, few of us are paid the salary we deserve and seldom is recognition given when it's deserved. I think it would be a good idea for the managers to examine their behaviors around their employees and to make constructive changes before individuals decide to quit."

Essentially, the same message was delivered. Yet, reactions would likely be different. The **closed style** uses definite comments that leave little room for a reasonable response. Positive exchange is stifled because of its absoluteness, finality, forcefulness, and all-inclusive/all-exclusive language. Opinions stated as inflexible truths invariably foster a negative communication climate while the **open style** is refreshing and encourages discussion. One's point of view is stated in a flexible manner which invites a reasonable, positive response. Rather than offending or "turning others off," open communicators attract people and are more likely to develop and maintain healthy relationships.

To change the closed style to one of openness requires awareness of the three types of closed communication. Then it's a matter of following certain guidelines as you rephrase.

RECOGNIZING DOGMATIC TYPE.   Think of statements that sound "definitely definite," rigid, and inflexible. A **dogmatic** communicator sounds like a final authority and essentially expresses opinion as fact. Read the closed style example about the company not caring about its employees, and note that each of the statements is dogmatic. Incidentally, if the person had said, "This company does care about its employees," it would still be dogmatic! How a comment is stated, not its content, makes it dogmatic. Most people do not realize how definite their opinions often sound.

> *THINK OF SOME DOGMATIC STATEMENTS YOU HAVE USED OR HEARD RECENTLY.*

USING "I" STATEMENTS.   The basic technique of open communication is the use of **"I" statements**. These eliminate the dogmatic element and because a person is speaking for self, they are considered assertive language. "I" statements can be divided into two categories: actual "I" statements in which the word "I" is used within the phrase (see Table 2–1) and phrases that convey an "I" meaning (see Table 2–2). Notice that "I know" is not considered an "I" statement because if used correctly, it is fact, not opinion. Unfortunately and incorrectly, people do use it when expressing an opinion as in, "I know this company doesn't care about its employees."

TABLE   2 – 1 ▲ ACTUAL "I" STATEMENTS

I think	I like	I want
I believe	I consider	I feel
I feel that	I prefer	I am or was

Note: An opposite could be made of each by inserting don't or another appropriate word.

T A B L E   2 – 2 ▲ "I" STATEMENT PHRASES

In my opinion	In my way of thinking
As far as I'm concerned	My thoughts are
It seems to me	To me it appears/it appears to me

Actual "I" expressions or phrases that give an "I" meaning can be used at the beginning of a statement, in the middle, or even at the end. Be careful of the inflection in your voice when using an "I" statement. If you say, "*I* think" or "in *my* opinion," the value of the openness is lost.

> USE AN "I" STATEMENT TO CHANGE ANY DOGMATIC STATEMENT YOU HAVE USED OR HEARD.

RECOGNIZING COMMANDO TYPE.   A second type of closed communication is commonly used. The use of forcing, pressuring words and phrases such as "should," "have to," "must," "ought," and "need to" are typical of **commando** statements. They leave little, if any, room for alternatives. Notice the authoritarian, commanding nature of these statements.

> You should get a job.
>
> He needs to go to college.
>
> She has to apply to more places.

Consider how you generally react to forcing words especially when they are preceded by the word "you." Most of us become defensive. This type of statement can evoke unhealthy responses of defiance, resistance, or passivity. In the closed style example given earlier, the commando statement uses the word "should."

> THINK OF A COMMANDO STATEMENT YOU OR SOMEONE YOU KNOW HAS USED.

BEING TENTATIVE AND FLEXIBLE.   In order to avoid commando statements, the forcing word or phrase is eliminated, and the statement is reworded with a tentative phrase (see Table 2–3). Also, when giving an opinion, using an "I" statement is recommended.

In most cases, an "I" statement would precede the tentative phrase. Following are changes in the commando statements used earlier as examples.

> I think it would be to your benefit to get a job.
>
> It seems to me a good idea for him to go to college.
>
> I believe that it's wise for her to apply more places.

T A B L E   2 – 3 ▲ TENTATIVE PHRASES

It would be a good idea if...
He or she, they, or you could benefit from...
It could be helpful to...
You might want to consider...
It would be wise...

The same point can be made less demandingly and, importantly, in a manner that offers the other person a benefit.

RECOGNIZING GRANDIOSE TYPE.   The third type can be fun to identify. **Grandiose** statements can be exaggerated, all-inclusive or all-exclusive, and dramatic. Facts are typically distorted. Following are examples of grandiose words and statements.

everyone–no one

everybody–nobody

all–none

always–never

everything–nothing–anything

only

every

The *only* way to learn about computers is to take a class.

She's *always* late.

Nobody is paid enough.

You *never* get the recognition you deserve.

The last two statements are taken from the closed example about the uncaring company at the beginning of this section.

Grandiose statements are almost always inaccurate. For example, even though it may seem true to say, "*Every* time I wash my car, it rains," it probably isn't. However, if the grandiose word is accurate, you may use it. Perhaps it has actually rained every time! Incidentally, the next time you are tempted to say, "There was *no* way I could get to class or to work," hopefully, someone will remind you that there probably was a way. Awareness of grandiose use is the first step in improvement. Then you can make use of accurate words.

DO YOU RECALL YOUR USE OF ANY GRANDIOSE WORDS? WERE THEY USED ACCURATELY?

ADDING OR REPLACING WITH QUALIFIERS.   In order to be truthful, replace or modify the grandiose word with a qualifier (see Table 2–4).

TABLE 2–4 ▲ QUALIFIERS

almost	rarely	infrequently	frequently
nearly	often	hardly ever	some
many	most	several	quite a few
few	seldom	possibly	sometimes
usually	generally	probably	in general

If an opinion is being offered, an "I" statement is advisable. Following are the rewordings of the grandiose statements that were given as examples.

I think that a good way to learn about computers is to take a class.

It seems to me that she's usually late.

In my opinion, most employees here aren't paid enough.

I believe you rarely get the recognition you deserve.

Many times a statement will contain all three types. "Everybody should work awhile before going to college" is dogmatic because it expresses opinion as fact, the "should" indicates commando, and "everybody" is grandiose. A better way to get your point across and not change the meaning to any great extent is to say, "I think that it would be a good idea for most people to work awhile before going to college."

Open communication is worth the time and effort (a dogmatic statement, by the way; however, these are permitted in textbooks). To become an open communicator, carefully listen to yourself, then reword mentally and aloud any closed statements. After practice, open communication becomes natural. The activity in KEY STEPS (page 277) is good practice. As you pursue your career path, open communication will open doors of opportunity.

▲ Closed communication indicates a closed mind.

INCREASING YOUR VERBAL EFFECTIVENESS.

In addition to using an open style, you can improve your speaking by expressing yourself effectively. Old patterns can be discarded as you practice new ways of getting a message across. Being direct and straightforward by speaking in an assertive way instills trust. Using veiled statements or sarcasm shows your lack of communication skills. Also, effective communicators do not ask a question when a statement or request is more candid. "Why are you making so much noise?" is better replaced with "I would appreciate it if you would make less noise."

Ineffectiveness often results in confusion. Clarity comes from selecting your words carefully and being specific about what you think and want. The ability to verbalize in behavioral terms prevents misinterpretation or confusion problems. For example, you may say, "I want you to respect me." What does *respect* mean in behavioral terms? How do you and the other person know when respect is being demonstrated if you don't specifically describe it? Many words are ambiguous and have several meanings. Employers in many fields want their employees to be articulate and able to explain their procedures to customers, clients, or patients. Effective communicators attempt to be clear and precise when they want to make a point.

> *"Firefighting is a communicative profession. Being able to get your message across is a definite asset."*
>
> Mark Munger, Captain
> Lincoln Fire Department
> Lincoln, Nebraska

Effectiveness is decreased by hurting another person or appearing superior to others. Instead, you can be a supportive communicator by avoiding derogatory labels, sarcasm, unnecessary comparisons of two or more people, judgmental comments, and threats. Effective communicators are not out to prove points or win; instead, they want to be encouraging and promote understanding and good will.

Effective communication is also hindered by meandering, giving too much detail, and overusing of fillers. Making one's point efficiently is often the best course. Notice the distraction in the following.

> *Well, you know—I go to college—you know—and—uh—it's been a good experience—you know. Uh, I've really—like—you know—learned a lot— you know—and think I—uh—well—basically—you know—would be a good employee.*

From the playground to corporation conference rooms in all walks of life, the phrase *you know* is heard. *Uh, well, like,* and *basically* are also common. A **filler** is a word, phrase, or sound used for no other reason than to replace silence.

Actually, any word or phrase used repeatedly can be annoying. "I'm going skiing this weekend," she says. "COOL!" is the reply. "My significant other is going, too," she adds. "COOL!" is heard. "We may be able to stay in my uncle's condo there." "COOL!" again is the reply. Keep in mind that too many "COOLS" may cool the conversation! Another bothersome insertion of a word involves unnecessary qualifying words such as "kind of" often spoken as "kinda." Sandra was explaining her reasons for not handing in an assignment.

> *I kinda got involved in another project which took a lot of thought. So I kinda lost track of time. I want to make up the work if I can cause I'm kinda interested in making psychology my career.*

Is it any wonder that it was difficult to take seriously what she was saying?

Being descriptive can enhance conversations. However, too much unnecessary detail is inefficient and likely to bore a listener. In a job interview, Kate was asked about a past job. Ten minutes later she was still describing every specific duty and how she had learned to do each one. It was no surprise when the interviewer yawned. Effective communication takes thought and practice. The rewards are plentiful, and you will certainly have grateful listeners!

MONITORING THE CONTENT OF A MESSAGE

Spoken or written words and sentences make up **content**. Considering all your comments and conversations, think of all the topics you cover during the day. Even though some of these lack depth, to talk with others is a significant part of life. The words that come out of your mouth indicate who you are and what you are all about. This section can help you in providing information and in responding to others' comments.

BECOMING AWARE OF CONTENT.   The words we use reveal a great deal about our attitudes and personalities and directly influence others' impressions of us. A positive communicator is authentic and sensitive and wants to avoid potential pitfalls. Specific areas of difficulty follow.

Semantics, the meaning of words, is a challenging area that includes vocabulary, dialect, and specific word images. Building your vocabulary can prevent some embarrassing situations. Also, you can help others by being sensitive to the challenges of anyone who is learning English as a second language. In a career development class, a Vietnamese man looked disturbed when the instructor told the students how important it was to sell themselves to a potential employer. Later he said, "Selling myself is bad." His confusion was understandable. The many slang terms and multiple meanings of words and phrases can be baffling.

Within the same language, **dialect**, any speech that differs from the standard, can be confusing. If you have traveled, you have probably encountered differences in dialect. For those from the Midwest, it's hard to believe that not all Americans call soft drinks "pop." As long as the differences don't result in misunderstandings, they can be fun and interesting. Helpful in getting along with others is avoiding the assumption that your way of speaking is the right way. An American tourist was asked, "When you were in England, could you understand them? They just don't speak the 'right' English." The person was reminded that their English is the original!

Probably the most common source of confusion and misconception is each individual's image of the meaning of a word. The mental representations you have of words such as *trust* and *loyalty* may be quite different from those of someone else. "He isn't trustworthy," says a co-worker. What exactly does that mean? It's helpful if people use concrete examples for abstract terms and then paraphrase and clarify to ensure a common meaning.

> *WHAT DOES* HONEST *MEAN TO YOU? ASK A FEW OTHERS AND SEE IF THE IMAGES ARE THE SAME OR DIFFERENT.*

One of the surest ways to sabotage your chances for career success is to use language that indicates prejudice, bias, insensitivity, or lack of knowledge. Whether in a job interview or after employment, anyone who consciously or unconsciously demeans others is likely to suffer. Certain derogatory labels are usually known and can be avoided. What may be more challenging is to recognize more subtle ones. Some of these are calling adult women "girls" or "gals" and using "colored" to refer to any race.

Demonstrating an attitude of gender equality means that you use inclusive language instead of the masculine-dominated speech of the past. For example, *chairman* is more appropriately *chairperson* or *chair*, *fireman* is now *firefighter*, and *policeman* is *police officer*. Use of male pronouns to denote either sex and salutations that begin "Dear Sir," are no longer in vogue. Fair-minded men realize that they wouldn't like it if language reflected female dominance and are committed to the elimination of outdated sexist expressions.

A difficulty in sensitivity is that bias-free language changes and individuals may have their own preferred terms. Whether to use *African-American* or *Black*, *Anglo-American* or *White*, *Native American* or *American Indian* can be puzzling. Likewise, you may not know what title to use or whether to use a title at all. Is it Mrs. Smith, Ms. Smith, Dr. Smith, or just Mary? The wisest choice is to keep up with what is acceptable and then, if in doubt, to ask a person what she or he prefers.

Finally, an awareness of content can help you avoid emotion-packed lead-in phrases such as "When I was your age," "After you've worked here as long I have," and "Let me tell you," as well as checking your use of slang, vulgarity, and grammar. A common slang term often used in a job interview that sounds extremely unprofessional is *guys* as in "What do you 'guys' manufacture?" Another unprofessional word is *yeah* instead of *yes*. Many people are offended by vulgarity as well as by certain slang terms. Profanity becomes a definite habit, and you may find it difficult to control in professional situations. Errors in grammar can also be embarrassing and detrimental. "It don't make no difference," he said and found that it made all the difference in the world. He didn't get hired!

Effective communication goes hand in hand with the ability to speak and write a language correctly. Awareness is necessary; if your skills are lacking, do yourself a favor and take a basic course or use self-study resources to improve.

IDENTIFYING AND USING LEVELS OF CONTENT.   What we talk about can be categorized into levels related to depth. After you've read about these, check your understanding in KEY STEPS (page 278).

- *Superficial*. This is made up of conventional comments such as "How are you?" "Isn't the weather great?" and "Have a nice day." Much of our everyday conversation consists of this chit-chat. It's safe and easy, and life would be dreary without it.

- *Basic data*. We often tell facts about ourselves and about others. "I'm an instructor," "I'm married," "I was born in Alabama," are examples of self-disclosure; this is a safe and easy level. "She's the manager," "Mary is getting married next month," "Tom's birthday was yesterday" are factual pieces of information about others. As long as they're not gossip or rumors, these are welcome additions to conversations.

- *Preferences*. We also talk about what we like, don't like, and what we enjoy. "I like to use the computer," "I would rather read than watch television," "I don't enjoy spicy food" are self-disclosing examples. We can also tell about other people's preferences. "She doesn't like violent movies," "Mark would rather write his own reports" are preference statements. These, too, are fairly easy to use in conversations.

- *Ideas and beliefs*. Depending upon the situation and our own personalities, it can be more difficult to converse at this level. In the work environment, new ideas are often welcomed; however, it may be considered inappropriate to discuss certain personal beliefs. When people use "I" statements and make it clear that they are not trying to impose their beliefs on others, this level can be interesting and stimulating. Certainly in your personal relationships, discussing your opinions in nonthreatening ways is positive.

- *Feelings or emotions*. For many people, this is a challenging level. In general, we have probably been told to keep feelings to ourselves. Few of us have had positive experiences revealing emotions, especially ones of fear, anger, sadness, or disappointment. Because there are several benefits related to emotional expression (Hanna, 1995), learning to reveal, when appropriate, is in your best interests. "I'm concerned because you seem depressed," "I was disappointed when you didn't follow through on that project," "It was upsetting to me when she criticized her supervisor" are "I" statements of feeling that can be quite useful. Being able to share your emotions with others may not only relieve stress; it also can serve to enhance relationships.

> *THINK OF EXAMPLES OF YOUR USE OF CONTENT ON EACH OF THE LEVELS OF CONTENT. IF ONE LEVEL HASN'T BEEN USED, WHAT IS THE REASON?*

Content from a particular level is best used in appropriate situations and in reasonable amounts. People who discuss only superficial topics or who converse on the deepest levels with mere acquaintances aren't effective communicators. Your career journey will be much smoother if you are aware of content levels and use them to enrich your conversations.

VERBALIZING ABOUT ISSUES

When individuals agree, it's easy to discuss an issue. What if they don't agree or if clarification is needed? Learning about dimensions of awareness (Miller et al., 1988) and then verbalizing each of these to others are effective in discussions about issues. The five dimensions follow.

- **Sensation** is input we receive through our senses (what we see, hear, smell, taste, and touch). Inaccuracies may occur so it's important to explain what our input has been. Typically, sensation either is not verbalized at all or is poorly described.

- **Thought** is the meaning, interpretation, or conclusion from the sensory input. Thoughts are subjective rather than objective truths. Interpretations are not "the way things are." They are the way you make sense out of your input, and even though it's real for you, others who have the same input may come to very different conclusions. Too often, people give only their interpretation of a situation or issue and, to make matters worse, begin their statement with "you."

- **Feeling** is an emotional response. An emotion is neither right nor wrong; it just exists. Being able to connect with your feelings and then in many situations to describe them can be quite useful.

- **Want** is a desire or wish for yourself, for others, and for your relationship together. To agree on a common want is an invaluable step toward resolution.

- **Action** is behavior in the past, present, and future. To describe action is to tell what you have done, are doing, or will do about the issue. It demonstrates a commitment.

When you privately identify each of the five dimensions, you realize what the issue means to you. Then, it's a matter of picking an appropriate time and, with the use of "I" statements, telling the other person about each dimension. For example, your supervisor has criticized you for not completing your work in a timely manner. You could say:

(sensation)   *Yesterday you told me I wasn't being productive, and today you said, "If you can't keep up with the work around here, I'll find someone who will!"*

(thought)	*It seems to me that you are not at all satisfied with my ability to do the work.*
(feeling)	*I'm concerned about this.*
(want)	*I want to keep the job, and I definitely want to be productive so I'm hoping to clarify things.*
(action)	*I've rearranged my work schedule and would like for you to share with me any ideas of how you think I can be even more productive.*

You can begin with any dimension and word each in a way that is comfortable for you, as long as you remember to use "I" statements. For example, you could say

I'm concerned because it seems to me you are not satisfied with my ability to do the work. Yesterday and today the two comments you made about my lack of productivity and possibly finding someone who can do the job prompted me to rearrange my work schedule. I do want to keep this job and certainly want to do it well, and I'd like you to give me some ideas of how you think I can be even more productive.

THINK OF THE LAST TIME YOU DISCUSSED AN ISSUE. WHAT INFORMATION WAS RELAYED AND, MOST IMPORTANTLY, WHAT WAS LEFT UNSAID?

If you're thinking that this is too time-consuming and involved, consider how worthwhile clear communication and a positive communication climate are to you. A major problem in the process of communicating is our tendency to relay partial information and leave the person guessing about the rest. For example, in the previous scenario, an employee might say, "You're not satisfied with my work," which may be true but is quite incomplete. Check your skills in the KEY STEPS activity (page 279). Verbalizing dimensions of awareness is not necessary in every situation; however, in discussions of issues, a positive outcome is likely.

"Having excellent communication skills that indicate you are a 'people person' is essential for career success."

Sue Collins, Director
KinderCare Learning Center
Lincoln, Nebraska

UNDERSTANDING PARALANGUAGE AND BODY LANGUAGE

The meaning of a message is greatly influenced by other factors in addition to verbalizing styles and content. About 93 percent of an expression is conveyed by vocal changes and nonverbal behaviors (Mehrabian, 1968; 1981).

USING PARALANGUAGE.   Of utmost importance is **paralanguage**, which refers to the variations in the voice, not the words themselves. Meanings can be changed or enriched in a number of ways. One way is to vary the rhythm or accent a part of a word. "*I think*" or "*I believe*" destroys the openness of an "I" statement. Similarly, inflection, which is a change in pitch, can convey sarcasm or negativity as in "You did *that*?" Inflection can also change a statement into a question. "You like your job" can become "You like your job?" Robert Frost, the well-known poet, said, "There are tones of voice that mean more than words."

> *SAY, "OH, SHE'S REALLY LISTENING." DID YOU EMPHASIZE REALLY? WOULD YOU AGREE THAT IT SOUNDED SARCASTIC?*

Volume and speed are also a part of paralanguage. Consider the different impressions you have of people who talk too loudly versus those who speak quite softly. Meaning can be altered just by changing degrees of volume. The rate of speaking makes a difference in the degree of understanding as well as the interest level of the listener. People who talk too fast are often misunderstood or they overwhelm a listener while slow talkers can easily put people to sleep or be quite frustrating. Practice using a well-modulated voice at a moderate speed and then introduce appropriate variances.

Articulation or distinct pronunciation is critical. When a person either mumbles or doesn't enunciate properly, a listener is apt to be confused and annoyed. Over-articulating can give an unfavorable impression. Without intending to do so, you may be using an insensitive blend of loud volume and over-enunciation, especially when you speak to an older person. A receptionist who was guilty of this was reprimanded by a 70-year-old woman who said, "I am quite capable of understanding you and would like to be talked to in exactly the same way as the last person."

Listening to yourself and even hearing a recording of you in conversation are helpful. You may be expressing more or less than you think and conveying far different meanings than you realize.

IMPROVING BODY LANGUAGE.   Our nonverbal behaviors and demeanor known as **body language** probably account for more than half the meaning of a message being verbalized. Even by itself, body language relays a powerful message. Misinterpretations are bound to occur; yet, you can improve your communication skills by paying attention to the message your body is sending and working hard to communicate the one you want to give.

Presentation of self is an attempt to present to others what and how we want to be seen (Goffman, 1959), and much of this is accomplished through body language and dress. Jason came to an interview in a nice-looking, dark-gray suit, crisp-looking white shirt, and a fashionable tie. From his polished shoes to his neatly combed hair, he looked the part of a professional. He smiled confidently, looked directly at the interviewer, and responded to the outstretched hand with a firm handshake. He was off to an excellent start before he even said a word!

Personality traits are often assigned to us based on our body language. Just by watching a person's body language, you may think that he or she is aggressive, shy, poised, confident, open, closed, or cocky.

> *Ask someone how he or she would have described your personality before the two of you ever talked. Are you surprised?*

Three areas of body language can be monitored and analyzed. **Body movement** occurs when any part of the body is changed. Variations in facial expression, eye contact, nodding, and touching were discussed in the section on listening.

A common movement of the body associated with speaking is done with the hands and arms. Gestures can add to or detract from a message. If you have taken a speech class, you learned the importance of gestures and, hopefully, an appropriate use of them. Interviewers have commented that a stiff, nongesturing applicant is not impressive; however, they realize that gestures can be overdone. "By the time she finished flailing her arms and hands around, I was almost dizzy. I hardly remembered what she said," commented an interviewer. A moderate and appropriate use of hand and arm movements is recommended.

Certain gestures are likely to elicit a negative reaction. A common one is an index finger pointed at another, usually in an effort to accentuate a point. "Pointers" may not realize that this gesture is likely to negate whatever point they are trying to make. Are you aware that arm and hand movements carry different meanings from one society to another? If you plan to travel to or do business with people from other cultures, take the time to learn their meaning of common gestures.

▲ Body language tells its own story.

Body position is the second element of body language. Position or posture is how you sit or stand. You can reflect attitudes of agreement, disagreement, interest, boredom, respect, affection, dominance, subordination, passivity, openness, or closed-mindedness. The student or employee who may be interested, yet appears bored, is likely to be characterized in an unfavorable way.

Of extreme importance is the impression you give of openness. Without intending to do so, people can look closed by sitting or standing with folded arms. In professional situations, as well in most personal conversations, you look open when you don't cross your arms, have your feet on the floor (standing or sitting), look squarely at the person, and have a comfortable, yet erect, posture.

> *CONSIDERING JUST BODY LANGUAGE, WHAT IMPRESSION ARE YOU GIVING RIGHT NOW?*

A final aspect of position has to do with eye level. Try sitting and carrying on a serious conversation with a person who is standing. After a while, it usually begins to feel strange. "I don't like it at all," said one person. "I felt as if I was being 'looked down on,' which I guess I was!" Unless there is a reason to be in a different position, a tone of equality is set when two people are on a similar level.

Have you ever heard about invasion of personal space? The third area of body language has to do with **spatial relationships**, the distance between two or more people. Individuals vary in their personal-space preferences; yet, for the most part, you can follow those identified by Hall (1969).

Intimate (actually touching—1 1/2 feet apart)

Personal (1 1/2 feet to 4 feet apart)

Social (4 feet to 12 feet apart)

Public (12 feet or more apart)

For most conversations, the personal zone is appropriate. In formal or business situations, the social zone may be more comfortable. Keep in mind that you can position yourself too close and appear intimidating (or just annoying), or you can distance yourself from another person and appear cold and aloof.

If you are surprised about how much is involved in communication, you are not alone. A person remarked, "I never thought about how I appeared to others in terms of body language. I might have worried about how I looked, then I forgot all the rest. Amazing!" Not only is body language amazing, but it can spell the difference between success and failure in many interactions.

To help you evaluate both verbal and nonverbal behaviors, videotape can be used. As students in a career development class watch themselves during a "mock" job interview, the reactions are predictable: "Do I really look like that?" "I didn't know I did that!" "I'm going to have to sit on my hands." "I sure looked a lot more confident than I felt." If you have an opportunity to see and hear yourself as others see and hear you, take advantage of a special learning experience. The activity in KEY STEPS (page 280) is also useful.

Communication is much more involved than most people think. Because so little formal instruction is offered, it is up to individuals to examine their own verbal and nonverbal behaviors and to set out to develop or improve the skills they have. Since no other ability will probably play such a critical part in your career success, be sure to give communication the attention it deserves.

KEY POINTS

- Relating positively with others begins with an attitude of open-mindedness. Even though first impressions are important, you are wise to reserve judgment.

- Appreciation for both similarities and diversity and a commitment to rid oneself of stereotypic beliefs and prejudice are vital to career success.

- Forsaking aggression and passivity and developing assertiveness skills help build self-esteem. When you use assertive behavior, you gain the respect of others and present yourself as a person of value.

- Communication, a complex process of mutually exchanging messages, is the key to positive relationships.

- Positive communication skills can be learned.

- One of the most critical requirements in the work world is the ability to listen.

- Becoming a positive listener includes eliminating barriers, improving active listening skills, and using the appropriate type of listening.

- Using an open style of verbalizing fosters a positive communication climate, while being effective helps to ensure a clearly understood shared meaning.

- Paying attention to certain elements of content such as semantics and bias-free language is a characteristic of a positive communicator.

- To become an interesting conversationalist and to build relationships, you can use different levels of content.

- Verbalizing five dimensions of awareness is beneficial in clarifying and resolving issues.

- Paralanguage and body language make up a large portion of the meaning of a message and deserve attention.

- Career success is directly related to positive interactions which require interpersonal communication skills.

RECOMMENDED READING

Alberti, R. and Emmons, M. (1975). *Stand up, speak up, talk back*. New York: Pocket Books.

Alberti, R. and Emmons, M. (1995). *Your perfect right: A guide to assertive living*. San Luis Obispo: Impact.

Butler, P. E. (1992). *Self-assertion for women*. New York: Harper Collins.

Deep, S. and Sussman, L. (1993). *What to ask when you don't know what to say: 555 powerful questions for getting your way at work*. Englewood Cliffs, NJ: Prentice Hall.

Hanna, S. L. (1995). *Person to person: Positive relationships don't just happen*. Englewood Cliffs, NJ: Prentice Hall.

Miller, S., Miller P. A., Nunnally, E. W. and Wackman, D. (1991). *Talking and listening together*. Littleton, CO: Interpersonal Communication Programs.

Smith, M. (1985). *When I say no, I feel guilty*. Toronto: Bantam Books.

CHAPTER THREE

Getting What You Want

Adults are commonly asked, "What do you do?" Most respond with a job title or an answer that indicates occupation. Our self-identities are invariably connected to our choices in careers and jobs.

> *WERE YOU EVER ASKED, "WHAT DO YOU WANT TO BE WHEN YOU GROW UP?" WHAT WAS YOUR RESPONSE?*

When you consider how much time people spend pursuing their careers and actually working, it's not surprising that so much of what individuals think they are is related to work. The 40-hour week, which used to amount to about 10,000 days of our lives, has expanded for most people. A 1996 poll by Louis Harris and Associates revealed that the average American is working 15 to 20 percent more than 20 years ago and has anywhere from 32 to 37 percent less leisure time (*Lincoln Journal-Star, 1996*). The work world has been described as "leaner and meaner," and those who hold jobs are expected to work longer hours. For many, this also means taking work home. It is no wonder that much of life's satisfaction stems from our work.

SEEKING CAREER AND JOB SATISFACTION

Because careers are so significant and the relationship between job satisfaction and personal well-being is well documented, it's imperative that you carefully select a career and then exert the necessary effort to design a satisfying occupational path. A survey indicates that this attention has paid off. Sixty-one percent of people under 30 said they were pleased with their jobs and optimistic about the future (Reinemer, 1995). Earlier studies weren't so positive. In 1991 only 18 percent of workers said they enjoyed their hours on the job more than time off (Braus, 1992). A Gallup Poll found that while 89 percent expressed some level of satisfaction with their work, only 28 percent were completely satisfied. Half the respondents said that if they were starting out and could choose their life's work over again, they would choose a different line of work (Kalb and Hugick, 1990).

To avoid being among the group of discontents and help increase the satisfied numbers, you can take steps to determine what is right for you. Knowing the difference between career and job is useful. Whether you have decided upon a career field, you probably have had a **job** which consists of tasks, duties, and responsibilities that one does on a regular basis. A **career** is a category of possibilities, a field of endeavor. Within a career you may have any number of different jobs.

When you think about satisfaction, consider career and job separately. Giving serious thought to career choice comes first. In the past, this was often overlooked. For example, Jack became an electrician because his father had been one, and he was expected to take over the family business. Sue decided to be a secretary because a technical school was located in her home town, and she didn't have other aspirations. Charles wanted to remain in his home town so he took a job in a bank and made that his career. My father started with a job in a retail business while he was in high school, then ended up having his own store and staying in the same business all his career life.

While it seems that people are giving more thought to what will be satisfying, some still limit themselves. Females especially are apt to adjust their career aspirations to a male's life. One young woman said, "I always wanted to be a doctor. However, my boyfriend who is in college wants me to get through a two-year college and get a job so I've decided to be a medical assistant." Some men have their own set of challenges. The pressure to be financially successful may lead to career and job choices that aren't satisfying. Also, men, more than women, feel compelled to take over family businesses or farming enterprises even if they don't want to do so.

Simple geography, coupled with fear, can be a hindrance. How many people do you know who have no desire to even explore living anywhere other than where they were born and raised? If you limit where you will live, you limit your career opportunities. Fear is often the cause. Sherri was born and raised in the Midwest and experienced apprehension when her husband wanted to take a job in the East. He persevered and convinced her to move to New Jersey, within a half-hour commute of Manhattan. It proved to be a wonderful experience which she would have missed because of fear.

Not only are there possibilities throughout the United States, you can even think of international opportunities. One suggestion is to contact companies who have branches in other countries and find out if they can offer you any opportunities. You can find executive search firms and other agencies that specialize in worldwide placements as well as consult international employment listings in large-circulation newspapers, both national and foreign. Specialty publications such as *The International Employment Hotline* and *Transitions Abroad*, which cater to entry-level work, have hundreds of listings. The book *What Color Is Your Parachute?* (Bolles, 1996) has an excellent section on overseas possibilities. Any large library is a source of valuable information.

If you're fortunate, you could have an easy way to see if living and working in another country is for you. Susan jumped at the opportunity to participate in a yearlong position exchange with another employee of the same advertising firm. She went to Madrid, and her counterpart came to Chicago.

At least, explore other possibilities. In the public library you can find newspapers from major cities, and state and local governments will be happy to send you information. You can also write or telephone the chamber of commerce in any city. If possible, spend some time in the possible relocation area finding out whether you like the climate and the social opportunities. Learn about housing possibilities and costs, tax rates, health care, educational opportunities, transportation, cultural and recreational facilities and activities, and anything that could make a difference in satisfaction. After amassing all the data, you may decide to stay where you are or to seek new horizons.

Even though there are hundreds of occupational fields, many people lack awareness of them, which restricts their choices. Even within one career field, the numbers of different jobs are high. For example, the Occupational Profiles Database, updated regularly by the federal government, contains profiles of approximately 250 of the most popular occupations. Within those career fields are about 107 million jobs. Libraries have several directories of both careers and jobs. See the partial list at the end of this chapter. An excellent resource is *The Career Connection for College Education* (Rowe, 1994), which gives information on more than 100 college majors and 1,000 related occupations. However you make a selection, vow not to limit yourself only to occupations of which you are now aware.

As you are thinking about choices, try not to be pressured or to put limits on your possibilities. Also, keep in mind that career changes are certainly

> *"Think of hundreds of trees when you consider a career and then consider the vast numbers of branches as jobs. You may be much happier on one branch than another. Expand your horizons."*
>
> Susan Brown, Account Executive
> J. Walter Thompson Advertising
> Chicago, Illinois

possible and, in fact, are quite common today. Knowing yourself is essential. If you aren't sure who you are, you are likely to choose a career that isn't for you. Several aspects of self are involved. Think of this critical step of career development as putting together a jigsaw puzzle. Each piece makes a contribution.

MATCHING YOURSELF TO A CAREER

If you were asked, "What do you want to be?" what type of answer would you give? Most of us would give a title such as teacher, accountant, journalist, or automotive technician. In some cases, this provides information about career expectations; however, it doesn't necessarily spell out exactly what one actually does. When I was in high school, I wanted to be a nurse until a friend of mine reminded me that most of the duties of a nurse were not to my liking! Asking the more revealing question, "What do I want to *do*?" is an excellent step in selecting a career that can be satisfying. Being able to do what you enjoy creates a stimulating work experience. Keep in mind that it's unlikely that all your career responsibilities will be enjoyable; yet, if a high percentage of those 10,000 days are filled with enjoyable tasks, you'll look forward to your time at work.

> *WHAT ARE YOUR INTERESTS? DO YOU HAVE ANY PASSIONS? MAKE A LIST OF YOUR FAVORITE SUBJECTS, ANYTHING IN WHICH YOU HAVE A SPECIAL INTEREST. IN OTHER WORDS, "WHAT TURNS YOU ON?"*

A student said that he had not yet made a career decision; when asked about absorbing subjects, he replied, "Classic cars and airplanes." On his list of things he enjoyed doing were writing and traveling. He decided to research careers that could combine his passion and what he loved to do. An activity in KEY STEPS (page 281) can enlighten you.

Instead of interests, a number of students have in mind only a dollar sign. While money is necessary, you're much better off focusing on more than just wages. Dave Sonenberg, a director of career counseling, says that too often the first and only question a student will ask when told of a job is, "How much does it pay?" He challenges students with a scenario.

> *If I offer you $25 an hour to pick up litter around the campus, most of you could do it; you would all have the ability. My bet is that most of you would not do it for a long period of time. Why? The interest isn't there, and earning money won't motivate most of you beyond the "really bored" stage.*

Other factors deserve your attention. Values and what is meaningful will also make a difference in career satisfaction. If you put a high premium on money or on what it can buy, you will not be satisfied in low-paying professions no matter how much you like the work. If a high income matters a great deal, a good idea is to seek current information on career rankings by median annual earning, growth rate, job security, prestige rating, location of available jobs, and stress and strain level. In 1994 the top position was a computer analyst (Gilbert, 1994).

Having a strong moral code would make it difficult to work in certain career fields that would challenge your sense of ethics. Is prestige of high value? Sociologists have ranked careers on a prestige scale, and if this is of importance to you, acquainting yourself with the higher status career fields is recommended. If you value upward mobility, certain career fields offer more. How important is leisure and family time? Some careers afford less of this than others. If you feel strongly about a certain cause such as the environment, working in that field is likely to be meaningful.

Your self-esteem level indicates how highly you value yourself. Having a genuine regard for one's self is beneficial in all aspects of life and is well worth strengthening and bolstering. When you consider a career field, ask yourself whether your sense of self will be enhanced. One of the reasons Tim changed careers was because his average record in a high-powered sales career was diminishing his self-worth. "I decided to go into elementary teaching which doesn't pay nearly as much but is so much more rewarding to me. My self-esteem is strengthened several times a week."

RANK THE FOLLOWING VALUES IN THE ORDER OF IMPORTANCE FOR YOU.

income	moral code/ethics	prestige	advancement
self	meaningful causes	health	service to others
security	accomplishment	power	family/balance

HOW MANY ARE POSSIBLE WITHIN YOUR CURRENT CAREER CHOICE?

Related to values are work orientations (Derr, 1986). Check the following to see which are personally significant.

- Having *upward mobility* means you want a career field where you can advance and move "up the ladder."
- Being *secure* is a feeling that your job will last.
- Being *free* is a desire for independence and the flexibility to "do your own thing" at work.
- Being *high* is a feeling of excitement and challenge in a career field where risks are desirable.
- Being *balanced* is harmony between personal and professional life and adequate leisure time.

The last orientation is a significant one for most people today. Based on polls and interviews with 1,000 managers, MC Associates in Philadelphia found that a lack of balance between work and personal life was one of the top six reasons new managers fail (Shellenbarger, 1996). Feeling that your life is out of balance is a factor in poor job performance. Even though jobs within a career field can offer more or less of each of the work orientations, knowing what you want before selecting a career is advisable.

"Knowing that I am really making a difference in helping people improve their lives by improving their health satisfies my need to feel that my work has a deeper purpose."

Lori Hall, Director of Education and Community Programs
American Heart Association
Southfield, Michigan

Personality type plays an instrumental role in a satisfying career. The Myers-Briggs Type Indicator reveals preferences that apply to career choices. For example, someone with an intuitive (N) preference will be much more satisfied in a career field that offers variety and opportunities to use creative ideas. The person with a sensing (S) preference enjoys working with facts, figures, and details, which lends itself to particular careers.

One preference can provide some insight; yet, it is the combination of the four preferences, what is called type, that is most enlightening. Ryan Turner, Harvard Business School in Boston, described characteristics of combined MBTI preferences necessary to prosper in the financial world. "To succeed, a person must be well-organized, responsible, good at time management, detailed-oriented, and assertive. He or she also has to have excellent communication skills, a high level of professionalism, and be able to manage expectations for self and others," he says. Knowing what personality characteristics you possess and which are needed in career fields will help you make a successful match. For a particularly insightful understanding of personality type as it relates to careers, read *Do What You Are* (Tieger and Barron-Tieger, 1995). The authors devote a chapter to each of the 16 personality types for a thorough look of what would be satisfying and why, as well as a description of each type's strengths and weaknesses on the job. Finding out my type and then reading satisfying career choices confirmed what I already knew: I love teaching!

Your emotions are an integral part of the self and play a major role in career satisfaction. As indicated in the MBTI personality typing, a number of individuals prefer to make decisions based on feelings. While this can be advantageous in certain situations, it creates stress in administrative decisions, especially those involved with hiring and firing. And even though empathy is a desirable trait, those who are overly empathetic usually agonize over everyone's problems. Because Beth was very caring and had a clear feeling preference, she thought counseling was the best career choice. Her adviser pointed out some potential problems. Could she leave her client's problems at work or would she carry them with her everywhere? Would she be so empathetic that she would forgo logical suggestions? Similarly, sales careers require people to accept "no" without taking it as a personal rejection, which requires use of the thinking preference. You are able to shift to the weaker preference when appropriate; yet, some people find that extremely difficult.

Related to emotionality is your ability to withstand pressure. Constant deadlines may not fit your personality. Similarly, high levels of stress are "part of the territory" in some career fields. Individuals vary considerably in their coping styles. For example, Jon was a laid-back individual who didn't like pressure and externally imposed deadlines. His first job in a busy printing company was an invaluable learning experience. He developed stress-related migraine headaches and ulcers before he realized that he didn't want to cope with the high-speed world of printing technology.

How much pressure can you stand? Does your "pressure point" fit with your chosen career field?

Obviously, an important consideration in satisfaction is matching your skills and abilities to a career. Even if you enjoy doing something and it matches your values and personality, if you are not adept in this field, you are likely to dislike it. Chris said he enjoyed writing and felt he had good ideas to offer. His personality type indicated that he would fit well into journalism. However, his writing was stilted, uninteresting, and full of errors. He could possibly improve his skills with effort; lacking that, career satisfaction would be unlikely. A computerized assessment program called "Discover" from American College Testing (ACT) factors in a person's skills, values, and interests and would be an effective tool in career selection.

The fire department in Lincoln, Nebraska, selects firefighters through a process that assesses physical abilities, mental aptitude, values, and personality. According to Deputy Chief Dean Staberg, this method works extremely well. "The firefighters who are selected experience a high degree of success, and we have an extremely low turnover rate. Employees don't usually leave until they retire or die."

Finally, commitment is a key element. How committed to a career will you be? Certain fields require more time, energy, and effort than others. A chief of a fire department caused a few eyes to widen in a class when he mentioned that a firefighting career means spending one third of your life away from family. It's possible to succeed in some careers with less time and motivation so, again, knowing yourself is essential. For example, people who aren't self-motivated seldom succeed in sales positions. Are you one who wants to someday own your own business? If so, do you realize the high degree of motivation and commitment that is required? A person may think, "I want to be my own boss so nobody can tell me what to do," and have no idea what owning a business means. For those of you who want to learn more about this, Chapter 6 has a section. Degree of commitment is a major factor to consider when you choose a career.

Matching Yourself to a Job

After a wise career choice, a specific job selection takes the spotlight. A career selection is similar to deciding what material possession to buy. Let's say you have decided that a new car is preferable to a new boat, computer, or furniture just as you might decide that your career field is architecture. The focus now is on what kind of car, just as the choice to make is which job in the field of architecture. If you're looking for the ultimate in satisfaction, you won't just look at a few of the usual possibilities. For example, the majority of psychology majors become counselors; however, many other possibilities exist such as teaching, research, consulting, training and development, marketing, and motivating athletes and others. Directories available in libraries list thousands of jobs in various occupational areas, so take advantage of them. Check the end of this chapter for the names of some. Finding the job that fits means putting together several more pieces of the puzzle.

As you specifically focus on a job, most of the same career choice aspects are relevant. Consider what you will *do* at work. Even though you select a career based on what you enjoy, it's possible that a particular job is full of less desirable tasks. For example, a creative drafter found herself in a job where she just copied others' drawings day in and day out. She dreaded going to work. After two years as a financial analyst, Ryan Turner is going to graduate school to open up other possibilities. He said, "I wish I would have done more homework on the day-to-day responsibilities of the particular job." Because this is so critical, a major question to have answered before accepting a job is: "What will I be *doing* in this job?"

Ethical considerations are critical, as well. In every career field there are businesses that use questionable methods. A young man said he quit selling automobiles for one firm because of expected sales techniques that, to him, were dishonest. If your standards and values are not in harmony with what is expected of you, it's unlikely you will be comfortable. Discussed earlier in reference to career choice, another aspect to consider is what you value. If you think it's important to do work that has personal purpose and meaning, a job that just requires routine labor will not be satisfying. For most people, health is a high priority. Studies have revealed that job satisfaction is directly related to the presence of wellness programs within a company (Epes, 1994; Violette & Violette, 1990; Wolfe & Parker, 1994). An activity in KEY STEPS (page 282) can help you match values with career and job selections.

A serious consideration is whether a particular job will offer adequate opportunities to raise or strengthen your self-esteem level. Chris realized that her self-worth was enhanced by seeing the end product of her work and from receiving recognition for her efforts. It wasn't difficult for her to understand why she was dissatisfied with a job where there never seemed to be an end to her many tasks for which she received little or no praise. She moved on to a different job because, as she put it, "I had high enough self-esteem to know that I deserved better!"

Before you accept a job, it would be a good idea to look over the work orientations described earlier. How many of the ones you value are aspects of this particular job? For example, a career in journalism or advertising calls for creativity and will usually afford freedom. However, certain jobs within those fields could limit your independence and not provide enough flexibility. Because your job occupies so much of your daily time, having your values and work orientations in harmony with the job description is of immense importance.

Knowing your personality type can be most helpful in job selection. A drafting job for Scott was particularly frustrating. "I just get started with one project, and my supervisor pulls me off that and puts me on another. I hate leaving one thing undone and going on to another!" His clear sensing preference required the chance to complete one task before moving on to another one. The interruption and change in routine were disconcerting. He found a different job which allowed him to stay with a project until it was completed.

Degree of pressure can vary from one job to another. Even though most jobs have times when deadlines must be met, some seem to be nothing but one deadline after another. On the other extreme, Craig found himself in a "laid-back" job that demanded little of him, and he was bored because his threshold for pressure was much higher.

Another factor is how well you cope with stress. All jobs can be stressful; yet, certain ones are loaded with stress producers. Finding a job that produces **eustress**, the amount and type of stress that is healthy and good for you, is well worth your time and efforts. Jeanne Baer, president of Creative Training Solutions, said, "Even though most jobs today demand a great deal and can be quite stressful, there is a point when a person really is wise to say, 'Enough! It's not worth my health.'" Ideally, you can find a job that provides you with eustress and, if you find yourself in one where you are constantly "on edge," you will make a healthy decision to leave. Incidentally, the *Jobs Rated Almanac* ranks as most stressful the job of U.S. President, one that few of us will ever consider. Following are firefighter, senior corporate executive, Indy class race-car driver, and taxi driver (Capell, 1995).

The size and personality of the company deserve attention. A study revealed that people with low self-esteem do best in larger, more decentralized firms. Those with a high need for achievement and recognition do best in a reward-for-performance environment (Turban and Keon, 1993).

A job may fit in all other ways and still not work for you because of money. Preparing for a job search means figuring how much salary you eventually want and what is presently required. If you have an up-to-date budget, the information is there. If you don't, a good resource is *What Color Is Your Parachute?* (Bolles, 1996), which provides an easy-to-fill-out monthly expense form in an excellent chapter on salary negotiation. You can come up with a realistic appraisal of what compensation is needed and then eliminate jobs that don't provide that amount.

> *DO YOU KNOW HOW MUCH MONEY YOU NEED EACH MONTH? IF YOU DON'T, DECIDE TO FIND OUT!*

A major factor to consider is whether the job contributes to your career design. According to Larry Hubka, Ph.D., dean of Business and Mass Media, Southeast Community College, applicants often do not differentiate between just a "job" and a position in their career fields. Assessing the learning opportunities in any job to determine if they contribute to your career goals is advised by Professor Linda A. Hill, Ph.D. of Harvard Business School (1994).

Lastly, some jobs demand more than others. Commitment and dedication go hand-in-hand. You may be expected to "go the extra mile" which could mean putting in extra hours, coming in on weekends, or assuming additional tasks. If you are not that committed, it's best to avoid those jobs.

> *"I looked upon the first few years as being in 'boot camp.' Putting in 60 hours a week wasn't unusual; the time and effort spent were worth it to me."*
>
> Lisa Patterson, CPA and Senior Manager
> Ernst and Young LLP
> Los Angeles, California

Several young career professionals report that the workload is heavier than they expected and that one person is often expected to do the work of two. "The 'real world' *is* different," said Mary Dixon, an administrative assistant in a major accounting firm. This is not expected to change in the foreseeable future. "A person is often required to perform multiple functions or have dual roles. Versatility, adaptability, and career commitment will prove invaluable in a crowded field," says Jody Horwitz, director of human resources, Turner Broadcasting System, Inc., Los Angeles. No matter what job you choose, more will probably be expected of you than in years past; yet, because of variation in necessary commitment, you will have some latitude in your selection.

Being Realistic and Practical

Getting what you want, in a sense, is following your dream. However, dreams do not become realities if certain realisms aren't considered. "I've wanted to be a firefighter since I was a little kid. It's all I've ever wanted," said Jeff who had just found out that his visual deficiencies were such that he would not realize his dream. Being realistic about your own limitations, as long as you don't restrict yourself unnecessarily, is essential.

Practicalities are also important. While predictions are risky, it is clear that certain occupations will be hard-pressed to survive in the next millennium. The U.S. Department of Labor Statistics foresees that 234,000 farm operators and managers along with 153,000 farm workers will be out of work by 2005 (Gest, 1995). Successful career designers keep an eye to the future when making decisions. For example, the expanding elderly population will create a demand for health-care workers and people with expertise in gerontology. Personal and home-care aide is the fastest growing occupation; its ranks will increase by 119 percent by 2005. Also predicted is a rise in retail sales jobs, computer careers, health care, education, and child care fields (Lewis, 1996a). Any attempt to peer into the future depends upon several assumptions, and some predicted jobs may never materialize. Yet, those who can program, service, and work with computers are quite likely to have a secure future.

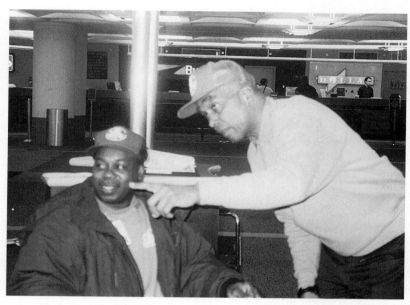

▲ Individuals who value being of service to others find satisfying careers in helping professions.

As you think about your future, consult the most recent publications. For example, projections into the next 10 years are made by government offices and are available in most libraries. It's also better to learn what several experts think and not just take the word of one.

Another realistic consideration is where you want to live and the type of lifestyle you wish to maintain. If you wish to own your own above-average home, look at whether your career path will support that. Find out what housing will cost in your favored geographic location. Some of the highest home costs today are found in Honolulu, San Francisco, and Los Angeles. Wherever you want to live, check to see what income will provide your desired lifestyle, then, if necessary, make adjustments either in your career, desired lifestyle, or geographic location. Even though men are more apt to consider these factors, doing so is highly recommended for both sexes. For example, during college at UCLA my daughter Lisa decided that she wanted to live in Los Angeles with an above-average lifestyle and, along with other considered factors, decided to become a certified public accountant. Her position as a senior manager with a large accounting firm makes her lifestyle possible. Often, women believe that someone else will always provide for them or at least with them; in today's society, that is definitely taking a risk.

VISUALIZE THE LIFESTYLE YOU WISH TO HAVE. WILL YOUR CAREER CHOICE AND AVAILABLE JOBS SUPPORT THIS?

An excellent book, *Getting the Lowdown on Employers and a Leg Up on the Job Market* (Kight, 1994), provides information on occupations, industries, and companies including a number of current and projected figures and listings of the fastest growing occupations and jobs. A revealing section discusses compatibility between a company's personality and that of an employee. Ratings of the best companies in different categories are included. Another unique part of the book focuses on the geographical aspects. If you want to locate in a certain area, taking a look at this information will be quite helpful. Bookstores and libraries have other books featuring certain localities. A feature article in *Time* (Greenwald, 1997) described states and cities that are expected to remain superhot job spots until at least the end of the decade. It also identified 15 of the hottest occupational fields.

If this sounds involved, that's because it is! Yet, when you consider how many other life choices are influenced by career and job satisfaction, the relationship between professional and personal satisfaction, and the actual time spent at work, your attention to these choices is imperative. How much satisfaction you get from your career and job will directly affect all other aspects of your life. Designing your career means knowing yourself well, considering and exploring all feasible choices, then choosing wisely. If you have put the puzzle pieces together correctly, you will enjoy the end result and certainly are deserving of a high level of satisfaction.

ACHIEVING YOUR GOALS

Most people have heard so much about goal setting, they tend to "tune out." Hopefully, you won't because if you are going to get what you want, you will have to set and achieve goals.

GETTING MOTIVATED

Most of us carry around a collection of internal messages about goals: "You should have goals," "You'll never get anywhere if you don't set goals," and "It's a good idea to have goals." Then we also have specific goal messages such as "My goal is to become a pharmacist," or "I should go into business." The language of goal setting makes a difference. Notice that some of the messages sound forcing and pressuring and lack a sense of personal commitment. Replacing words such as "should" with "want" generates motivation and enthusiasm. If you *want* to graduate from college, you are more likely to do so and enjoy the process than if your thoughts and words are "I should" or "I have to."

In a career development class, Daryl Rivers, president of Rivers Metal Products, said, "Human beings will if they want to and won't if they don't. I want employees who want to work and will be enthusiastic about it." Personal desire for a goal creates a powerful motivating force. Instead, the goal may belong to someone else, as in the case of Michael. "My parents always wanted me to go into engineering, and even though I don't really want to, I went along with them. After three years in college, I was even more convinced it was a poor choice for me. It's hard to disappoint them though." Yet, in order to experience career and job satisfaction, you must set and pursue your own goals.

Assessing Goals

Once you are sure that you really want a certain career goal, analyze it realistically. In addition to asking whether the goal is yours, can you answer the following with a "yes?"

- Is the goal in accord with my values and beliefs?

- Is this goal compatible with what I want in my personal life?

- Do I have enough motivation to achieve it?

- Is the goal realistic and attainable?

- Do I have the capabilities it requires?

- Is the goal focused and well-defined?

In designing a career you will have a major career goal related to the occupation you choose and other goals to help you get there. A goal of graduating from college will lead to a position in a career field that can, eventually, enable you to achieve your ultimate career desire.

Figuring Out the "How"

This is the stage where so many falter. Setting a goal is easy compared to carrying it out. A career development student completed a goal-setting exercise by writing, "I'm going to be rich and retire by the time I'm 35." I smiled as I wrote, "Good luck," and then added, "HOW?" It's wonderful to have wants and goals; however, if you don't know how to achieve them, they can easily become frustrations.

Eliminating obstacles.   Even if people have an idea as to "how," they may be hindered by self-imposed obstacles (Brinkerhoff, 1994). Some of these follow.

- *Pessimism*. If one's attitude is one of "gloom and doom," feelings of hopelessness and helplessness prevail, and little is done. Developing a strong internal locus of control, discussed in Chapter 1, is beneficial.

- *Optimism*. Strangely, the opposite mental attitude can be a detriment. "I can do anything" isn't realistic, and if a person is overly optimistic, the results are usually disappointing.

- *Procrastination*. Putting off activities until later is a serious problem if it's a chronic behavior. Learning why you procrastinate, the repercussions for doing so, and then taking necessary steps to accomplish even the small bits are remedies for this destructive habit (Hanna, 1995).

- *Lack of money*. Conducting a job search isn't terribly costly. However, it does require funds, and this isn't the time to "pinch pennies." For example, why order cheap paper for a résumé instead of the heavier weight, which is usually only a few cents more? If your money is limited, try to cut costs for a while in other areas such as fewer soft drinks, alcoholic beverages, candy, and cigarettes. Your health will benefit as well!

⊚   *Lack of time.* Remember that we all have the same amount of time—24 hours a day. Instead of using this as an excuse for inaction, figure out how you can take time away from other activities and use it on your job search. Fifteen minutes here and there really add up.

Feeling overwhelmed by a lofty goal is another major obstacle. An especially helpful technique is to pinpoint, or set goals with realistic numbers attached (Schmidt, 1976). Breaking the goal into attainable, measurable action steps converts a towering mountain into a small hill. Likewise, having a way to measure accomplishment can spell the difference between success and failure. For example, just saying that you want to exercise is less likely to bring about results than, "I'm going to walk a mile a day." The realistic numbers in pinpointing also include completion dates for both the goal and each action step. Being able to chart your progress and reward yourself for smaller achievements along the way will be energizing.

ACTING ON A GOAL.   A plan must include measurable actions if a goal is to be achieved. Thinking about writing this book was somewhat overwhelming even though I'd already written one. Knowing that the plan would have to be action-driven, a key initial step was to write an outline. That achievement then motivated me to begin the actual manuscript. "Little by little" can move mountains so don't sabotage yourself by feeling overwhelmed and failing to act. Think of a goal and do the activity in KEY STEPS (page 283) to show you understand the process.

The following plan has an ultimate goal of sending out 25 résumés.

⊚   I will look through a directory of employers and compile a list of at least 25 possible addresses and telephone numbers by January 31.

⊚   I will write or telephone each of the companies and request information about the company and get the name and address of the person to whom résumés are sent by February 7.

⊚   I will gather the needed information to develop a résumé by February 15.

⊚   I will compose the first draft of my résumé by February 18.

⊚   I will have Stephanie read my résumé draft and make suggestions to me by February 25.

⊚   I will contact my references and ask permission to use their names by February 25.

⊚   I will type the final copy of my résumé by March 1.

⊚   I will select résumé paper and have 30 copies made by March 2.

⊚   I will compose a draft of a cover letter by March 3.

⊚ I will have Stephanie read my cover letter and make suggestions to me by March 7.

⊚ I will type addresses of 25 companies on envelopes by March 7.

⊚ I will type the 25 individual cover letters by March 14.

⊚ I will take the résumés/cover letters to the post office, have each weighed to ensure sufficient postage, and mail by March 16.

If you miss an intermediate date on the way to the final goal, simply revise it and stay on task. Of benefit is to write these steps in a checklist format. Marking each completed step provides satisfaction that is motivating. This may seem a bit tedious; however, you are much more likely to achieve the goal by March 16 than if you carry around the nebulous idea to begin a job search. Remember, you can let time slip away by not doing what is necessary to reach a career goal, or you can begin to take those essential action steps.

> *IN THE RÉSUMÉ-SENDING PLAN, FIND EACH ACTION WORD AND THE MEASURABLE PINPOINTS.*

RESEARCHING CAREERS, JOBS, AND EMPLOYERS

After you have become familiar with yourself and have a good idea of a desired career, yet before you set specific job-seeking goals, learn all you can about that career field, the jobs that are available, and the employers. As in all major decisions, people who amass information are in a better position to make sound judgments. House buyers usually spend a great deal of time and effort learning all they can. Your career decisions deserve as much, if not more, consideration.

WHY RESEARCH?

Information can confirm your career choice or reveal meaningful questions. Research will clarify job expectations and let you know what is required of you. Because job satisfaction is so critical, you want to match yourself to a job. How can you do this without research? Additionally, finding out about potential employers helps you narrow your list of desirables so you can focus on the jobs you really want.

Most importantly, employers are impressed by applicants who have taken the time to find out about their businesses. "When a job candidate shows me that she or he knows about us, that's a major plus. Those who know nothing are unimpressive," said an interviewer. Downsizing makes the job market more competitive. Hopefully, you will be like some motivated job seekers who are well-prepared, knowledgeable, and persistent in their approach because it will spell the difference between getting what you want or settling for less. Knowledge really is power.

The answer to the question "How do I get information?" could be, "Anywhere you can!" However, some sources are more creditable than others.

A library, especially at a college or university, contains numerous resources such as the following. Typically, there is a special career counseling or development area.

- Directories such as the *Occupational Outlook Handbook, Dictionary of Occupational Titles, Encyclopedia of Business Information Sources*, and *Standard and Poor's Register*, which provide trends, definitions, and profiles of occupations and information about companies

- Books on career development, specific parts of the job search such as résumé writing, and specific career fields

- Trade journals and magazines about all aspects of career development

- Newspapers from major cities

- Videotapes about careers and job-seeking skills

- Software that can provide occupational outlooks, job-seeking suggestions, and job-search tools

- Actual human beings who are career counselors there to provide services, often free, if you are a student of that particular institution

Spending several days in a library may sound grueling, yet it will pay off in many ways. The book *Help! My Job Interview Is Tomorrow* (Templeton, 1991) explains how to use the library to research an employer. Other books to guide your research are listed at the end of this chapter.

An increasingly bountiful source of career information is online. The Internet, often called cyberspace, offers information and new ways of conducting a job search. You can interact with experts, read job postings, list your résumé, and even interview using a computer system. You can explore what seem like endless sites on the World Wide Web in search of information. For example, JOBTRAK (http://www.jobtrak.com), used by over 150,000 employers, offers job listings and company profiles. Another online opportunity is to enlarge your contact list through chat rooms, forums, and special interest groups.

Online services offer their own resources. For example, America Online's Career Center has, among other offerings, job listings, candidate résumés, online professional counseling, and occupational profiles. Another feature is Employer Contacts, a collection of information on over 6,000 American employers. Also, within the center is the Career Resource Library, which contains materials that can help you select a career goal and conduct a job search as well as articles aimed at personal understanding and enhancement of career opportunities. Most services are free with some optional for-sale items. The book *The On-Line Job Search Companion* (Gonyea, 1995) is an excellent guide to using a computer in your job search.

An added benefit of using cyberspace in your job search is to learn about it. If you are unfamiliar with the superinformation highway, the sooner you discover it, the better. Many employers today expect applicants to be well-versed in this area. If you don't have your own computer system, you may have a family member or friend who does. Most schools provide students with access to the Net. As a last resort, you can pay for time at a specialty store. However you do it, being able to navigate in cyberspace either keeps you up with the competition or, if you're fortunate, gives you an added advantage. Check the end of this chapter for a partial list of both library and online resources.

> *HOW MUCH DO YOU KNOW ABOUT THE INTERNET AND ONLINE SERVICES?*
> *IF YOUR EXPERIENCE IS LIMITED, WHAT CAN YOU DO TO CHANGE THAT?*

Another source of information is a company itself. You can write to or telephone a company and ask for information to be mailed. Most will provide you with brochures or packets of material. Very important for future use is to get a copy of the job application and ask for details about the job-seeking process for this particular company. Be sure to volunteer to pay for the postage.

It may be even better to go in person to get information. Conducting what are called **informational interviews**, designed solely to learn about the business and your career field of interest, is highly recommended. Having visual and auditory information, in addition to written materials, can be especially beneficial. Also, you are in an excellent position to make a positive impression in a much less formidable situation than a job interview. For a required career development course project, Steve visited an architectural firm and talked with the head of the drafting department and two other employees. "It was great," he reported. "I learned so much, and I think they were impressed. The head of the department asked me to contact her when I was ready to graduate."

Steps in conducting an informational interview include:

- Decide on businesses in which you have a keen interest.

- Identify the individuals whom you want to interview.

- Write or telephone for appointments making it clear that your only purpose is to learn. Find out how much time the person has available. You may also request a tour if that is appropriate.

- Prepare questions. These are to be related to the company, products, and the career field of interest. You can find a sample of questions in the KEY STEPS section (page 284). Refrain from asking questions that have obvious answers or seeking information which you can readily find elsewhere. Often, the interviewee is willing and even pleased to offer information about his or her own career path and give advice. You will want to request names of other companies and individuals who would be valuable sources of information.

- Conduct the interview. Dress as you would for a job interview. Record the information you receive either in writing or with a tape recorder or both. If you want to record, be sure to get the person's permission. It is advisable to bring out a résumé only if the person requests one. Because this was set up as an information-gathering interview, obvious job seeking will probably diminish your credibility. Stay within the time limits and express your sincere appreciation for this opportunity.

6 Follow up with a thank-you letter to the person you interviewed. Also, you benefit yourself by sending either a letter or a note to anyone who was helpful, such as a receptionist or a tour guide. If you were impressed by the interviewee, an excellent idea is to write a letter of praise to his or her supervisor or to the owner of the business.

Informational interviews take time and effort, yet probably no activity is more conducive to a successful job-search conclusion.

Even more informative than a short visit is **job shadowing,** spending a day or so observing a person on the job. Obviously, this will be scheduled ahead of time, and it's imperative that you not interfere with the person's work. Being a "shadow" means maintaining a low profile as you gather valuable information. Whether you conduct an informational interview or spend a longer time in job shadowing, send a sincere thank-you note.

A unique information-gathering suggestion was offered by Mary Conway, instructor of a career development course. "Conduct observational research by being in the parking lot at the end of a work day. You can glean a great deal from watching the employees. Do they seem happy, energetic, worn out, discouraged? It's interesting!"

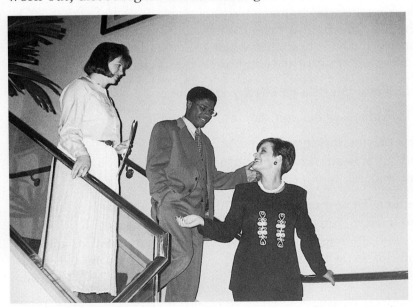

▲ A tour of a company provides valuable first-hand information and contacts.

If the company is a public corporation, you can get an annual report from investment services and brokerage houses. The Better Business Bureau in the particular city is also a source of information about the company's reputation and record. The more than 22,000 trade associations, representing different industries and occupations, can be contacted. The *Encyclopedia of Associations* and the *National Trade and Professional Associations of the United States* list various associations. Information is also available from reporters and journalists who write in business and trade-industrial fields and through labor unions.

Word-of-mouth is a commonly used resource. Talking directly with employers and employees can yield helpful information. You might also talk with customers or clients of particular businesses; however, be cautious of personal opinions and assessments. Other people's ideas can be enlightening; yet, restricting your information to word-of-mouth is not recommended. Later you will read about using personal contacts to actually help you find a job.

PLANNING AND CONDUCTING YOUR JOB SEARCH

Imagine this scenario. It's Sunday morning, and Tony is reading through help-wanted ads. He is disgruntled because there are only four interesting ones; he circles each in red ink. On Monday morning he makes a telephone call as directed in the advertisement and mails three résumés. Then he waits—and waits—and waits. He may play a waiting game forever in today's world of work.

> *"Job seekers have to take the initiative and be very resourceful."*
>
> Jeanne Salerno, Director of Professional Development
> Kutak Rock Law Firm
> Omaha, Nebraska

Learning actual job-seeking skills is one of the best investments you can make. You may have the highest qualifications of any candidate yet be overlooked because of poor job-search methods. Make a commitment to become proficient in job-seeking skills. Reading and applying the ideas in this book is one way to do so. Other possibilities are courses, seminars, workshops, and by reading other books listed at the end of this chapter. Expect to invest time and energy in this endeavor, which is the preliminary stage.

> HOW MUCH JOB-SEARCH TRAINING HAVE YOU HAD? WHAT HAVE YOU READ? YOUR ANSWERS CAN TELL YOU WHAT YOU MIGHT NEED TO DO.

Getting to the actual search, you may have heard the advice of many in the career development field: Make your job search a full-time job. Recommended is 35 to 40 hours a week if you are unemployed (Lock, 1992). Yet, how many people do you know who work at least eight hours a day at job seeking? Regardless of the time spent, the key to a successful job search is activity. Of course, random or frivolous activity is pointless as in the case of Matt. He spent hours mailing 150 résumés, what is called the shotgun approach; then he settled in to wait. "I put in lots of time and effort," he said, "and all I have to show for it are two rejection letters and three that say they'll keep my résumé on file. The rest didn't even respond." This type of activity proved fruitless and resulted in a depressed young man.

Even though experts once recommended sending as many résumés as possible with the idea that a certain percentage would generate results, the reality is that the results are "slim to none." Mailing out hundreds of résumés doesn't lead to a job for 92 out of every 100 job hunters who try it (Bolles, 1996).

To help make your job search seem like a job, set the stage. Successful job hunters have a "professional spot" even if it's just a desk where everything pertaining to the search can be found. Spend time there every day as you would on a job. Be sure you have a telephone line that is seldom used except by you plus an answering machine with a professional-sounding personal message. When making return calls from applicants for my husband's company, I was appalled to hear, "Hey, guy, be cool. This dude's out doin' some damage. Catch ya later!" I'm not sure who "caught him" later; he definitely did not hear from us again!

What kind of activity leads to success? If you haven't yet formulated goals and objectives, it's time to do so. Knowing what you want limits your list of potential employers, which saves you time and effort. The shotgun approach may sound good; yet, if 50 of those companies don't have what you want or if you don't have what they want, you have wasted your time. Having goals and objectives also shows that you are in charge of your career.

Finding Potential Employers

After researching and deciding what you want, it's time to take the initiative. Action is key. You might think that Tony in the scenario at the beginning of this section took the initiative and acted when he responded to four advertisements. The problem is that this was all he did. Later you will read more about newspaper advertisements.

An action step is to develop a list of employers from your research. Then you can focus all aspects of the search on this particular group. The list contains those you want to work for and ones who have reason to hire you in order of priority. If an employer fits both criteria, it ranks at the top of your list. Don't overlook small companies. Many job seekers limit their job search to names they recognize. The number on your list is up to you; however, be reasonable because you can always add to it. This list can come from a variety of sources (see Table 3–1).

As a practical matter, have an organized system for your employers' list such as index cards. Relevant data include name, address, telephone and other numbers, name of the person in charge of hiring, and a brief profile of the business. In addition to cards, accordion-file folders with a slot for each potential employer can hold brochures and other information. If you have not yet contacted the employer directly to request materials, this is the time to do so.

The more alert and curious you are, the more possibilities you will find. Before graduating from a desktop publishing program, Tom saw an article in the

TABLE 3–1 ▲ SOURCES OF EMPLOYMENT LEADS

- ◎ directories of employers
- ◎ directories available from a chamber of commerce
- ◎ career development books
- ◎ trade publications, newsletters, and magazines (advertisements and articles)
- ◎ newspapers from any location of interest (news articles, business advertisements, and classified ads)
- ◎ classified telephone directories (yellow pages from any desired location)
- ◎ online sources
- ◎ college career and placement services
- ◎ college program or department
- ◎ career days or fairs at colleges and universities
- ◎ government reports and listings
- ◎ word-of-mouth

newspaper about a new printing company opening soon. He sought further information, then mailed a résumé and cover letter (mentioning how he knew about the company). His reward? He was one of the first local people hired! Most of the sources in Table 3–1 are self-explanatory. A few merit special attention and some explanation.

Seeking Help In Your Job Search

If you are a student, definitely take advantage of the college placement office. The services can include help with developing a list of prospective employers, matching employer to applicant, résumé writing, and other job-seeking skills. According to Sally Beck, placement specialist at a community college, her office will help fine-tune a résumé and even create an original on a high-quality printer. She advises students to become acquainted with placement services before they are needed. She said, "One student came in the second week he was on campus seeking information about his career field and available jobs. Unfortunately, other students, even at the time of graduation, don't even know the placement office exists."

A major service of a college placement office is to connect employers with job seekers, and numerous employers contact the placement office when they're hiring. If you're not registered with your college placement service, you could be missing out on a major opportunity, says Sally Beck, a placement specialist who does all she can to provide students and alumni with desirable job referrals. A placement staff person can be an invaluable ally because he or she, as a representative of the college or university, wants you to find a job. Not all placement services are free; however, in most cases, the fee is nominal and certainly could be well worth the expenditure. Incidentally, if you use the service, remember to send a thank-you letter.

Most placement offices are a part of a larger career counseling department. According to Dave Sonenberg, director of Career Counseling and Placement at Southeast Community College, his staff tries to match students' interests, values, and skills with career areas through informal discussion and inventories. A popular instrument is the Career Assessment Inventory, which creates a lengthy report in response to a person's answers.

Usually, a college program or department can provide contacts and job leads. Be sure to let the program or department chair and other faculty know you are seeking employment. Typically, employers are in contact with these people and may even be serving on advisory committees for the program. Don Mumm, head of an environmental laboratory program, commented, "The employers with whom we're in contact are actually 'standing in line' for candidates. In the past six years close to 100 percent, if not 100 percent, of our graduates found jobs in their field, and most of them were directly through our program." Take advantage, as well, of special events such as career days or job fairs. Usually, employers are there in person to offer information firsthand, and you have an opportunity to personally talk with representatives.

IF ONE IS AVAILABLE, HAVE YOU REGISTERED WITH YOUR COLLEGE PLACEMENT OFFICE? HAVE YOU DISCUSSED EMPLOYMENT WITH A PROGRAM OR DEPARTMENT CHAIR, A PROFESSOR, OR AN INSTRUCTOR?

Government agencies can be valuable sources of leads. For material published by the federal government, make a request of the Government Printing Office or contact specific agencies of interest. States and cities, eager to attract residents, will assist you in finding potential employers. Writing or calling the

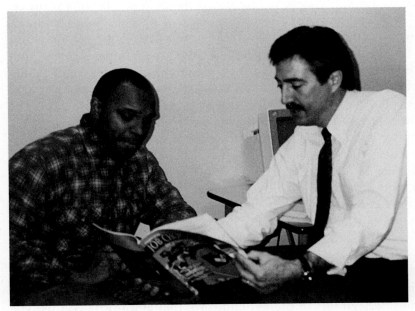

▲ Difficult career decisions are easier with the help of a professional college placement officer.

mayor or city manager's office will probably be well worth your effort. Janet had decided she wanted to relocate to a warmer climate and chose a city in Arizona. She requested information about the area and specifically regarding employment and said she was overwhelmed with the response. "I really felt as if the city wanted me to move there, and I already feel welcome."

Have you ever received a name of a potential employer or a job lead from a personal contact? This question is almost guaranteed to be answered "yes." Word-of-mouth is by far the most prolific source of information about employers and is a successful way of actually getting a job. Approximately 85 percent of all openings get filled by word-of-mouth (Baron, 1996). A list of possible contacts is given in Table 3–2.

> AS YOU READ TABLE 3–2, MAKE YOUR OWN LIST OF ANY NAMES THAT COME TO MIND.

To increase your contacts, suggest that each person mention your job search to others. No matter whom you are with, mention career and job aspirations. Leads can come from anywhere!

USING YOUR NETWORK

Personal contacts can become even more beneficial if you are **networking**—establishing contacts who may be helpful. Even before the job search begins, you can meet new people and ask for business cards or at least their names, addresses, and telephone numbers for professional reasons. Ted, whose career field was accounting, had a file of 82 names before he graduated from college. One of the ways he met so many people was by joining and participating in professional organizations, a highly recommended way to increase your network.

Networking can help you get a desired job, advance in your career, and change directions. The old saying, "Who you know, not what you know, makes

TABLE 3–2 ▲ WORD-OF-MOUTH POSSIBILITIES

- immediate or extended family members
- friends and friends' family members
- other students (college and high school)
- members of a church
- teachers, instructors, professors
- former employers and supervisors
- co-workers
- acquaintances such as an insurance agent, banker, attorney, dentist, dental hygienist, doctor, nurse, hairdresser, minister, priest, rabbi, real estate agent, sales clerk
- members of special-interest groups such as bowling teams, hobby clubs, or craft groups

a difference" is not entirely true; however, the first part, "who you know," certainly is. One man proudly asserted, "I don't want to be hired because I know somebody; I want to be hired on the basis of my abilities alone." He was assured that even Albert Einstein found a job after graduation through the father of one of his classmates (Fisher et al., 1977). Besides, you are unlikely to be hired, even with the best personal contact, unless you are qualified. The "what you know" is a necessary part of being hired for most positions. The key is to get "your foot into the door" which a person can often do for you. Finding the person who can hire you through your contacts has the highest job-search effectiveness rate of 86 percent (Bolles, 1996).

Additionally, those in your network can provide career education, information, and encouragement and be utilized as role models and references. If someone gives you a job lead or if you think you may want that person to serve as a reference, ask permission to use her or his name. Whether you get actual ideas for jobs, each name you collect could reap benefits in the future. Get active in the networking process!

FINE-TUNING YOUR INFORMATION

Once you have an initial list of employers with information about each one, scrutinize it carefully. If you don't have the name of the person who could hire you, call the company and ask for the name. This is usually the supervisor or head of the area in which you want to work. You may be told to apply or send your résumé and cover letter to human resources (formerly called personnel); yet, you want to make sure the person in charge of the final decision also has your information. Using the name of the human resources director is a "nice touch." Definitely use the name of the hiring person. Be sure to get the correct spelling of each one's name even if it's common. Even "Smith" can be spelled "Smyth" or "Smythe."

Then study each potential employer and identify reasons you would be needed and ways you can help the business achieve its goals. This is one of the most basic elements of successful job seeking and the one that is too often overlooked. Employers are most likely to hire an individual who will be of benefit to the business. Generally, job seekers fill their minds with, "What can the company do for me?" instead of "What can I do for this company?" In a competitive world employers want employees who will give them an advantage,

---

Accent Enterprises	Owner: Mark Caldwell
334 South Rose Street	Telephone: 612-728-1940
St. Paul, MN 55111	e-mail: accent@aol.com

Small company of 16 employees involved in real estate management and renovation of houses

Needs: office organizational skills, computer word processing and spreadsheets, and renovation estimate expertise

and if you want to be hired, you must convince them that you can do this. Be sure to write the reasons for each employer similar to the following. The more you know about the employer's needs and how your abilities will match, the more likely you are to be hired.

SELECTING REFERENCES

You may have thought about this before; however, once you know more, specifically what employment you plan to seek, you are in a better position to select your references. This critical part of the job search deserves serious thought followed by appropriate action.

References can be divided into two general categories: professional and personal. Following are suggestions for each.

PROFESSIONAL REFERENCES.   Select people who know of your work capabilities—attitude, abilities, and performance. A final group of three, four, or five is satisfactory; however, you may want a larger pool from which to draw. If your research has been complete, you will know which ones are likely to be most impressive to which employer. As a result, you may not use the same group of references for each applied position. Continue to update this list as you make more professional connections.

Obviously, if you have demonstrated skills necessary in the job for which you are applying, anyone who can document this is a top reference candidate. Even those who are aware of your transferable skills can be quite helpful and would be included in the top group of possibilities. Think of:

- past or present supervisors
- co-workers
- those you have supervised
- customers or clients
- professors, instructors, and teachers

USING THE LIST OF POSSIBILITIES, THINK OF SEVERAL REFERENCES.

Other professional references could be people with whom you have had business dealings or have worked with in a professional or volunteer organization such as bankers, sales representatives, insurance agents, and community leaders.

PERSONAL REFERENCES.   Sometimes requested on an application are personal references, those who can attest to your character and can document certain desirable characteristics. Preferably, these individuals would have credibility in their profession or in the community. Most important is to know ones *not* to select. Do not use relatives, people you have known less than a year, clergy unless you have worked with that person which would qualify her or him as a professional reference, or significant others. In checking references, an employer called and talked to what sounded like a young female. He asked,

"How do you know this applicant?" She replied, "Oh, he's my boyfriend." The unimpressed employer was left with the question, "Is this all he could do in terms of a reference?" Unless an application specifically asks for personal references, use only professional ones.

CONTACTING AND USING REFERENCES

After you have a list of possible references, the next step is to contact each one personally and ask permission to use him or her as a reference. This point cannot be overemphasized. Even if you inform the person later, not asking first is a major mistake in the job search. Not only is it considered impolite, it can backfire. A career counselor told of receiving a telephone call about a former student who had used her name without permission. "I honestly could not recollect anything about the person so I couldn't help. In fact, I'm sure it hurt the person's chances." An aspect to consider is whether you can expect a positive recommendation. If you don't know for sure, ask about the quality of the recommendation. KEY STEPS (page 285) encourages you to make necessary contacts.

To effectively use your references, here are additional ideas. Keep in contact. When you apply for a position, share your research. Their knowing specific job requirements can make a significant difference. Donna had received permission to use me for a reference. She stopped in a few weeks later and gave me a copy of her résumé and cover letter, a job description of a position

I'm delighted your wife wants you to work, but do you
have any other references?

for which she had just applied, and a brochure about the company. She did the same with each of her references. Being prepared when I was called made a major difference as my comments about Donna related specifically to the position. I wasn't surprised when she was hired.

Many job seekers collect letters of recommendation and supply these to potential employers. While these can be helpful, they aren't as effective as an unsolicited letter directly from the reference. Before being contacted by an employer, a reference can either call or write a letter of recommendation. Be sure not to ask one person to do this every time you apply; however, if there is a position you especially want, this is appropriate.

These references can also be used on an application and with a résumé and cover letter. Will a person always be contacted? The honest answer is no, not always. Yet, in many instances, they will be. Strong, positive recommendations from respectable individuals can spell the difference between being considered and hired or being just an applicant who eventually is rejected.

MAKING DIRECT CONTACT

Even if an employer doesn't appear to be hiring, the direct approach is highly recommended because it works. The idea is to be ahead of the competition or at least at the same level. Most effective is to arrange to see the person who can hire you. This is done by using your contacts—either having the appointment set up for you or using the name of the person to get "your foot in the door." Because most employers aren't impressed when someone just appears at the door, you are advised to telephone or mail résumés and cover letters to well-targeted employers or both. Follow-up is definitely recommended.

If you have excellent telephone skills and want to contact employers quicker, you may opt to use an effective three-step method. To begin, if you don't know who is answering or if it's obviously an operator or receptionist, introduce yourself by name and then ask to speak to the person who could hire you (use this individual's name which you would already know). If the person is not available, you are better off finding out what time to call again. Leaving your name and telephone number may yield nothing, or the person may call back when you are not there or not in a position to talk. Julie had left her name and telephone number, and when the potential employer returned her call, she was embarrassed because her two children were both crying loudly in the background. Another reason is that throughout the job search, a good idea is to "keep the ball in your court"; in other words, you want to stay in control as much as possible.

When you are talking to the person who can hire you, proceed as follows through the three steps.

1. *Greet the person by name and then give your name.* "Hello Mr. (or Ms.) Ross. This is Kevin Grant."
2. *Mention at least one of your assets (a reason why the person would be interested in hiring you) and, if you can, the contact person who is the connecting link.* "I will graduate in June with a degree in landscape architecture and have worked throughout college for Jacobs Landscape Design in Seattle and understand that you are

expanding in this area. The creative work I've been doing, I think, would be of interest to you. Jane Larson thinks it would be a good idea for us to talk." Or, you can lead in with: "Jane Larson, my previous employer, suggested that I call you."

3. *Tell the reason for your call.* "I'm very interested in a position with your company in the area of landscape design."

Some might question the reason for the second step. "Can't I just introduce myself and tell the person why I'm calling?" Certainly you can; however, what you have to offer is most significant. Another practical reason has to do with memory. If a person receives several calls a day, specific information is likely to be remembered. "Oh, yes, I remember. He said he worked for Jacobs Landscape Design, and that company hires only the best."

Just as important as what to say is what not to say. One of the worst openings is also one of the most common. In any of these variations, *don't* begin with:

⊚ Do you have any openings?

⊚ Are you hiring?

⊚ Do you have any positions (or jobs) available?

Those questions are quite likely to get a response of "no." When you make a direct contact, you don't want to provide an opportunity for an easy rejection. And even if an employer had an opening, the caller has done nothing to be impressive. A day care center director put it bluntly, "If I pick up the phone one more time and hear, 'Do you have any openings?' I think I'll just scream."

The three-step direct method will result in one of several replies. Because you have exerted time and effort to make this telephone call, you don't want to go away empty-handed. Following are employer replies (given from most to least positive) and a recommended response.

1. *Employer:* I am in need of someone in the near future and would be interested in discussing the position.
   Applicant: Except for Mondays and Wednesdays when I have classes, I'm available at your convenience. In the meantime I'll mail you a copy of my résumé.

2. *Employer:* Your qualifications sound great; however, we aren't hiring right now.
   Applicant: I'm sorry to hear that; I'd like to send you my resume to keep on file for future openings.

3. *Employer:* We aren't hiring right now, and I don't see any chance of it in the foreseeable future.
   Applicant: I'm sorry to hear that because I'm very impressed with your company. Do you know of anyone else who might be hiring in the near future?

The request for another contact may sound strange, yet employers also network and are usually willing to be helpful. If you do get a name, ask if you can tell how you received it. Practice this method in KEY STEPS (page 286).

No matter which reply you receive, you can be pleased that you did get something for the time. Also, you may be like Sally who was told that the hospital was not hiring in her field and probably wouldn't be in the foreseeable future (the third reply). Two weeks after she made the call, she received a call from the head of the respiratory therapy department.

Sally, if you haven't yet taken a position, I'd like to talk to you about employment. I just received a surprise one-month notice from a technician who is moving to another city. I was quite impressed with our telephone call and remembered your qualifications. Now I do want your résumé and would also like to schedule an interview.

If Sally had not made direct contact or had just asked if the hospital had openings, this would not have happened.

Other types of direct contact are through the postal and carrier services, computer e-mail, and fax machines. The next chapter covers presenting yourself in writing.

USING ADVERTISEMENTS

Remember Tony and his Sunday morning circling of classified ads? When most uninformed individuals decide to look for work, this is how they proceed. The numbers of job seekers who look for work by answering or placing advertisements has almost doubled since 1970 (Ports, 1993), and a 1995 study indicates that newspaper classified ads are still the most popular way to look for a job (Giobbe, 1995). While it would be foolish not to use the classified ads, some facts are good to know. One is that about 80 percent of jobs available are not even advertised (Jackson, 1992), which means you are missing out on most opportunities. Many employers don't need to advertise, and commonly they don't want to deal with the usual overwhelming response. Classified ads are costly for smaller companies so they, too, would rather find applicants other ways.

▲ A common, yet usually ineffective, way of finding a job is to rely only on newspaper advertisements.

Another reason not to rely on this method comes from thinking about what others are doing on that same Sunday morning. Picture hundreds of others circling the same ads as Tony. When you respond to an ad, you have a great deal of competition. The higher the level of job, the less effective is this method. Even ads in professional or trade journals within one's field have a success yield of only 7 percent (Bolles, 1996). Besides the degree of competition, employers probably won't be as impressed by a responder as they will be by an activator.

> CHECK A CURRENT CLASSIFIED-AD SECTION TO SEE HOW MANY JOB OPENINGS WOULD BE OF INTEREST TO YOU.

Online job postings also have the same handicaps although the competition may not be as intense. Possibilities lie in the Help Wanted-USA and E-Span employment databases. You may search by (1) career or skill area such as law enforcement or accounting; (2) geographical location such as city, state, or region; (3) job title or position although companies use different job titles; (4) job elements such as duties, qualifications, or salary; (5) company name. Sites are identified in special Internet or online search books; some are listed at the end of the chapter. As one of several job lead sources, be sure to include cyberspace.

You can even place your own advertisement either in a newspaper, trade publication, or online. A position-wanted ad in the classified section of a newspaper is probably the least effective of the three. It's definitely more effective to pursue other strategies that don't cost as much money as advertising.

> WRITE A SHORT AD ABOUT YOURSELF THAT TELLS WHAT YOU HAVE TO OFFER. THEN ASK SOMEONE TO EVALUATE ITS EFFECTIVENESS.

UTILIZING PLACEMENT SERVICES

Different types of services are available, each with advantages and, in some cases, a few drawbacks. Even though the already discussed college or university placement service will not guarantee you a job, its effectiveness is fairly high, successful about 27 percent of the time (Bolles, 1996). You have nothing to lose, except a small amount of money if the service is not free, and everything to gain by registering. You're advised to make contact several months before your anticipated graduation date and check with the office on a regular basis.

What are commonly called employment agencies are of two general types: public and private. Depending upon the agency, you could receive help in identifying potential employers, researching companies, improving specific job skills such as interviewing, determining appropriate salary figures, and preparing for employment tests.

Public agencies, operated by state and local governments, offer free services. These are part of a federal network called United States Employment Service, and Job Service is a typical name for the agency. Registration involves paperwork. This may be well worth your time although you will want to use it as only one source. Most agencies have current job listings and hot lines you may call; most importantly, they will put you in contact with any employer who is looking for help.

Private agencies are in business to match employers with applicants. They are paid by either employers or applicants or by both, and you'll want to know who is liable for the fee. Read carefully and ask questions about any contract before you sign. Applicants pay only if they accept positions through the agency. Typically, the fee is a percentage of your salary. Avoid signing a contract that demands "exclusive listing or handling" which binds you to a fee even if you find a job elsewhere (Lock, 1992).

Agencies are similar to real estate agents who are paid by a homeowner when a house is sold. Most claim they can find applicants better jobs at higher salaries faster. If this is so, it could be a worthwhile investment of money. The Current Population Survey of 1991 reported that nearly one fourth of job seekers found jobs through private agencies, and it ranked as the most successful single strategy for finding a job (Bortnick and Ports, 1991). Others disagree as to its effectiveness. Of those who walk in the door of a private agency, the average placement rate is only 5 percent (Bolles, 1996). If the employer pays the fee, the applicant obviously has no cost; however, in these cases, the agency is working for the employer, not the applicant. This could mean an agency will try to pressure you into taking a job just to collect a fee.

Is it wise to use a private employment agency in your search? An advantage in using it as one method is that you have control over acceptance of a job and, thus, ever having to pay for the services. If you are in a hurry to find a job, you may opt to use an agency immediately, or you can save it for a last resort, especially if there is a fee. Regardless, research the agency and be sure it has a good reputation in the area. You can check either *The Directory of Executive Recruiters* or *Directory of Personnel Consultants*, which list those who are certified.

After you have been on the job for a while, you may be contacted by an executive-search firm staffed by what are called **headhunters**. These firms find employees for companies; however, if you are well-qualified and seeking higher-level positions, you may take the initiative and contact one.

If you are not successful in finding full-time employment or even as a way of gaining invaluable information, you can consider a temporary-help agency. Temporary work is the fastest growing segment of the economy with over 1.5 million people working as "temps" each day, according to *Career Opportunities News* (1995). Job seekers benefit in many ways. The most obvious is that you are being paid while getting both information and experience. Having access to all the different companies serviced by a temporary agency can help a job seeker decide which is most desirable. For example, Nicole wanted a job in the entertainment business. She "temped" and had the opportunity to work several months at NBC followed by assignments at CBS and ABC.

A major benefit is that a temporary job can become a permanent one especially if you demonstrate what you can do for the company. For the best opportunities, you want to choose an excellent temporary agency. Ted Milner, president of Executive Temps in Burbank, California, contends, "Individuals are carefully selected to work through this agency. After six months with us, you would have a full-time job unless you are extremely picky." Other temporary work that has value is summer employment or a part-time job during the school year, ideally in your career field. However, any job you do well adds to your credentials. Additionally, the fact that you are using your time productively will impress a potential employer.

Seeking Internships, Volunteer Work, and Special Program Help

Whether you're still in school or actively seeking work and having no success, you can take advantage of methods that have worked for many. **Internships**, sometimes called work-study programs, are cooperative efforts between employers and schools. For the potential job candidate, they provide opportunities to gain experience, valuable information about the career field and companies, and excellent contacts. In most cases, you also get scholastic credit. "Internships are a great way to gain 'real-life' career experience to see if you really like that type of work," says Lori Hall, director of Education and Community Programs with the American Heart Association.

> *"Students are wise to look upon internships and other part-time employment as a long-term investment in their future rather than just as a way of earning money."*
>
> Marcia Phelps, Ph.D., Associate Director, Career Services
> University of Nebraska
> Lincoln, Nebraska

Even if you are like Tanya, who participated in a yearlong work program and discovered that early childhood education was not for her, you have gained valuable information. Obviously, paid internships are preferable; however, don't disregard an unpaid opportunity which could reap major dividends later. Another benefit is explained by Marcia Phelps, who helps place students in positions at the University of Nebraska. "If the internship or any type of student employment is related to one's major, it can lead to the student's enhanced academic performance and persistence in that field." She recommends that students start applying for intern positions early and, ideally, work in more than one during their college career. This has what can be a "funneling effect." A student may begin with a broad career goal such as accounting, and through related work experience eliminate certain type of work in that field. Eventually, she or he can focus on exactly what type of accounting is desired.

Volunteer work, whether when you are still in school or when you are having difficulty finding exactly what you want, has the following advantages.

- You can improve skills and learn new ones.
- You will add to your experience. Incidentally, employers today are likely to assess unpaid work in the same way they do paid experience.

- You can make valuable contacts.
- You can develop helpful references.
- As with temporary work, you could get a paid position.
- Employers are almost always impressed by volunteerism.

The last reason was underscored by a deputy chief of a city fire department when he told a class, "If I don't see any indication of volunteer work, you have fallen a degree in my estimation. Obviously, volunteer firefighting is preferable; however, I'm impressed by any type of volunteer activity."

In order to locate volunteer activities, check for a community volunteer clearinghouse or center or find names of nonprofit organizations in the yellow pages. You are unlikely to get or keep even a volunteer position unless you are qualified and eager to work. Most organizations know that a poor volunteer is worse than none.

Special programs that provide information and help are available through local, county, or state governments, community colleges, universities, and organizations. If you are middle age or older, the American Association of Retired Persons (AARP) has member programs that either put people to work or sponsor workshops that foster job opportunities.

HANDLING REJECTION

Almost certain in any career is being told or receiving in writing: "Sorry, but your qualifications and the position were not the best match. Good luck." It may be worded differently yet the meaning is the same—you were not considered or selected. What is your reaction? Most of us struggle with rejection.

So what can one do? Accept the idea that nobody wants to be rejected. Instead, most people believe that always getting what they want makes life wonderful. The reality is that life will never be that way, and we wouldn't be truly happy if it were. The line of life is a series of ups and downs, and well-adjusted individuals learn to use the low spots to enhance the highs. Valuable lessons are learned in the trenches, the dips of life (Hanna, 1995).

> *BEFORE BEGINNING A JOB SEARCH, EXAMINE HOW YOU HANDLE REJEC-TION. ASK YOURSELF HONESTLY: ON A SCALE OF 1 (VERY POORLY) TO 5 (VERY WELL), WHERE WOULD YOU RANK YOURSELF? IF THE ANSWER IS A 4 OR 5, YOU ARE PROBABLY READY TO STRIKE OUT ON YOUR QUEST. IF IT'S LOWER, YOU WOULD BE SPENDING YOUR TIME WISELY BY LEARNING HOW TO DEAL WITH A REBUFF. NOT DOING SO CAN LEAD TO DEPRESSION AND OTHER UNPLEASANT EMOTIONS, GIVING UP, OR BECOMING DESPERATE AND ACCEPTING ANY JOB TO AVOID THE PAIN OF FURTHER REJECTION.*

As in life, rejection in a job search is usually inevitable, appearing at any step of the process. In general, not getting interviews from telephone and written attempts is disappointing but not as potentially devastating as a later rejection. After an interview, applicants are more likely to take it personally. Similarly, not getting a bite while fishing can be discouraging, yet having a big fish on the line then losing it is enough to make a person weep!

If, after an interview, you don't get a job you really want, cognitive restructuring techniques can transform negative feelings into hopeful ones. Instead of thinking, "Because they didn't hire me, something is wrong with me," change it to: "Just because they didn't hire me doesn't mean something is wrong with me. Evidently, in their minds the position and I didn't match. The company missed an opportunity to get a first-rate employee." Then choose to move forward to a better job selection.

Another useful technique is described in *Guerilla Tactics in the Job Market* (Jackson, 1993). Visualizing the job search as a series of "no's" followed by a "yes" is not only realistic, it's hopeful. Also comforting is to realize that this is the path almost every effective job hunter follows.

Getting what you want in a career and jobs requires a great deal of initiative, time, thought, and activity. Determination in the wake of rejection is essential. Those who are willing to invest in the effort are likely to succeed and feel satisfied with this extremely important aspect of their lives.

KEY POINTS

⊚   Because so much time is spent on your career and because career satisfaction is closely related to life satisfaction, you are well-served by spending time and effort on its development.

⊚   A career is a broad field of endeavor while a job consists of tasks and duties on a day-to-day basis. In both, satisfaction is essential.

⊚   Individuals can limit career and job choices and are benefited by expanding their range of possibilities.

⊚   Through self-understanding and career research you can match yourself to both a career and a particular job.

⊚   Having realistic and practical aspirations and keeping up-to-date on various occupational fields increase your chances for career success and satisfaction.

⊚   Getting motivated, assessing your goals, and then acting upon them are instrumental.

⊚   Research into careers, jobs, and employers is a critical part of total career development.

⊚   Numerous sources of information exist, and an effective job search takes advantage of as many as possible. A library holds a vast store of career material; online sources are also plentiful.

⊚   Using a school's career counseling and placement services and your own program or department is effective in making career decisions and job searching.

- From a potential list of employers, making direct contacts is highly recommended. Responding to advertisements, while not effective on its own, is still advisable.

- Seeking and making use of references and networking can lead to job leads and career advancements.

- Temporary work has benefits that include experience and potential permanent jobs.

- Students can benefit from internships and other types of employment while in school.

- Volunteer work is a definite asset.

- Learning to handle rejection is necessary because most job searches include some negative results.

RECOMMENDED READING

Bolles, R. N. (1996). *What color is your parachute?* Berkeley, CA: Ten Speed Press.

Bounds, S. and Karl, A. (1996). *How to get your dream job using the Internet.* Scottsdale, AZ: Coriolis Group.

Caple, J. (1994). *Finding the hat that fits.* New York: Plume.

Edward, P. and Edward, S. (1996). *Finding your perfect work.* New York: G. P. Putnam's.

Gonyea, J. C. (1995). *The on-line job search companion.* New York: McGraw-Hill.

Hammer, H. (1991). *Complete guide to U.S. civil service jobs.* New York: Prentice Hall.

Hanna, S. L. (1995). *Person to person: Positive relationships don't just happen.* Englewood Cliffs, NJ: Prentice Hall.

Goldenkoff, R. & Morgan, D. (1991). *Federal jobs for college graduates.* New York: Prentice Hall.

Jackson, T. (1992). *Not just another job.* New York: Time Books.

Jackson, T. (1993). *Guerilla tactics in the job market.* Toronto: Bantam Books.

Kennedy, J. L. and Morrow, T. (1994). *Electronic job search revolution.* New York: John Wiley.

Kight, L. K. (1994). *Getting the lowdown on employers and a leg up on the job market.* Berkeley, CA: Ten Speed Press.

Michelozzi, B. N. (1996). *Coming alive from nine to five: The career search handbook.* Mountain View, CA: Mayfield Publishing.

Sinetar, M. (1989). *Do what you love, the money will follow.* New York: Paulist Press.

Strasser, S. and Sena, J. (1992). *Work is not a four letter word.* Homewood, IL: Business One.

Templeton, M. E. (1991). *Help! My job interview is tomorrow.* New York: Neal-Schuman Publishers.

Tieger, P. D. and Barron-Tieger, B. (1995). *Do what you are*. Boston: Little, Brown.

Tracy, D. (1994). *Take this job and love it*. New York: McGraw-Hill.

DIRECTORIES AND REFERENCE BOOKS

The Almanac for International Jobs and Careers

Dictionary of Occupational Titles

Directory of American Employment Agencies

Directory of American Firms Operating in Foreign Countries

Dun and Bradstreet Million Dollar Directory

Encyclopedia of Associations

Encyclopedia of Business Information Sources

Job Seeker's Guide to Private and Public Companies

Mac Rae's Blue Book

Moody's Complete Corporate Index

National Directory of State Agencies

National Trade and Professional Associations of the United States

Occupational Outlook Handbook

Polk's City Directories

Standard and Poor's Register of Corporations, Directors, and Executives

Thomas' Register of American Manufacturers

ONLINE RESOURCES

America's Employers: http://www.americasemployers.com

CareerPath: http://www.careerpath.com

JOBTRAK: http://www.jobtrak.com

The Monster Board: http://www.monster.com

Connect-Time: http://www.connect-time.com

CHAPTER FOUR

You in Writing

The ability to present yourself positively in writing is the most critical part of your job search. Unless you go in person or speak to the person who can hire you by telephone, your first impression will be a written one. If you don't succeed at impressing the reader, this particular job search is over. Résumés, cover letters, and applications are key elements in "getting your foot in the door." And, even if these methods aren't your initial way of approaching, presenting yourself in writing will, at some time, be expected. Generally, an employer will not take the time to interview you unless you, in writing, have set yourself apart from the competition.

DEVELOPING YOUR RÉSUMÉ

Entire books have been written on this subject, and you are encouraged to read several. Then it will be up to you to decide exactly what advice to take. From years of researching résumé writing, one thing is clear: There is different advice, and, in some cases, disagreement among the experts. In this section you will read suggestions from different sources and have access to this textbook's recommendations. The rest is up to you!

WHAT IS A RÉSUMÉ?

You can think of a **résumé** as a promotional piece or an advertisement for yourself. In the academic field, a résumé is called a vitae and includes all published works, which usually makes it longer.

Résumés are not autobiographies and are definitely not personal in the sense of describing your private life. The purpose of a résumé is to impress a potential employer and get you an interview, which is accomplished by clearly stating what you can do for the employer. Anything that could possibly hinder or detract from this should not be included.

REASONS FOR RÉSUMÉS

Today, most job seekers know that a résumé is a necessity. Understanding a résumé's benefits has merit. Most employers either require or at least expect a résumé. In order to be competitive, yours needs to be at least as impressive and preferably more so than others. In the unlikely case that a résumé is not required, your having prepared one will likely put you ahead of the competition.

Another benefit is that a résumé forces you to gather and clarify self-information. You will then be much more prepared for other aspects of a job search. Also, a résumé, unlike an application, lets you present yourself in the most favorable way. Have you ever considered why you take notes in classes or for what reason you might write a person's name in order to remember it later? Something in writing that one can refer to later jogs the memory. Employers use résumés for the same reason, and having one on file helps you be remembered. An interesting benefit is that résumé preparation can raise one's confidence. Said Todd, "After I read all the things I can do and have done, my self-esteem is higher."

Additionally, you can use your résumé as a written advertisement with your entire group of contacts. Ask each one to try to give it to someone who might be interested. With knowledge of its many benefits, look on résumé writing as an opportunity to present yourself in the most favorable way, realizing that what you are is worthy of pride.

RÉSUMÉ REQUIREMENTS

Even though employers aren't necessarily in agreement about all aspects of résumé writing, certain "absolutes" are clear.

- The résumé has a neat, professional appearance. It must be typed using either a computer or a typewriter, and other layout guidelines, covered later, are to be followed.

- No negative information is given.

- All words are spelled correctly. Spell-check functions in word processing programs will not catch certain errors such as the word "to" used for "too." Have someone with excellent spelling skills proofread your résumé. In addition, using correct grammar, punctuation, and sentence construction shows that you are adept in the language and that you care enough to be error-free. As an employer put it, "Employers conclude that if you make errors in your written communications before you are hired, you will make even more mistakes on the job." Even though perfection may be hard to achieve, a résumé should be perfect.

- The content is brief. Experts differ on whether a one- or two-page résumé is better; however, it's rare if anyone suggests longer than two pages. A vitae which is used in academia could be an exception to this if you have a number of published works.

- The writing is clear, concise, and easy to read.

- All information is the truth. Dishonesty on a résumé is a guaranteed way either to not get hired or to be fired if the truth is learned, and it usually is.

- It is evident what the candidate has to offer the employer. Self-serving résumés are a waste of time.

- A poor résumé is worse than no résumé at all. Decide that yours will be excellent.

> *"A tiny lie on a résumé can destroy all credibility. A misspelled word or grammar error shows lack of thoroughness or pride in one's work."*
>
> Lois Kemble, Cooperative Education Coordinator
> Southeast Community College
> Lincoln, Nebraska

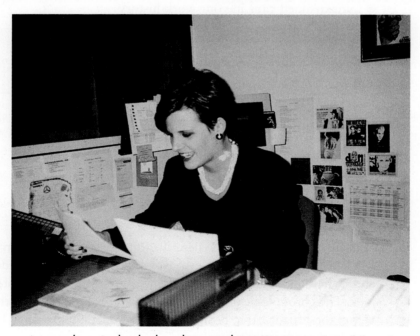

▲ An employer's shocked and amused reaction to a résumé is not what a job seeker wants!

TYPES OF RÉSUMÉS

Even though a résumé is one's own unique creation, successful job seekers select and then follow a certain prototype. The **format** is the way a résumé is laid out or organized. An important early decision is which format to use. The differences are primarily ones of order of listings and emphasis.

CHRONOLOGICAL RÉSUMÉ.   As the name implies, a chronological résumé emphasizes dates and follows a time sequence. Positions are described beginning with the present or most recent, regardless of how relevant they are. Following your job history, you tell when and for how long you were employed. Following are reasons you would choose this format.

- Because it is the most common one, employers are comfortable with it. Many believe that dates are valuable information, and they expect to see them.

- If your work history is stable with jobs of average or longer duration, this format focuses on a major asset.

- If your progression has been steady and in the direction of career objectives, achievement is evident.

Knowing the reasons you would want to consider another format is quite useful. A chronological résumé is *not* in your best interests if you have had:

- several jobs (number varies depending upon your age)
- jobs of short duration
- unexplained gaps in your work history

> *THINKING OF YOUR OWN HISTORY, DOES IT INCLUDE ANY OF THE REASONS TO AVOID A CHRONOLOGICAL RÉSUMÉ? IF NOT, THIS FORMAT IS PROBABLY THE BEST CHOICE.*

FUNCTIONAL RÉSUMÉ.   This type emphasizes experiences and skills, not dates. The order of listing is not chronological so the résumé writer can prioritize the value of the experiences and describe those first. Following are its advantages.

- You have an opportunity to highlight what you can do.

- The potential employer is not "hit in the face" with chronological liabilities. If you have unexplained gaps or several jobs of short duration, this is not evident.

- Relevant experiences can be described first even if they occurred early in your work history. For example, Kevin was applying for a job in radio broadcasting, and he had once had a similar position. Since then, he had worked at two other jobs. The chronological format would force him to describe the unrelated jobs before the broadcasting position. Using a functional résumé, he could begin with his broadcasting experiences.

Chronological format

KELLY L. HALL
2226 Parham Place
Ann Arbor, Michigan 48104
(312) 770-5546

OBJECTIVE   *Youth psychological counseling*

QUALIFICATIONS
* *Youth counseling certification*
* *Counseling experiences with children aged 6–17*
* *Desire to continue to learn and expand current level of expertise*

EXPERIENCE

1994–present   **Counselor**
Youth Services at Larchmount Clinic
Ann Arbor, Michigan
* *Counseled 16–20 children a week.*
* *Trained two new counselors.*

1990–1994   **Teacher Aide**
Early Childhood Education Center
Columbia, Missouri
* *Guided young children in development and craft activities.*
* *Provided art therapy sessions for five children.*

EDUCATION

1994   *B.A., Psychology*
University of Missouri, Columbia, Missouri
GPA: 3.98, graduated with high distinction

1993   *Assisted with research on teenage drug abuse.*
University of Missouri, Columbia, Missouri

1992–1993   *Served children with special needs in summer internships*
Camp Hope
Columbia, Missouri

◉   Any skills gained from various jobs that are assets for the position being applied for can be grouped together. This gives more validity to your qualifications.

> *CAN YOU THINK OF ANY REASON A FUNCTIONAL RÉSUMÉ WOULD BE A BETTER CHOICE FOR YOU?*

COMBINATION RÉSUMÉ.   As the name suggests, this format is both functional and chronological. Skills and experiences are functionally highlighted and followed

Functional format

MICHAEL A. NEWTON

5424 Forest Avenue   (310) 552-2624
Santa Monica, California 90276   (310) 842-7229

OFFICE MANAGEMENT
- *Established procedures to improve office efficiency.*
- *Maintained payroll and tax records.*
- *Communicated with customers personally and by correspondence.*
- *Scheduled three crews on a weekly basis.*

ACCOUNTING
- *Set up and maintained a computer accounting system.*
- *Prepared tax returns for a 20-employee company.*

SALES
- *Sold computers and related products for large electronics firm.*
- *Earned recognition for outstanding sales record in one year.*

SUPERVISION
- *Promoted to supervise three other crew members in pouring and finishing concrete for residential driveways after one month of employment.*

EDUCATION
Associate of Science Degree, Business Management, 1996
Valley Community College
Riverside, California
GPA: 3.78

HONORS AND ACTIVITIES
Who's Who in Junior Colleges
President of Student Senate, Valley Community College
Dean's List (all semesters)
Volunteer, Red Cross

by a brief chronological listing of employment history and education. The advantage is the opportunity to emphasize what you can do for an employer while not avoiding what most want to know—dates and duration.

TARGETED RÉSUMÉ.   Introduced in the book *The Perfect Résumé* (Jackson, 1981) and described in *Guerilla Tactics for the Job Market* (Jackson, 1993), this format clearly identifies what you can do in relation to a particular position. It also documents past achievements to support your claims and includes at the end a brief list of employment history and education. Designed to be highly specific, the major disadvantage is its limitation to just one position. If

Combination format

M A R Y A. M A R T I N O

4432 South Patton Avenue   *(802) 445-3829*
Montpelier, Vermont 05156

OBJECTIVE: *FIREFIGHTER*

EXPERIENCES

- *Volunteer firefighting experience for six years*
- *Leadership experience as head of firefighting team*
- *EMT certified and advanced CPR training*
- *Associate of Applied Science Degree with Highest Distinction*
  Fire Protection Technology
  GPA 4.0
- *Relevant coursework in psychology, sociology, and interpersonal relations*
- *Volunteer experiences at rehabilitation center and with Meals-on-Wheels*
- *Customer relations responsibilities for large insurance company*
- *Retail sales with record for highest productivity for two consecutive years*

EDUCATION

Associate of Applied Arts Degree with Highest Distinction   *1996*
Fire Protection Technology
Rosemount Community College
Montpelier, Vermont

EMPLOYMENT

Customer Service Representative   *1990–1994*
American Life Insurance Company
Montpelier, Vermont

Salesperson   *1988–1990*
Beller's Department Store
New Haven, Connecticut

---

this is the job you want, the targeted résumé is the best choice because it focuses on your directly related assets. Examples of these different formats are found at the end of this section, and you can find numerous samples in books listed at the end of the chapter.

ELECTRONIC RÉSUMÉ.   Effective job seekers develop another résumé that is computer/scanner friendly and which may never be seen by human eyes: an electronic résumé. These résumés are scanned, placed into a computerized database, and accessed only through the use of key words which are terms, words, and phrases that a worthy candidate would be expected to use (Beatty,

Targeted résumé

ROBERT WONG
2466 North 92nd Street
Lincoln, Nebraska 68520

(402) 477-6898   *rwong@aol.com*

JOB TARGET: EMERGENCY ROOM STAFF NURSE

EDUCATION: *Associate of Applied Science Degree in Nursing,*
Southeast Community College, Lincoln, Nebraska
C.E.R.N., 1995
Active license as a registered nurse in Nebraska

CAPABILITIES: *Emergency medical treatment*
Patient assessment
Successful patient rapport
Staff supervision
Training and development
Ability to think quickly and withstand pressure

ACHIEVEMENTS: *Performed all emergency room functions in a 12-bed*
emergency facility.
Assessed patient trauma in cardiac, respiratory, and
psychiatric cases.
Supervised 5 emergency room staff members.
Provided continuing education to new personnel.
Treated serious injuries as a member of first-response
ambulance team.

WORK HISTORY: *September 1995–present*
Staff R.N., Emergency Room
Bryan Memorial Hospital, Lincoln, Nebraska

March 1988–September, 1995
Emergency Medical Technician
Foster Ambulance Service, Lincoln, Nebraska

1995; Gonyea, 1996; Washington, 1996). For example, for a sales position, some possible words are *sales representative, accounts, marketing, profits, quotas,* and *increase.* During your research, ask whether this employer is one of many who scans résumés. If so, yours must include the expected key words, or it will not be accessed. If you do not know whether résumés are scanned or read, a good idea is to send an electronic résumé along with the traditional type. Attach a note labeling the scannable one.

JOT DOWN SOME KEY WORDS YOU THINK WOULD APPLY TO A POSITION IN YOUR CHOSEN FIELD.

The following points about electronic résumés are emphasized in *Résumé Power* (Washington, 1996), which has an excellent chapter on the subject.

1. Use a 12-point font; you may use 14- or 16-point font for your name and other headings.

2. Print your résumé on a high-quality laser printer. Definitely do not use a dot-matrix printer.

3. Use a sans serif typeface such as Arial, Helvetica, Univers, or Century Gothic. These are ones without little strokes in parts of each letter; each letter stands alone.

4. Keep lines 80 characters or less. Using a 12-point font and leaving margins of 1.25 to 1.5 inches on both sides will usually ensure this. To be safe, you can count each letter and space to stay under 80.

5. Use white or light-colored 8 1/2 × 11 paper and print on only one side. Black ink on white paper is preferable.

6. Do not fold the résumé. Send it in a large envelope.

7. Avoid the use of italics, underlining, fancy fonts, shading, columns, boxes, and vertical lines.

8. Use standard spacing between letters and lines.

9. Unless requested, do not send by fax; also, send a scannable résumé to arrive as soon as possible.

More information is available in books and online. A scannable cover letter also uses a 12-point, sans serif font. When sending an electronic résumé and letter, it's a good idea to also send additional ones in the conventional way.

DECISIONS AND STEPS IN RÉSUMÉ WRITING

After deciding about the type, you will be faced with still more choices. This section presents different questions and information to guide you in your answers. In some cases, a definite recommendation is given; however, you are the one responsible for your own résumé. KEY STEPS (pages 287–88) offers

▲ "That is a very creative résumé. What else do you have to offer our company?"

questions and suggestions. After decisions are made, action is key. Assembling information, making a draft or what is more likely, several drafts, and then refining the information into a perfect piece will take plenty of time and energy, all of which can be one of the best investments you will ever make.

    ◎   How will I head the résumé?

Every résumé must have your name, address, and telephone number on it. You may also include a second telephone and fax number and e-mail address if these seem appropriate. Your name should stand out somewhat. Centering it and using all capital letters and a slightly larger and bolder font is one possibility. Another is to leave a space between each letter so that instead of:

JANET R. STERLING

it is:

J A N E T R. S T E R L I N G

Many computer programs offer single-line and other interesting heading formats.

    RECOMMENDATION: It is not necessary to use "Résumé" in your heading. Clearly the reader will know what this is! Be sure your name is the most obvious part of the heading; however, don't make it so much larger than the rest of the information that it looks "overdone." If possible, use computer technology to create an impressive heading.

    ◎   Do I use a career or job objective?

Not everyone agrees about this. Many career development experts recommend an objective in order to let a potential employer know what you want and to appear focused. Yet, some employers say to eliminate it. "An objective wastes space that could be better used for other information," said Ed Rasgorshek, a senior vice president in the farm credit industry. "A candidate is better off stating an objective in the cover letter rather than the résumé, and it should specifically focus on your unique strengths for the targeted position. It's important that it not sound as if it were copied from a book," says Marcia Phelps, an associate director of career services at a university. Ted Milner, who owns his own executive temporary-help agency, put it bluntly, "Objectives aren't impressive."

    A disadvantage of an objective is that it can limit your résumé, and if almost no information is conveyed, an objective doesn't help. Little is gained by writing, "To pursue a career in advertising utilizing my skills as an artist." However, there are advantages. If you know exactly what you want or if you are sending your résumé to a human resources department, a clear objective is appreciated, and there are many employers who look for one. "It's helpful to know if a person wants an office or technical position; if you know exactly what you want, use a career-specific objective in either the résumé or cover letter," says Lyn Patterson, human resources administrator, Turner Broadcasting System, Inc., Los Angeles.

    RECOMMENDATION: If you believe an objective in the résumé will save the reader time or help you get the interview, write a clear, original one. Otherwise, use a cover letter to define relevant goals.

❻   After the heading, what comes next?

You may begin with one of the main categories or an eye-catching brief summary of your qualifications and skills. In a targeted résumé, this synopsis is placed directly below the name. For an electronic résumé, this section incorporates those recognizable key words. Use common industry-specific terms and jargon that describe your credentials (Weddle, 1994). Regardless of format, having a short, readable section of what you have to offer calls attention to your assets immediately and saves time for the reader. Because of its position on the page, a summary has to be exceptionally well done. See later sections and the samples for recommended language and layout.

RECOMMENDATION: Write an easy-to-read, concise section that immediately lets the reader know what you can do for his or her business. For an electronic résumé, make use of any key word you think an employer would use to access résumés from a database.

❻   Do I begin with work history or education?

The answer to this question is a quick, "That depends." A common mistake of job applicants is to simply follow a format from a résumé sample. That may not be the best choice. Remembering that this is your way of impressing an employer, describe your strongest area first. In some cases, strength is determined by how recent was the education or work. In the following scenarios, see if you can decide "which comes first" for the applicants.

> *Kelly has been in the work place for seven years after earning a degree in psychology. For the past five years she has counseled in a hospital drug-rehabilitation program. She is seeking a similar position in a private clinic.*

In Kelly's case both her education and work experience are relevant. However, because she has had a position similar to the one she is applying for and her degree was earned seven years ago, work experience would be described ahead of education.

> *John will graduate soon with a degree in economics and wants a position as a financial analyst. During college he worked in retail sales in a large department store.*

Because John has not had a job in his career field and his education is so recent, he would first cover education.

> *Tina has just earned an Associate of Applied Science Degree in Fire Protection Technology. She seeks a firefighting position in a metropolitan fire department. For the past year she was an assistant in the state fire marshal's office and a member of a volunteer fire department.*

This one is not as clear because both her education and experiences are relevant and timely. In this case, as part of her research, Tina should find out which is more important to the fire department. If that doesn't give her an answer, it comes down to which, in her opinion, is her stronger asset. Because she is strong in both, it probably will not make a major difference.

> ## WHICH OF THE TWO CATEGORIES IS YOUR GREATER STRENGTH?

RECOMMENDATION: Consider this carefully and don't just follow someone else's format. If the two are similar, find out which will be more impressive to a potential employer.

⊙ Is there a certain type of wording to use?

Most experts say to avoid the word "I." Rather than writing in complete sentences, the use of **telegraphic phrases** is highly recommended (Greene and Martel, 1992). Such a phrase begins with an action word such as *designed*, *sold*, or *instructed* and leaves out unnecessary words such as *the*, *a*, and *also*. The phrase sounds crisp and leaves the distinct impression that you have been active. Select action words carefully (see Table 4–1 for examples). A thesaurus can be an excellent resource. Marcia Phelps, Ph.D., an associate director of career services at a university who has had several years of experience in human resources, says, "Employers today are most interested in what skills you can bring to the position. The most effective résumés are skill-based rather than experience-based."

If a résumé will be scanned, the language is somewhat different. Most résumé-tracking systems tend to key in on nouns, and these words must be the ones an employer has identified as desired qualifications (Beatty, 1995).

RECOMMENDATION: Avoid "I" and complete sentences. Use telegraphic phrases with specific action words. Anyone can use general words such as *worked*, *served as*, or *participated*. It's better to write specifically what you did. Another way to be specific is to include figures that favor

T A B L E   4 – 1 ▲ ACTION WORDS

Achieved	Consulted	Identified	Reported
Acquired	Coordinated	Increased	Researched
Acted as	Created	Informed	Reviewed
Addressed	Delegated	Inspected	Revised
Administered	Designed	Installed	Saved
Advanced	Developed	Interacted	Scheduled
Advised	Devised	Invented	Selected
Analyzed	Diagnosed	Maintained	Sold
Answered	Directed	Managed	Solved
Arbitrated	Edited	Marketed	Sorted
Assigned	Employed	Mediated	Studied
Assisted	Engineered	Monitored	Summarized
Balanced	Estimated	Negotiated	Supervised
Budgeted	Evaluated	Operated	Taught
Built	Filed	Ordered	Tested
Communicated	Formulated	Organized	Trained
Composed	Gathered	Recorded	Updated
Computed	Generated	Redesigned	Utilized
Constructed	Hired	Reorganized	Wrote

you. Instead of "Serviced customer accounts," it is more impressive to write, "Serviced 165 customer accounts." Avoid "responsible for" as a lead-in because it does not describe action. Strive for consistency in verb usage rather than switching from past tense ("wrote articles") to present tense ("instruct students") when describing the same position. Instead of abbreviating, write the word completely unless you are absolutely sure the reader will know what you mean as in the case of college degrees. Even though postal abbreviations for states are commonly used, the more professional approach is to write the entire word. Any complete word will eliminate confusion and show that you can spell. If your résumé will be scanned, include key words and acronyms such as *RN* along with registered nurse.

⑨ **What is to be included in the education category, and what is a good heading?**

If you are using the chronological format, the year or years will be included and are usually placed in the left margin next to the relevant information. Because the potential employer is most interested in your level of education, place first the degree or diploma earned followed directly by your major, then the name and location of the institution. Generally, you can abbreviate the degree as most people are familiar with the common ones such as B.A., B.S., M.A., M.S., and Ph.D. If your degree is not a familiar one, write it out completely.

Even if you have not completed the requirements for a degree or diploma, write: "Completed ___ hours in (course of study)," or you can write: "Will receive B.A. in May 1999." For a thorough look at ways to describe your specific educational experiences, a recommended book is *Résumé Power* (Washington, 1996). Listing a high school diploma isn't necessary because employers know that if you are in college, you completed high school. The exception is if you are a recent high school graduate with an exceptional record either in academics, leadership activities, or both.

Most experts recommend that you include your GPA if it is high enough (3.0 or higher on a 4.0 scale) and any recognition or honors related to academic achievement. Another possibility is to include relevant coursework especially if education is your strongest asset or if the class taught specific necessary or desired skills. For example, naming specific software courses and an interpersonal relations class lets employers know of valuable training and will likely make a difference.

> *THINK OF ALL RELEVANT EDUCATIONAL EXPERIENCE YOU WOULD INCLUDE.*

RECOMMENDATION: Begin with your highest degree. Include any educational experiences that are assets, and almost all are. If your GPA is high and you have coursework that is especially relevant, mention these. The simple heading of *Education* set off in capital letters and, perhaps, bold font is recommended.

⊙ What is to be included in the employment section and what is a good heading?

This section has four main purposes (Washington, 1996):

1. describes duties and responsibilities
2. highlights results and accomplishments
3. shows career progress
4. reveals where you've been and for whom you've worked

If you are using the chronological or combination format, it also tells when and how long you have been employed. You may use just years employed or months and years although some wonder about rounded-off dates (years only). A key point is that in the chronological format, you begin with your present or most recent position and describe your jobs in reverse order.

When you arrange the information, consider what the reader will most want to know. What you have done rather than for whom you have worked is usually of more interest. The descriptions of job duties and responsibilities are where the reader will concentrate to see what you have actually done (duties) and the employer's level of trust and expectations (responsibilities). Résumés that are quickly readable are impressive. Scanning down rather than left to right is easier. Note the difference in the following descriptions.

> Have taught courses in English and speech, developed new writing projects, and advised students; worked on a special team to improve teaching methods; provided expertise to a student debate team; made presentations to organizations.

versus

- ▲ Taught English and speech to diverse groups of students.
- ▲ Developed four innovative writing projects.
- ▲ Advised 50 students each semester regarding course schedules.
- ▲ Contributed creative ideas to a team designed to improve teaching methods.
- ▲ Led and provided expertise to a student debate team.
- ▲ Presented various programs to organizations.

The second one is easier to read and uses specific numbers.

An electronic résumé will use more nouns than verbs. For example, a job title or position such as "office management" is a better choice than "managed an office." On any type of résumé, leadership or supervisory experiences and any advancement in responsibilities and positions are to be emphasized.

RECOMMENDATION: Emphasize your job title by putting it first followed by employer name and location (exact address isn't necessary). Do an excellent job of describing duties and responsibilities by using specific action words and telegraphic phrases for a conventional résumé. Arrange and set the phrases off so they are easy to read. Use key noun words for electronic résumés. On all, include any evidence of leadership and advancement. If you use months, write out the word. If you use years only, be prepared to be more specific in an interview. Possibilities for a heading are *Employment, Employment History, Employment Experience, Work Experience, Professional Experience*, and *Experience*.

⊚ What is a good way to highlight the information in both the education and employment categories?

Highlighting or emphasizing can be accomplished by listing the most relevant information first and using capital letters and different fonts (i.e., bold, italics) to emphasize essential information such as job title. Placing "bullets" in front of each telegraphic phrase catches a reader's eye.

    RECOMMENDATION: Because an employer will most want to know your level of education and job positions, place them at the beginning of the descriptions and highlight them in some way. See the samples for possible ideas.

⊚ Besides education and employment, what else can be included?

Membership in professional associations related to your career can be included under such headings as *Professional Affiliations, Affiliations, Professional Memberships*, or *Memberships*. Most employers are impressed with volunteer activities. They are also looking for indications of teamwork and leadership such as in college and community activities. Exceptions are any that indicate religious, political, ethnic, and social affiliations or others that might concern a potential employer unless they are specifically job-related. Listing social fraternities or sororities is not advisable unless you believe this is necessary to show strong leadership.

> *WHAT ORGANIZATIONS CAN YOU INCLUDE? CONSIDER JOINING ONE OR MORE THAT WOULD ADD TO YOUR CREDENTIALS.*

    Honors that indicate special expertise or leadership are quite relevant. This type of information can go in a separate section called *Relevant Experiences, Relevant Activities, Activities, Awards, Noteworthy Accomplishments, Accomplishments, Honors*, or *Activities and Honors*. Keep in mind that a potential employer is interested only in the ones that are assets for this position. If you were Girl Scout of the Year when you were in grade school, be proud of that; however, do not include it! Because so many candidates have similar educational and work backgrounds, supplementary information such as volunteer work, athletic pursuits, and elected offices can set you apart.

    Licenses or certification are assets, as well, and could be included under one of the categories mentioned earlier, if appropriate, or under a separate heading of *Licenses* or *Certification*. If you have written articles or books that have been published, most employers will be impressed. In certain fields such as education, being published is a definite asset. These can be listed in a section called *Publications*. A thesis or dissertation can be placed in the education category. Special skills such as a second language or training in transferable areas such as interpersonal communication could make the difference in your getting an interview. If beneficial, you can indicate willingness to relocate or, preferably, write this in a cover letter.

RECOMMENDATION: Check your list of assets and include as many as possible. Know what the position requires and definitely include any experience that would document important characteristics and skills. Remember that a résumé is a promotional piece that stresses what you have to offer this employer.

⊚ What about references?

This is an area of mixed opinions. Generally, you will find authors recommending that you add to the end of your résumé the statement: *References Furnished Upon Request.* Because this is so common, as well as virtually useless at this point in the job search, you can, instead, include your references on a separate sheet headed *References*. This page is not a part of the résumé. Consider the following reasons.

▲ Your references may help at this stage. For example, one day I received a telephone call from a man I knew from a volunteer organization. He owned his own printing company. He said, "I don't usually call references at this point. However, I saw your name and since I know you, decided to get your opinion right away." My positive comments about the candidate led to an interview which may not have occurred otherwise.

▲ Networking may work. If a name is recognizable and also especially creditable, it will likely be particularly impressive. When reading a list of references, I saw the name of a prominent citizen who was a top professional in the same career field as the applicant. This led me to be more interested in the résumé than I might have been.

▲ Including references makes the potential employer's job easier. Instead of having to contact you and get your references, the list is right there. Incidentally, most employers don't bother to get an applicant's references unless he or she is one of the final candidates. So unless you include the names, your impressive list of references may do you no good.

One author opposed to an inclusion of references mentions the danger of the slightest bit of negative information keeping you from getting an interview (Beatty, 1995). Certainly, if you have even the tiniest concern about a reference, you would be foolish to present this name. Yet, if you are confident the comments will be to your benefit, the danger disappears.

You may want to vary the names depending upon the company and the actual position you are seeking. Following is a recommended way to list a reference.

Angelo Edwards, District Supervisor
United Industrial Products, Inc.
924 South 28th Street
Anchorage, Alaska 99502
(907) 486-2715

As a professional courtesy, you would use a home telephone number only with permission.

RECOMMENDATION: Selection of references was covered in Chapter 3. Include three to five references with your résumé on a separate page headed *References*. Mention in the cover letter their inclusion. Use only professional references and include name, title, business address, and telephone number.

⊚ Should I include personal data such as age?

Although you will still find a few who say to include information of a personal nature, most strongly advise not to do so. Besides your age, such personal data include marital status, children, religion, vital statistics such as height, weight, race, sex, and condition of health. Ask yourself, "How will this information help me?" Any piece of personal information is just as likely to be considered a liability as an asset. Even though health is an asset, most employers know that nobody is likely to admit to less than excellent health. Your space is best used in other ways.

Perhaps, the most significant reason to avoid personal data is to show awareness of the law. If you include age or marital status, an employer is apt to wonder where you have been in recent years. This type of information is, in most cases, illegal for an employer to ask or to consider as criteria. Also, any candidate who would try to get hired on the basis of personal data is probably not the best applicant.

RECOMMENDATION: Do not include any personal data.

⊚ What else is to be avoided?

The following are on the list of "to-be-left-out."

▲ salary history or expectations

▲ reasons for leaving past job

▲ photograph (could be part of a portfolio for a modeling or acting position, but not on a résumé)

▲ hobbies and leisure time activities unless these are definite assets (if so, could be included when listing skills or accomplishments)

▲ social security number

The basic criterion for inclusion is simple: Will this information enhance my chances for this position? If not, leave it out. Even then you may have too many assets to fit on two pages. Then it's necessary to prioritize to keep the résumé brief. Another question to ask is: What impression will this make on the potential employer? If you aren't almost certain that it will be a positive one, leave it out.

RECOMMENDATION: Remember that the prime purpose of a résumé is to convince the potential employer to give you an interview, and you have a limited amount of space to do so. Not only does the information on the "leave-out" list take up valuable space, it could actually be detrimental.

◎ How can my résumé have the best-possible appearance?

Your final copy is to be done on a quality typewriter, word processor, or computer. If you don't have access to any of these, you will need to find someone or a company that can provide the service, or you can rent computer time. A quality printer such as a laser or ink-jet is necessary. Again, if you don't have one, take a diskette to someone who does.

White space makes a résumé more appealing. The page is to have at least one-inch margins on all four sides and adequate spacing between sections. A page completely full of print will turn off most readers. Accent lines and paragraph or page borders can enhance the look of the résumé. If you don't have software that can transform a plain typed page into an attractive piece, have it done for you. Several firms are in business to provide layout and copying service. Typically, they charge a one-time fee for layout with small charges for future modifications. However it is done, your original is to be camera-ready, which means ready to be copied.

At this point, you will have some choices to make. One is selection of a reputable business firm that provides quality photocopying. Prices can vary considerably. While you are unwise to base your decision on which is the cheapest, there is no reason to pay a much higher price to a company that doesn't offer any higher quality than a less expensive one.

The next decision has to do with paper. Even though some people want to show creativity in a résumé by cleverly done brochures, a wiser choice is to stick with standard size paper. Choose a heavier-weight stock from the company's selection of professional résumé papers. These are available in a variety of colors. Avoid anything other than light, conservative hues of white, ivory, or beige. For electronic résumés, white paper with black ink is best. The company is likely to make copies of your résumé so white or very light colors are much better. Avoid parchment papers; a textured or linen weave is acceptable. A wise idea is to purchase extra sheets for your cover letters and other correspondence.

If you are responding to an advertisement which gives a fax number, send a copy that way. "Speed is of the essence," says Lyn Patterson, human resources administrator, Turner Broadcasting System, Inc., Los Angeles, "and a fax that's clear and concise in content will quickly put the information in the employer's hands." You can also send a paper copy immediately.

RECOMMENDATION: Your résumé is usually a potential employer's first impression of you. Consider what degree of quality you want to present. Follow the suggestions about producing the highest quality résumé. This is no time to be frugal if spending a little more will buy you a highly professional résumé.

How many copies of the résumé should I order?

There is no absolute answer. Ask yourself how many copies of the résumé you plan to use within a short period of time. If you plan to send out 50 résumés, get 55 copies so you have a few extra. It's foolish to order too many more than you will use right away. You can always get additional copies as you need them. Consider the case of Karla. "Out of excitement I had 150 copies made. I mailed out 25 the first week then got word from the telephone company that our number would be changed within a month!" If any information on your résumé changes, it is obsolete.

RECOMMENDATION: Order only the number of résumés you plan to use within a few weeks.

What else in a résumé might be important?

Fine organization is a major plus in a résumé. Readers want to recognize a logical sequence. What is called parallel structure is worth checking. For each job description, are you providing information in the same order? Are you consistent in verb tense unless there's a reason to switch?

What about using the Internet?

Today's sophisticated job seeker will also use the superinformation highway. If you are requested to respond to an opening online or find an employer to access in this medium, you can send a résumé and cover letter in cyberspace. Using the Internet will undoubtedly become much more popular than it is today when one estimate of its effectiveness in getting a job is only 3 percent (Bolles, 1996). Instructions are available online. As an interesting way of presenting yourself, give it a try!

KEY ADVICE

WHAT DO YOU LIKE OR NOT LIKE ON A RÉSUMÉ?

Architecture and Drafting: *"The format must permit a quick review. Don't get too cute or too artsy because this can cause difficulty in reading and be detrimental."*

Lynn Jones, Chairman, Davis Design

Drafting: *"Direct it toward the job you are applying for; don't be too generic. Make it clear that you have goals and have participated in school and community activities."*

Mike Petersen, Supervisor of Drafting Services, Lincoln Electric System

Machine Tool: *"Don't get any past employment dates mixed up and be 'to the point' in describing your experiences. I definitely like to see references included."*

John Buse, President, Precision Machine Co., Inc.

Firefighting: *"I like to see evidence of experiences that contributed to positive character development such as worthwhile activities and organizations."*

  Darrell Eastin, Beatrice, Nebraska, Fire Department Chief

"Put your personality into the résumé. I want to know you, not a professional résumé designer."

  Mark Munger, Lincoln, Nebraska, Fire Department Captain

Communications: *"I prefer a short one-page résumé with bulleted points that make for easy reading."*

  Doc Chaves, Assistant Vice President, Ameritas Life Insurance Corp.

Automotive Technology: *"A résumé needs to contain all the necessary information relating to your qualifications, be typed, neat and easy to read, and not overly long."*

  Bob Batt, Owner, Auto Tek Service Center, Inc.

Printing Technology: *"Be honest and provide complete information."*

  Bill Payzant, President, Capitol Graphics

Child Care: *"Make it brief and include only current information."*

  Sue Collins, Director, KinderCare Learning Center

Lending and Banking: *"I like to see a very organized and concise résumé that has dates. Unexplained gaps in work history concern me."*

  Ed Rasgorshek, Senior Vice President, Farm Credit Services
  of the Midlands

Health Care: *"Résumés of length get lost in the shuffle. Details and listing every seminar you've ever attended are unnecessary."*

  Nancy Brown, R.N., Program Manager, State Department of Health

Human Resources and Development: *"I want an easy-to-read and well-organized résumé that has a neat and clean appearance. I don't need to know about hobbies and definitely don't need to see personal data."*

  Jody Horwitz, Director of Human Resources, Turner Broadcasting
  System, Inc., Los Angeles

"Limit accomplishments to the most significant. Don't include every detail. Leave 'white space.'"

  Jeanne Salerno, Director, Professional Development, Kutak
  Rock Law Firm

A résumé to be read by an actual human being will continue to be expected. As you look at the following examples and samples from other sources, make decisions that will be best for you. Proudly create a résumé that reflects the best of you in writing.

"Get rid of the idea that there is absolutely one right way to develop a résumé. The 'right way' for you is the way that most effectively presents your skills and qualifications relative to the type of job you are seeking."

Marcia Phelps, Ph.D., Associate Director, Career Services
University of Nebraska
Lincoln, Nebraska

If you are ready to throw up your arms in despair because you don't think you can write an excellent résumé, consider asking a friend or family member with more expertise to do much of it for you or look into using a professional résumé-writing service. A disadvantage of the latter is that these are often easily spotted by people who receive many résumés; in order to make yours unique, be the major consultant on the résumé-writing project. "Make it your own," is the advice of Carolyn Olsen, an instructor of employment techniques for business students. In doing so, make it tasteful and professional.

If you opt to use a service, be sure to get references from others and shop around for a fair price as well as quality service. Most will offer a free consultation session. A desirable résumé service would have had a minimum of one or two years experience and at least 1,000 resumes (Provenzano, 1995). Also ask about the service's success rate. Above all, be satisfied with the writing style and the way in which you are presented to a potential employer.

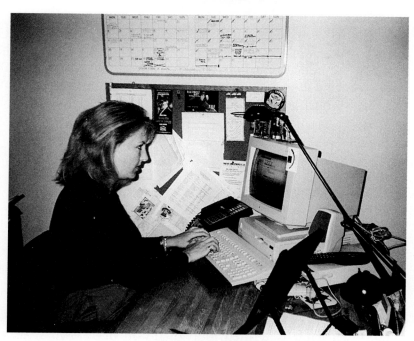

▲ A computer is an invaluable tool in drafting a résumé.

Use a typewriter or printer to address the envelope and be sure to include a return address. The employer's address will look exactly like the inside address, which usually requires four lines. A question is whether to fold a résumé to mail. To present a neater appearance, the use of a larger envelope and an unfolded résumé is advisable. If the résumé will be scanned, definitely don't fold it. What is not open to question is a hard-and-fast rule: Do not send a résumé without a cover letter. This leads to the next critical aspect of "You in Writing."

WRITING A COVER LETTER

As difficult as you may think it is to develop a résumé, writing an excellent cover letter can be even more challenging. And, even more than a résumé, it may determine whether or not you get an interview. Why? Each cover letter is a creative endeavor. You may use the same résumé for several positions while a cover letter is customized to the particular potential employer. A good way to destroy your chances for an interview is the obvious mass production of a cover letter. That is one reason Sue Collins, director of a KinderCare Learning Center, said she isn't interested in the cover letter. "They seem to all come from the same book." Obviously, you will want yours to be uniquely your own—and one that will arouse interest.

Another reason for a letter's importance is that employers realize that your résumé could be the product of a professional résumé-writing service. However, in most cases, applicants write their own cover letters. Because the cover letter is usually read before a résumé, it becomes the first impression.

WHAT IS A COVER LETTER?

One day in class after I had been talking about the importance of a cover letter, a student asked, "This may be a dumb question, but what is a cover letter?" As an educator who doesn't believe that any question is dumb, I was happy that he asked! Specifically, a **cover letter** is a letter that accompanies a résumé. Its purposes are:

- to introduce the writer and the résumé,
- to indicate a knowledge and interest in the particular employer and a desire for a position,
- to explain briefly what you have to offer,
- to request an interview.

Your cover letter may be exploratory in nature, often called unsolicited, or be solicited such as in response to an advertisement. You could be writing because of one of your networking contacts. If this is the case, be sure you mention the person in your initial paragraph.

GUIDELINES FOR COVER LETTERS

While each letter is written individually in one's own style, there are general guidelines. Unless absolutely impossible, the most important requirement is to send the letter to a specific person; in other words, use a name. Not doing so will

KEY ADVICE

WHAT ARE YOUR RECOMMENDATIONS ABOUT COVER LETTERS?

Communications: *"Send a 'killer' cover letter. This can be more important than the résumé."*

    Doc Chaves, Assistant Vice President, Ameritas Life Insurance Corp.

Architecture and Drafting: *"Address it to the proper individual. The personal touch helps. Be very careful about grammar and spelling as this is your opportunity to make a good first impression."*

    Lynn Jones, Chairman, Davis Design

Drafting: *"Know who you are writing to and show that you know what product or service the company provides."*

    Mike Petersen, Supervisor of Drafting Services, Lincoln Electric System

Automotive Technology: *"Introduce yourself, refer to the job you are seeking, ask that you be considered, and request an interview at the convenience of the employer. This should not be a long and involved letter, and I don't feel that salary requirements should be mentioned."*

    Bob Batt, Owner, Auto Tek Service Center, Inc.

Health Care: *"A cover letter reveals a person's ability to write clearly and accurately. Writing skills are very important."*

    Nancy Brown, R.N., Program Manager, State Department of Health

Machine Tool: *"Don't over-use the word 'I.' Other people helped you get where you are now."*

    John Buse, President, Precision Machine Co., Inc.

Human Resources and Development: *"Make it short with no errors. Do not describe in the letter what is presented on the résumé. Be sure to save information for the interview."*

    Jeanne Salerno, Director, Professional Development, Kutak Rock Law Firm

"A cover letter is very important. I want to know immediately how and why this resume is coming to me. Is it a referral? What is the person looking for? Be sure you have names and titles correct and no misspellings."

    Jody Horwitz, Director of Human Resources, Turner Broadcasting System, Inc.

most likely place your letter and résumé behind the other candidates who did. Even if an advertisement directed you to send a résumé to a search committee, find out the name of the head of the committee and give yourself an advantage. How do you find names? If you don't know who these people are, call and get the names and the correct spelling. If finding out the name of the person who is hiring is not possible, the next best choice is to send your cover letter and résumé to the human resources director. Again, use a specific name unless impossible.

The letter, like the résumé, is to be typed or printed from a computer. Using one half to three fourths of the page is preferable; this letter should not be more than a page long. Perfection is again the key so be sure you have no misspellings, grammatical or punctuation errors, or incomplete sentences. It's best to have someone else read the letter, as well, to check for errors and to see if the content is clear. Margins are to be at least one inch on each side, and there should be plenty of white space. One recommended format is to use single spacing with each line starting at the left margin. Double space between the paragraphs and don't use any indentations. Check to find out which form of a business letter is currently most preferred.

Contents of a Cover Letter

If you look at different samples, you will see various ways of heading and ending cover letters. A professional touch can be achieved by having your name, address, and phone number printed in a personal letterhead at the top. You can create your own letterhead on a computer. Other possibilities are to type your address and date at the top or begin with only the current date and at the end, type your address under your name.

After the date, there is a quadruple space (four line spaces) then the inside address. The first line of this address will preferably be a person's name followed by a title. The next three lines contain the name of the company, street address, and city, state, and ZIP code. For the greeting you may use a title before the last name such as: *Dear Dean Steinberg, Director Carlson,* or *President Bowen,* or the customary *Mr. Thomas* or *Ms. Herrara.* At this stage of the search, using a first name is not recommended. What can you do if you are responding to a blind ad or have tried and been unsuccessful at getting a name? You may use either: *Dear Hiring Authority* or *Dear Human Resources Director.* Never use: *To Whom It May Concern, Dear Sir,* or *Gentlemen,* which implies that only men are in positions of power, or *Dear Madam.* End with a professional closing phrase such as *Sincerely* or *Respectfully* and four spaces below that, your full name. Use a colon (:) after the greeting and a comma after the closing phrase.

If you aren't using personal letterhead paper, typing your address and telephone number under your name makes it easily accessible to the reader. Two spaces below that, type the word *Enclosure,* which indicates that a résumé is enclosed. The samples give you an idea of how this looks.

> *IF YOU HAVE A COMPUTER, EXPERIMENT WITH PERSONAL LETTERHEADS.*

The main contents of a cover letter will vary somewhat depending upon whether you are responding to an advertisement or taking the initiative. In both the solicited and unsolicited situations, the conventional letter has three sections; each is usually one paragraph long. The purpose of each section follows.

1. *Introduction:* Attracts the reader's interest and makes clear why you are interested and why you would be an asset. According to Lois Kemble, college instructor,

the first 20 words are the most important. Your research should be evident; preferably, you express positive information about the business. The samples indicate some ways to do this. If your résumé doesn't have an objective, be sure to include this. It will be clear to the reader why you are writing.

2. *Body:* Documents your assets; makes a strong connection between what you have to offer and what the business needs or what the position demands; calls attention to your résumé. If you are responding to an advertisement, this section will convince the reader that you can handle the job. If you are initiating a search, it will point out why the employer would want to hire you. This part creates a desire to learn more about you.

3. *Closing:* Restates keen interest in and regard for the specific business; requests a meeting at the employer's convenience; provides a way of contacting you; tells what you will do as a follow-up. If you are responding to an advertisement, a follow-up comment may not be appropriate; instead, you can acknowledge agreement with whatever procedure was described. While many experts suggest that you write, "I will call to arrange an interview," you might consider a slightly different, and less directive, statement such as, "I will call to discuss setting up an interview." See the samples for other ideas. This last part requests action and shows without a doubt that you intend to play an active role in securing employment.

If you are responding to an advertisement, provide all requested information. Responding to "salary desired or expected" or a salary history request can be disconcerting. If the employer wants a full salary history, you may submit a separate sheet with an appropriate heading. Otherwise, you can include information about desired or expected salary in your letter. Ideally, your research will give you an idea of the exact wage or range for the position, or you can find lists of average starting salaries in various publications. If you don't have this information, decide what range is acceptable to you such as "$35,000–$40,000 a year" or use a general amount such as "upper $30s a year." Do not offer any salary information unless it is specifically requested.

Of extreme importance is to sound enthusiastic and sincere. "An excellent cover letter conveys confidence and enthusiasm in its wording," says Tony Reimer, claims superintendent, State Farm Insurance, Rocky Mount, North Carolina. Writing a rough draft as if you were talking directly to a person is a good way to start. Once something is on paper, you can polish the contents. Employers usually do not like letters that are filled with well-worn phrases and sound like everyone else's. Neither is it desirable to be overly clever such as: "How would you like to hire the best employee anywhere in the world? You have that opportunity if you choose yours truly!" Probably, only a few would find this amusing and want to meet the writer.

"Don't just re-state what is in your résumé. The phrase, 'As you can see by my résumé,' is a turn-off. Tell me something I don't know."

Marcia Phelps, Ph.D., Associate Director, Career Services
University of Nebraska
Lincoln, Nebraska

September 22, 19XX

Marcella A. Butler, Director
Early Childhood Learning Center
787 Prescott Road
Freeport, IL 61032

Dear Ms. Butler:

Your advertisement in the *Freeport Journal-Standard* attracted my attention. Because my career objective is to contribute to a child's optimum development and your center is considered one of the finest in this area, I would like to talk with you about the teaching position.

The job description intrigues me as the four-year-old age group is my favorite. During my graduate work at Oklahoma State University, I taught in the child center and researched language development. Evaluations from professors indicated that the children and I easily developed rapport and documented my successes in encouraging and guiding their progress.

I would like an opportunity to meet with you and discuss what I can offer to your already outstanding center. Since my current job necessitates a great deal of travel and you may not be able to reach me, I will telephone you during the week of September 29, 19XX to see that you received my résumé and the other enclosed materials and discuss the next step. Your time and attention are appreciated.

Sincerely,

Elizabeth L. Neale
2822 N. Harrison
Freeport, IL 61032
(815) 232-8999

Enclosure

You can also overdo a cover letter by writing too much. Just as a movie review is written to arouse interest in the film and not tell the whole story, you only want to motivate the reader to read the résumé. "Tooting your own horn" too much will likely achieve the opposite effect. Carolyn Olsen, who teaches employability skills to business students, suggests that writers limit the use of "I." "An employer wants to hire a team member, not a 'hot dog'," she

4420 Hawthorne Lane
Springfield, Massachusetts 49015
April 25, 19XX

Ted Bowers, Senior Manager
Hallstead Accounting Firm
9046 Rayburn Place
Redondo Beach, California 90278

Dear Mr. Bowers:

Your accounting firm is held in high esteem by Nathan Goodwin, my uncle.
Immediately after my graduation from the University of Massachusetts on May 10,
19XX, I am moving to the Los Angeles area and am eager to explore the possibility of
making a contribution to your company.

Having paid for my tuition through scholarships and employment during the past four
years, I look forward to beginning my career. The enclosed résumé briefly explains
what I have to offer. A few of my accomplishments are:

- 3.8/4.0 GPA while working 20 hours a week.
- Vice-president of Delta Theta Pi Business Fraternity.
- Big Brother program working with disadvantaged youth.

I will be in Los Angeles on May 12, 19XX, and will contact you. If you would like
any more information, you may reach me through e-mail or by telephoning me collect. I look forward to meeting you.

Respectfully,

Terry R. Mack
(413) 289-6447
trmack@prodigy.com

Enclosure

says. Your letter will create a positive impression if it's brief, readable, error-
free, and sounds like you—the "best of you in writing."

The cover letter and résumé are always mailed together. A mistake that
some job seekers make is to send this material with insufficient postage.
Imagine what chance you will have if the employer is asked to pay for additional postage! Take each mailing to be weighed for sufficient postage. You can

use certified or registered mail although this could add up if you are sending several. Use the examples of cover letters for ideas, remembering not to end up with a letter that sounds like everyone else's.

WRITING OTHER LETTERS

The cover letter is undoubtedly most important because it either "gets your foot in the door" or it doesn't. Other pieces of correspondence also play a valuable role in the job search.

> *"In person you have another chance to correct a poor impression. In written communications you have only one chance."*
>
> Leonard F. Murphy, CPA, Partner
> Baird, Kurtz, and Dobson
> Lincoln, Nebraska

FOLLOW-UP LETTERS

Potentially, the most constructive letter is written following an interview. You can even consider sending one after a telephone conversation. Called a follow-up or thank-you letter, its main purpose is to show professional appreciation and, practically speaking, to place your name in front of a potential employer one more time.

The same guidelines, related to the inside address, greeting, and signature at the end, apply. One difference is that this letter is shorter. Similar to a cover letter, the follow-up has three parts.

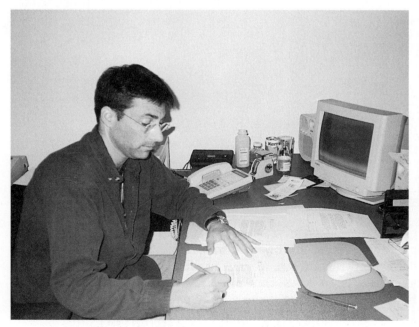

▲ Several drafts are necessary in order to produce a perfect letter.

October 24, 19XX

Marcella A. Butler, Director
Early Childhood Learning Center
787 Prescott Road
Freeport, IL 61032

Dear Ms. Butler:

After our interview yesterday, I was even more impressed with the Early Childhood
Learning Center. I appreciated the opportunity to discuss the position of teacher for
your four-year-old group. The tour and the positive experience of talking with several
of your teachers were most beneficial.

The children were delightful, and I am very interested in and enthusiastic about being
a part of their growth and development. They seem especially well-suited for the language empowerment program in which I have had extensive experience. Since you
indicated that this was a part of your future plans, I am confident I can provide quality
instruction in this endeavor.

The Early Childhood Learning Center and you surpassed my expectations, and I
would be pleased to contribute to its fine reputation. I look forward to hearing from
you within a week.

Sincerely,

Elizabeth Neale
2822 N. Harrison
Freeport, IL 61032
(815) 232-8999

1. *Introduction:* Whether the follow-up is after a telephone conversation or an
   interview, this short paragraph thanks the interviewer for her or his time and
   attention. This is stated simply and sincerely, and gushiness is to be avoided.
2. *Body:* This part reinforces your interest in the position, shows any positive
   impression of the employer, and briefly calls attention to what you have to offer.
   Again, the emphasis is on what you can do for the company; as a result of your
   research or the interview, you probably know precisely what is needed.

4420 Hawthorne Lane
Springfield, Massachusetts 49015
May 30, 19XX

Ted Bowers, Senior Manager
Hallstead Accounting Firm
9046 Rayburn Place
Redondo Beach, California 90278

Dear Mr. Bowers:

Even though I was disappointed when I received your letter telling me that someone else was selected for the accounting position, I want you to know that the opportunity to interview was a valuable learning experience. I realize that competition in the Los Angeles area is keen, and being one of the final candidates was a confidence-booster for me.

If your busy schedule permits, I would appreciate any advice you could offer as well as names of other potential employers. My positive impression of your firm has motivated me to continue in my career search. I appreciate the opportunity you gave me.

Respectfully,

Terry R. Mack
(413) 298-6447
trmack@prodigy.com

3. Closing: At the end, either in a separate paragraph or in one sentence at the end of the body of the letter, the closing indicates the next step either on your part or the employer's.

A key point is to mail the follow-up letter the day after you speak with the person. The same day may give an impression of desperation. Follow-up letters are not written by all job seekers. If yours is impressive, it could make a definite difference. Use the examples in this section for ideas.

After-rejection Letters

As strange as it may seem, writing a letter after you have not been offered a position can be quite advantageous. The overt purpose is to thank the employer for being considered; however, demonstrating an out-of-the-ordinary professional courtesy will leave a positive impression. Depending on the circumstances, you may also ask for another possible job source.

Examples of these unique types of letters can be found in this section and in several of the books listed at the end of this chapter. Critical in any type of written communication are accuracy, neatness, clarity, honesty, and sincerity. If a letter is error-free, readable, and genuinely represents you, it will enhance your chances of being interviewed and, ultimately, hired.

Filling Out a Job Application

Years ago an application for a job was probably the only writing expected of an applicant. In today's world of work, many companies still rely on applications to get the information they want and to scrutinize you as a potential employee. In these cases, even though you submit a résumé and cover letter, you will also complete an **application**.

Others do not expect you to apply in writing at all, or a résumé may be sufficient. Still others require an application; however, it's used only to check quickly to see that you have the minimum requirements. Your research should indicate exactly what is expected of you. If hired, the application usually becomes a part of your permanent file. Regardless of how it is used, if an application is required, take pride in yours and make it *perfect*.

Essentially, an application differs from a résumé in one primary way. The résumé is created by you so it's your choice of what and how much to reveal. On an application, you have no choice; an employer has decided what you are to provide. Because an application will usually ask for more information, just having a copy of your résumé isn't enough. Having more information is much preferable to not having enough. Being prepared is essential.

If you can get a copy or copies of the application in advance, do so. You may be able to fill it out at home; if so, you will probably have a choice of typing. Be sure to check the directions. Typing is fine although it can be challenging. Corrections are not to be noticeable, and you may have difficulty staying within the allotted space. If a final copy is done at home, you will either mail it or return it in person. An employer may require you to come in person to fill out an application; if so, it helps to have an already-completed application to use as a guide.

Application Information

In whatever form, it's a good idea to have in writing the following information.

- *what position is available or which one you want*
- *relevant personal data such as complete address including ZIP code, home and work telephone numbers, and social security number*

You may wonder about anyone who wouldn't remember this information. However, "horror stories" from applicants reveal how easily memory can slip at critical times. You may even be asked for addresses in the past five to ten years, and your social security card may need to be photocopied.

⑥ *complete education record including name and address of the school plus dates of attendance and graduation*

Some may even ask about elementary school.

⑥ *complete employment record including names, addresses, and telephone numbers of present and past employers, names of supervisors, dates started and dates left, hours worked per week, total time of employment, pay at start and at end, duties, and reasons for leaving*

As you can see, applications may ask for information that is inadvisable to put on a résumé. Space is usually limited so you will need to be able to explain your duties briefly. Action words are best. You may also be asked about military and volunteer experiences. A challenging question is reason for leaving. Avoid anything that sounds negative such as "personality conflicts." If you were fired, it's best to be honest, and writing "terminated" or "laid off" sounds less negative. Give positive reasons for voluntarily leaving such as "wanted advancement opportunities," "desired more hours," "returned to school," or "better position offered."

What if you don't remember some of the called-for facts? The answer is simple: You do everything in your power to find out. As one employer bluntly put it, "When it seems as if the applicant is too lazy to find a telephone number of a former employer, his or her application isn't considered." You can call schools and past employers to retrieve any forgotten information. In fact, it makes sense to call just to check for accuracy. "One of the most critical aspects is accuracy. Many times we see incorrect information," said Mark Munger, a fire department captain.

You will probably be also asked about citizenship, a past conviction of the law other than a minor traffic violation, and if driving is required as part of the job, your driving record. The key is to be honest. This type of information can be easily checked, and dishonesty will probably be considered worse than what an applicant is trying to conceal. You might consider typing a brief summary of the circumstances of a conviction leaving the impression that you learned from the experience. Matt, a young man, asked me after class one day, "What do I do about a minor in possession charge? It happened six years ago when I was 16, and the juvenile records are sealed. Yet the application asks whether I have *ever* been convicted." After conferring with several employers, my advice was to be totally honest, add a few lines about it as a learning experience, and emphasize a clean record since. Six months later Matt called to tell me he had been hired by an employer who told him he had been quite impressed with his candor. The person told him, "Before I was old enough to drink legally, I could have had one of those myself; I was just lucky."

Another difficult question asks salary expectations. If your research has revealed the salary figure or range, then your answer is easy—just write that figure or figures. If it hasn't, the best options are to write "within the salary range," "prevailing wage," or "open to negotiation."

Most applications will also ask for a list of references. If not specified, use only professional references such as employers or instructors. Because some also want personal references, be ready with these, as well. Information needed includes name, title, business address and telephone number, and length of acquaintance. These references are most likely to be contacted so be sure you have selected wisely and then asked for the person's permission in advance, as discussed in selection of references in Chapter 3. Immediately after submitting an application, contact your references and give them specific information about this particular company and position. Then, their comments can be even more beneficial. If one of your references is a present employer, you have a choice understood by future employers. You may ask that the company not be contacted until you give permission which may be during the final stages of hiring or after you have given notice.

Other possible questions on applications have to do with skills, activities, memberships, honors, licenses or certifications, and available employment starting date. If you are presently employed, be sure to indicate you will give the employer notice. One more application went into the "dead file" when my husband read that an applicant who was currently working for another company could start immediately.

Occasionally, an application will give you an opportunity to answer some open-ended questions about additional experiences or skills, the reason for an interest in the company, and specific qualifications. Whether required or optional, the worst thing you could do is leave this part blank. This indicates disinterest, laziness, or inability to convey in writing what you have to offer—all negatives. The second worst thing would be to poorly present yourself. Make sure you read the directions carefully. You may be told to print the information. If nothing is specified, choose to print or use cursive writing, depending upon your penmanship. Also, use your space effectively. A good idea is to take a tablet with you so you can first write a rough draft.

Does this sound like a lot of preparation? Instead of bemoaning the fact that there is so much required information, look upon it as an opportunity to impress a potential employer.

GUIDELINES FOR APPLICATIONS

Besides the data itself, applications can reveal other information to a potential employer. Even though you have filled out countless numbers of applications, treat each one as the difference between being hired or not. Create a perfect application. Following are further guidelines.

- *Be prepared.* If you go in person, dress as you would for an interview as you will be creating a first impression on at least one person. Take your own quality pen, an erasable one that writes in black. Blue ink may be acceptable; black always is. A good idea is to take two pens. Walking in and asking to borrow a pen creates an impression of being unprepared.

⊚ *Read the entire application before you begin writing.* This can help you avoid several problems. Have you ever almost completed an application then discovered you were writing on an incorrect line? Pay close attention to what you are to write where. "Take your time at this stage," cautions Sue Collins, day-care director. "Sometimes even yes-no questions can trick you."

⊚ *Follow directions exactly.* Common mistakes are made in the following areas:
  ▲ information in the wrong place or writing in areas where it says not to write

  ▲ order of information such as first or last name and employment history

  ▲ too much or too little information especially about employment history as the application may ask for the past 10 years (or more or less)

  ▲ type of writing so instead of printing, an applicant writes in cursive

  ▲ color of ink or whether typing is permissible

⊚ *Be complete.* Anything left blank is open to suspicion and concerns such as:
  ▲ didn't have the information

  ▲ didn't know how to answer or what to write

  ▲ just forgot or was careless

  ▲ didn't want employer to know

Would any of these reasons impress a potential employer? Blanks on application lead to blanks in the job search. How do you avoid a blank? In some cases, you write a simple answer such as "no" or "none." For example, if the section is about military experience which you don't have, indicate that with the word "none." Writing *NA* which means "not applicable" is appropriate if the question truly doesn't apply. An example would be: "Have you ever been convicted of a crime other than a misdemeanor?" to which you answered, "no." The next question of when and where is an appropriate *NA*. Writing "See résumé" is also not recommended as it can indicate laziness or taking the easy way out. Additionally, it makes the job harder for the person who is reading the application.

⊚ *Be honest and accurate.* These two coincide because a potential employer won't know whether the reason for the incorrect information is dishonesty or inaccuracy. This guideline is significant as any falsification on the application is cause for dismissal even after employment.

⊚ *Write legibly and neatly.* Poor writing can be misread so wrong information can be conveyed. If the application is difficult to read, most employers will be annoyed. Neatness deserves attention for other reasons, as well. An employer said, "If your application looks sloppy, I'm guessing you will do sloppy work." Either neatly erase any mistake or start over so that the end result looks perfect. Similar to a résumé and cover letter, an application creates an initial impression.

⊙ *Show excellent writing skills.* An advantage of being prepared with the written information you need is the opportunity to check for any writing errors. Poor grammar and misspellings can lead an employer to think that you don't care enough. As on résumés, try not to abbreviate unless space demands it, and you are sure the reader will know what you mean. For example, NE as an abbreviation for Nebraska is fine if you don't have the space for the entire word. However, A.A.S. for the degree Associate of Applied Science may not be understood.

⊙ *Recognize illegal questions and know how to respond.* As a result of federal legislation, certain information is not to be considered as grounds for employment. Questions in any of the following areas are off-limits, and you have the right not to answer them.

- ▲ age

- ▲ sex

- ▲ race, ethnicity, national origin

- ▲ religion

- ▲ physical or mental conditions unrelated to the job

- ▲ marital or family status

The information in Table 4–2 provides a thorough list of legal and illegal questions. Laws can change so it is recommended that you check the most recent regulations with an agency such as the Commission on Human Rights or a government office.

If an application asks a question in any of these areas, what can you do? Some applicants, who are willing to reveal this information, think their chances might be diminished by not answering so they do. However, another course of action may be better. Instead of leaving a blank, you can write *NA*, or more clearly, "not relevant" or "unrelated to job qualifications." Or, you can write "see attached," and include a brief, tactful paragraph pointing out that this is an inappropriate question. An employer may be unaware of certain illegalities and even be impressed by your knowledge. If you are concerned that you might sacrifice your chances by pointing this out, consider whether you want to work for employers who might discriminate or who do not want mistakes called to their attention.

The final step in filling out the application is to sign your name. You will usually date the application, too. Amazingly, candidates do forget this all-important part of the process.

T A B L E 4 – 2 ▲ SOLVING THE PUZZLE OF ON TARGET INTERVIEWING

	ON TARGET	OFF TARGET
Name	a) To ask whether an applicant's work records are under another name, for purposes of access to these records.	a) To ask the ethnic origin of an applicant's name. b) To ask if a woman is a Miss, Mrs. or Ms. c) To request applicant to provide maiden name.
Address/Housing	a) To ask for applicant's address, phone number, and/or how he or she can be reached.	a) To request place and length of current and previous addresses.
Age	a) After hiring: to require proof of age by birth certificate. b) To indicate minimum legal age for specific type of employment.	a) To ask age or age group of applicant. b) Before hiring: to request birth certificate or baptismal record.
Race/color National origin	a) To indicate that the institution is an equal opportunity employer. b) After hiring: to ask race and/or national origin for Affirmative Action plan statistics.	a) To make any inquiry that would indicate race, color, or national origin.
Gender	a) To indicate that the institution is an equal opportunity employer. b) After hiring: to ask gender for Affirmative Action plan statistics.	a) To make an inquiry which would indicate gender unless job related. (Such jobs require written state government approval.)
Religion/Creed		a) To ask an applicant's religion or religious customs and holidays. b) To request recommendations from church officials.
Sexual Orientation		a) To inquire about sexual preference.
Citizenship	a) To ask whether ALL applicants are legally authorized to work in the United States.	a) To ask for date of citizenship or whether applicant is native-born or naturalized citizen. b) To ask whether parents or spouse are native-born or naturalized. c) Before hiring: to require proof of citizenship.
Marital/Parental/ Family Status	a) After hiring: to ask marital and parental status for tax purposes. b) After hiring: to ask name, relationship, and address of person to be notified in case of emergency.	a) Before hiring: to ask marital status. b) To ask the number and/or age of children, who cares for them, and if applicant plans to have more children.

	ON TARGET	OFF TARGET
Military Service	a) To inquire into service in the U.S. armed forces. b) To ask about branch of service, rank attained, and any job-related experience.	a) To request military service records. b) To ask about military service in armed service of any other country. c) To ask about type of discharge.
Education	a) To ask whether the applicant has the academic, professional or vocational training required for the job, and to ask which institution provided it. b) To ask about language skills such as reading and writing foreign languages, if job related.	a) To ask the racial or religious affiliation of schools attended. b) To ask how foreign language was acquired.
Criminal Record	a) To inquire about convictions if the reason for the inquiry is a business necessity.	a) To inquire about arrests.
References	a) To request general and work references not relating to race, color, religion, sex, national or ethnic origin, age, disability, or marital satus.	a) To request references specifically from clergy or any other persons who might reflect race, color, religion, sex, national or ethnic origin, age, disability, or marital status.
Organizations	a) To inquire about professional organizations, union memberships, and any offices held.	a) To request listing of all clubs to which applicant belongs or has belonged.
Photographs	a) After hiring: to require photographs for identification purposes.	a) Before hiring: to request photographs.
Work Schedule	a) To ask about willingness to work the required work schedule. b) To ask if applicant has military reservist obligations.	a) To ask about willingness to work any particular religious holiday.
Physical Data	a) To require proof of ability to do manual labor, lifting, and other written physical requirements if necessary for the job.	a) To ask height and weight, impairment, or other non-performance related physical data.
Disability	a) To ask whether the applicant is capable of performing the essential functions of the job with reasonable accommodation.	a) To exclude disabled applicants as a class on the basis of their type of disability. (Each case must be determined on an individual basis by law.)
Other Qualifications	a) To inquire about any area that has direct relevance to the job.	a) To inquire about political affiliation. b) To make any inquiry not related to a bona fide requirement of the job that may present information permitting unlawful discrimination.

With permission of Affirmative Action and Diversity Programs, University of Nebraska, Lincoln, Nebraska

> *"Of 90 applications for one position, 80 were 'weeded out' by minor writing errors. It was a quick, easy way to screen out those who really didn't seem to care."*
>
> Doc Chaves, Assistant Vice President
> Ameritas Life Insurance Corp.
> Lincoln, Nebraska

Too often, applicants do not take applications seriously. Individuals come in totally unprepared and then, in a lackadaisical manner, partially complete the form. They don't get the job. Instead of doing a less-than-excellent job, the successful applicant realizes that an application, because it's a company product, is to be taken seriously and is an integral part of pursuing a desired position. Hopefully, you will be like a former career development student who, after being hired at a major printing company, said, "One of the first questions I was asked in the interview was where I had learned to fill out an application. The person said 'It's the best application I've ever seen!' I think it had a lot to do with my getting this dream job."

USE THE APPLICATION EXAMPLE IN KEY STEPS (PAGES 289–92) AS A WAY OF PREPARING FOR A BASIC PART OF THE JOB SEARCH.

Writing skills matter a great deal during the job search and after you are hired. You will be expected to present yourself in writing in several ways. The inability to excel in these efforts will severely deter you in your job search.

KEY POINTS

- How you present yourself in writing usually makes the difference between getting an interview or not.

- A résumé is a short promotional piece highlighting an applicant's qualifications, educational and employment background, and accomplishments. It is designed to create interest in you as a potential employee.

- Even though there is no one "right" résumé, certain guidelines are to be followed.

- Résumé formats include chronological, functional, combination, and targeted. Electronic résumés are used for easier computer scanning. Your choice depends upon the most positive way of presenting yourself.

- Being aware of decisions and steps to follow in developing an effective résumé and reasons for differences will help you choose the best résumé for you.

- A cover letter always accompanies a résumé and, as such, is as important, if not more so, to most employers.

- Other letters are indicators of your interest and professionalism, as well as your writing skills.

- Even though all employers don't require a written application, learning how to fill one out is necessary.

- Typically, an application will indicate your ability to follow directions and also provide information about you.

- In all forms of written communication, honesty, readability, neatness, and accuracy are essential.

RECOMMENDED READING

Beatty, R. H. (1992). *175 high-impact cover letters*. New York: John Wiley.

Beatty, R. H. (1995). *The résumé kit*. New York: John Wiley.

Fournier, M. and Spin, J. (1993). *Encyclopedia of job-winning résumés*. Ridgefield, CT: Round Lake Publications.

Fry, R. (1992). *Your first résumé*. Hawthorne, NJ: Career Press.

Gonyea, J. C. and Gonyea, M. (1996). *Electronic résumés*. New York: McGraw-Hill.

Jackson, A. (1993). *How to prepare your curriculum vitae*. Lincolnwood, IL: VGM Career Horizons.

Jackson, T. (1996). *The new perfect résumé*. New York: Doubleday.

Kennedy, J. L. and Morrow, T. (1994). *Electronic résumé revolution*. New York: John Wiley.

Michelozzi, B. N. (1996). *Coming alive from nine to five*. Mountain View, CA: Mayfield Publishing.

Provenzano, S. (1994). *The guide to basic cover letter writing*. Lincolnwood, IL: VGM Career Horizons.

Provenzano, S. (1995). *Slam dunk résumés...that score every time!* Lincolnwood, IL: VGM Career Horizons.

Tipper, R. (1992). *Power résumés*. New York: John Wiley.

Tipper, R. (1992). *Résumés for college students and recent graduates*. Lincolnwood, IL: VGM Career Horizons.

Washington, T. (1996). *Résumé power*. Bellevue, WA: Mount Vernon Press.

Weddle, P. D. (1994). *Career fitness*. New York: Cadell & Davies.

Weddle, P. D. (1994). *Electronic résumés for the new job market*. Manassas Park, VA: Impact Publications.

CHAPTER FIVE

You in Person

An interview for a position ranks among the highest anxiety-provoking experiences of life. Yet, you can congratulate yourself for reaching this stage and view it as a supreme opportunity. Being fully prepared for the interview can considerably lower the anxiety and set the stage for a successful outcome.

PREPARING FOR AN INTERVIEW

In actuality, the entire job search up to this point has been preparing you for interviews. Ideally, you have conducted several informational interviews and have amassed valuable knowledge while polishing your communication skills. Of utmost importance is to realize that your first conversation with a potential employer to arrange an interview is critical. Be open, adaptable, and positive!

Once a meeting is arranged, two invaluable pieces of information are the length and type of interview. One hour for an interview is typical although this can vary. As to type, will you be talking to just one person, and if so, is this person in the human resources department, which would be a screening interview, or is it a supervisor of the position? This information will help you prepare in terms of what questions to expect and which ones to ask. You will also want to know, if possible, how many interviews will be required before a hiring decision is made.

Another type of interview is conducted by a group. Not expecting this can create panic at the time of realization. In actuality, a group interview has its advantages. For example, if five people are on the team, you will need to impress only three of them. Additionally, eye contact may be easier because you aren't required to keep focused on just one person. Knowing what to expect and having the maximum amount of information increase your sense of control. The best advice is to practice. Employers, such as two in the firefighting field, concur.

Captain Mark Munger:

The most important piece of advice I can give is for a person to practice for an interview. Too often, individuals show up and have never considered how or what might be asked of them. That's the wrong way to go.

Fire Chief Darrell Eastin:

Practice for an interview cannot be over-stressed.

Ideally, you would go through a "mock" videotaped interview. The students in college career development classes find that this experience, while a little frightening, is extremely valuable. "I didn't know I did that" was a comment about a specific gesture. "I liked the way I answered that question. I'm going to remember to use it" was another. According to Mary Conway, an instructor, "Many times the confidence of students increases after watching their videotaped interviews." If videotaping isn't possible, you can still practice interviewing skills with someone else and learn a great deal from the frank appraisal of the "mock" interviewer or a person who acts as an observer. Ideally, being able to see yourself on videotape exactly as the interviewer sees you is the best learning experience of all.

PREPARING YOURSELF MENTALLY

Most candidates approach this stage of the process by thinking: "I want to impress the employer so he or she will offer me this position." Even though this is a worthy goal of a successful interview, a preferable attitude is: This interview is a mutual exchange of information during which I will decide if this position is right for me. Realistically, because the interviewer will be deciding if you are right for the position, being impressive is essential. Yet, placing yourself in the position of an equal partner in the interview can lower intense pressure, eliminate a feeling of desperation, and elevate your confidence. Thinking about this interaction as similar to any in which you want to let yourself be known, get to know another person, and, hopefully, impress each other, will help you be more comfortable. Another thought that can provide a psychological boost is to realize that the interviewer wants to be impressed by you. Trying to find the right person for a job is difficult, and you are in a position to make this easier. In reality, the interviewer would like to hire you!

Determining a goal for the interview is a critical part of mental preparedness. Would a logical one be to receive a job offer at the end of the interview?

▲ A practice videotaped interview even without professional attire is excellent preparation.

Remember that any employer who would hire you "on the spot" may be too hasty in decision making (you may be fired just as quickly) or is desperate. Neither of these types would make a worthy employer! A more realistic goal is to impress the interviewer so that you are a top contender.

KNOWING WHAT EMPLOYERS WANT

What qualities do almost all employers seek? Two individuals, because they work closely with employers, know what is wanted. "Strong oral and written communication skills, interpersonal skills, responsibility shown in attendance records and quality of work, computer literacy, and, in several cases, a foreign language," says Marcia Phelps, associate director of career services at a university. Jeanne Baer, a consultant to many employers, says: "Flexibility, being open to change, commitment, problem-solving abilities, and evidence of being a team player." The following ideas are from employers and college program chairs.

KEY ADVICE

WHAT DO YOU THINK EMPLOYERS WANT?

- *enthusiasm, energy, loyalty, verbal skills, humor*
  Mark Munger, firefighting captain

- *mechanical aptitude; formal education; physical endurance and agility; knowledge of fire prevention, rescue, and supervision practices; ability to establish and maintain effective working relationships*
  Darrell Eastin, firefighting chief

- *work ethics, honesty, education, open-minded to change*
  Bill Payzant, printing and graphics design

- *enthusiasm, quiet confidence, ability to work with people and communicate, knowledge of job tasks, honesty, and ethics*
  Lynn Jones, architecture and drafting firm chairman

- *desire to help the company, commitment, innovative ideas, initiative*
  David Hanna, insurance regional office manager

- *willingness to learn and take on challenges, ability to start tasks with limited direction, flexibility so that you can work in a multi-project setting, punctuality, and the ability to work with others; a "people" person*
  Mike Petersen, drafting supervisor

- *a balanced ego so you believe in yourself but are not brash, basic communication skills, compassion about work, ability to interact with others, and taking what you do seriously but not taking yourself too seriously*
  Doc Chaves, communications vice-president

- *communication skills, maturity in judgment, commitment, efficiency, professional manner*
  Jeanne Salerno, law office development director

- *honesty, experience, flexibility*
  John Buse, machine tool company president

- *conscientious attitude, a sense of pride in what is done, ability to follow directions, innovative ideas and initiative yet caution in how to proceed, dependability, responsibility, and ability to relate well to others*
  Bob Dinkel, construction company owner

- *good attendance, positive attitude, ability to work safely*
  Jerry Baxter, manufacturing plant manager

- *ability to perform the tasks, pride in what one does, comfortable with change, self-motivated, quick to learn, strong "people" skills, ability to sell and attract clients*
  Lisa Patterson, accounting firm senior manager

- *commitment to the job, loyalty to the company, reliability, integrity, honesty, team spirit, flexibility, adaptability, and an ability to think "outside the box," (i.e., creatively and innovatively)*
  Jody Horwitz, media and entertainment human resources director

- *self-motivation, organization, interpersonal skills, and ability to prioritize*
  Laura Mann, sales representative

- *reliability, straightforwardness, organization skills*
  Ed Rasgorshek, banking vice-president

- *integrity, efficiency, personable, professional, effective communication skills*
  Nancy Brown, state health department program manager

- *training and education, dependability, reliability, good communication skills, flexibility, appropriate motivation*
  Alicia Baillie, child care program chairperson

- *punctuality, ability to get along with other people, technical skills*
  Janis Bible, medical laboratory technology program chairperson

- *professional attitude, willingness to learn new techniques, technical laboratory skills, responsibility*
  Don Mumm, environmental laboratory technology program chairperson

- *positive attitude of being a team player, problem solver, desire to help the company be profitable and grow, good attendance, motivation to achieve academically*
  Millard Carnes, machine tool technology program chairperson

- *technical skills, "people" skills, broad training background, flexibility*
  Linda Bettinger, computer technology program chairperson

- *dependability, technical skills, honesty, flexibility, able to handle stressful situations*
  Ruth Walsh, surgical technology program chairperson

- *self-confidence, preparation in field, open-mindedness*
  Jo Ann Frazell, office technology program chairperson

- *positive attitude, ability to problem solve, communication and interpersonal skills, dependability*
  Virginia Hess, nursing program chairperson

- *ability to use technology, creativity, problem-solving abilities*
  Dan Masters, drafting technology program chairperson

- *respect for the chain of command, positive attitude, sound problem-solving skills, honesty, "people" skills, dependability*
  Sue Asher, dental assisting program chairperson

- *good written and oral communication skills, customer relations skills which means ability to relate to others and treat them with courtesy and honesty, required job skills, and some past work experiences*
  Carolyn Olsen, business occupations program chairperson

If what you have to offer matches with an employer in your career field, use the interview as an opportunity to convey this.

Also enlightening is to know what keeps people from being hired. To find out, personnel directors were surveyed (Madry, 1988). Listed in order of importance, Table 5–1 reveals these characteristics.

TABLE 5–1 ▲ COMMON MISTAKES OF APPLICANTS

1. poor personal appearance
2. overaggressiveness
3. inability to express information clearly
4. lack of interest and enthusiasm
5. lack of planning for career; no purpose and no goals
6. nervousness, lack of confidence and poise
7. putting too much emphasis on money
8. unwillingness to start at the bottom
9. tendency to make excuses
10. lack of tact and courtesy
11. lack of maturity
12. condemnation of past employers
13. no genuine interest in job or company
14. failure to look interviewer in the eye
15. sloppiness on application form
16. little sense of humor
17. arriving late for interview
18. failure to express appreciation for interviewer's time
19. failure to ask questions about the job
20. giving vague responses to questions

Importantly, review your assets with a specific focus on the particular position. "What does this company need that I have to offer?" "What can I bring to this position?" If your research has not been complete, these questions demand attention. Essentially, interviewers are much more interested in what *they* want than in what *you* want (Richardson, 1992). Thus, a major goal of the interview is to directly address the employer's needs and convey how your skills and abilities match. Display the attitude that you have needed characteristics and skills that will be of great benefit to this business. Focus your attention on this employer's needs.

The most critical part of the preparation process is to learn how to interview. You may have exactly what the employer needs and still not be selected. The art of interviewing is just that—an art, and, as such, must be mastered if you are to be successful.

SELLING YOURSELF DURING THE INTERVIEW

What will make a positive difference during an interview can be determined from a quick look at the four developmental areas of self—physical, mental, emotional, and social—followed by other success tips and ways to communicate. This book has described the characteristics desired by employers. Several recruiters identified what they look for during job interviews (Richardson, 1992).

1. self-awareness and the ability to understand what the interviewer is seeking

2. being goal-oriented

3. being results-oriented

4. articulateness including good eye contact, a calm conversational speech pattern, and direct, nonevasive answers

5. flexibility

Selling yourself involves knowing what employers want and letting them know that you possess these qualities.

PRESENTING YOUR BEST SELF

The whole self will come across in the interview as a "total package." Yet, you can use knowledge of the four developmental areas to bring the best "you" to this important interaction.

PHYSICAL SELF. Preferably, several weeks before a scheduled interview, you will make decisions and take action regarding your physical presence. How you appear to an employer is a vital part of first impression and reveals a great deal about pride in self. Because attractiveness, especially for women, seems to continue to be a factor (Marlowe, Schneider, and Nelson, 1996), it is best to emphasize your positive appearance points and de-emphasize the negative ones. Three key aspects of appearance are essential: neatness, cleanliness, and appropriateness.

Being appropriately dressed demands expenditure of time and probably money. Consider it one of the best investments you will ever make. Appropriate means suitable for the occasion. A job interview is a semiformal event, and, and in most cases, to be appropriate, you must look professional. Dressing too casually or showing a lack of professionalism will dim your chances. Conversely, overdressing is inappropriate. Just as a man would not think of wearing a tuxedo to a job interview, a woman does not want to look as if she is going to a formal affair. Wearing a quality outfit is advisable.

A general "rule of thumb" is to dress one step above what you would wear to work. However, it could be two steps above. Research can help. During an informational interview, ask about interview attire, not just what you can get by with wearing but what will make the most positive impression. Unless one is applying for a manual labor or truck driving position, both men and women can safely dress in a business suit, and in most white-collar positions, this is expected. In some occupations, rather than a suit, a man could wear slacks and a dress shirt. An owner of a trucking company commented, "Even though I wear a suit, I might wonder about a person in a dressy suit applying for a truck driver position. He or she would need to be neat and clean, however."

"It impresses me when it's obvious the applicant has tried to be impressive in appearance."

Ted Milner, President
Executive Temps
Burbank, California

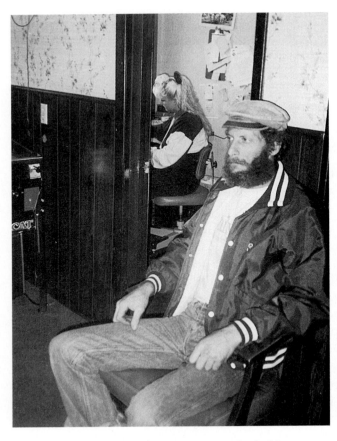

▲ Looking too casual isn't appropriate for an interview.

What about color? Gray or dark blue are preferred although other conservative colors are permissible. An interesting study showed that perceptions of women's employability were influenced by suit colors. Either black or red was deemed more appropriate than pink, green, or teal (Carter, 1993). As long as it's not overly bright or flashy, if a certain color is especially complimentary, that is a good choice.

Females should avoid low-neck blouses and very short skirts even if they are in style. One young female, after watching a videotape of a "mock" interview, commented, "Wow! I didn't realize how revealing that blouse is nor how much of my legs would show. I'm glad I saw this here first!" Jewelry is to be tasteful and not distracting. Also, a woman may want to consider taking an extra pair of hosiery along just in case there is a need for a change. For both sexes, shoes that go with the attire should be clean and polished and fingernails clean and trimmed.

Comfort and confidence are to be kept in mind. Wear the entire outfit before the interview so you can feel "at home" in it. If you've made a wise choice, your appearance should increase your confidence. Whatever you wear, interviewers will be impressed by a healthy, energetic look. Applicants who look tired, unhealthy, or apathetic have definite liabilities. Taking good care of yourself and aiming for wellness, getting a good night's sleep, then maintaining an

▲ Ideally, the applicant and interviewer will present similar appearances.

alert, interested, and pleasant facial expression will go a long way in enhancing your physical appearance.

An interviewer can be "turned off" for any number of other physical reasons. Two have to do with scent. Consider these scenarios.

> *Melanie looked the part of a career woman as she walked confidently in to be interviewed by Janet, the department manager. Unfortunately, it was not only her appearance that was noticed. The perfume that she had evidently doused herself with permeated the office. "The worst part about it," said Janet to a co-worker, "is that it's a scent I really detest."*

Melanie undoubtedly didn't realize that it's possible to smell a drop of perfume diffused throughout a small house!

> *Matt puffed nervously on his cigarette as he drove to his interview. After he left, the interviewer thought: "He smelled like he had been sitting in a smoky bar for hours before he came here. I wouldn't want to put up with that day in and day out."*

One of the strongest odors is cigarette smoke, and it's sure to be annoying to a nonsmoker. If you smoke, be sure you don't do so before an interview.

Certain other habits are bound to interfere with your interviewing effectiveness. These include gum chewing, nail biting, hair flipping, and knuckle cracking. Anything that creates noise or is visually distracting is to be avoided.

The reality of life is that human beings are judged somewhat on physical appearance. Ideally, you will not get a job just because you look a certain way; however, you could end up not getting a job because of poor appearance or physical habits that send a negative message. Use the checklist in KEY STEPS (page 295) before an interview.

> *WHAT CAN YOU DO TO IMPROVE YOUR PHYSICAL APPEARANCE?*

MENTAL SELF. Depending upon the position, certain intellectual skills are necessary. Even though you may assume that the interviewer knows your capabilities, you are responsible for pointing out all desirable skills. Probably more important than your grades is whether you were at a satisfactory level of achievement and if you worked up to your potential. "An average student who gets average grades is more employable than an above-average student who gets average grades," says Millard Carnes, head of a machine tool program. If you earned high grades, be sure this is known.

Regardless of the job, potential employers want to know that you can think clearly and solve problems. Additionally, desire and willingness to learn are key transferable assets. Alicia Baillie, chairperson of a college child development program, believes that mature judgment and decision-making skills are high on the list of employability factors. Similarly, Dan Masters, head of a college drafting technology program, says, "The industry wants creative drafters who are problem solvers."

A positive attitude is a "must." Whether or not this is discussed in an interview, your broad outlook on life will probably come across. Both verbally and nonverbally, we move through life as if we are carrying a lighted sign that flashes positive or negative. Body language cues and comments can influence an interviewer. "The applicant slumped in his chair, said little, and had a disinterested look on his face. His whole demeanor was negative," said one business supervisor. Adverse comments about past employers, supervisors, or co-workers will dampen any enthusiasm for you. Likewise, not taking responsibility for your past experiences and blaming others for problems indicate negativism. Candidates who have a professional attitude demonstrated in demeanor, willingness to learn new techniques, and a respect for chain of command have an advantage.

> *THINK OF AN EXPERIENCE IN WHICH YOU EXHIBITED A POSITIVE ATTITUDE. IN AN INTERVIEW THIS WOULD BE WORTH MENTIONING.*

> *"The ability to create and sustain a professional relationship with an employer along with a high level of integrity are definite assets."*
>
> Susan Asher, Program Chair, Dental Assisting
> Southeast Community College
> Lincoln, Nebraska

EMOTIONAL SELF.   Balance in emotionality is an asset. An interview is no place for total emotional expressiveness; however, the bland, seemingly unemotional individual is unlikely to be impressive. A proper balance is to appear relaxed and calm, yet enthusiastic and pleasant. Any feelings of frustration, dismay, anger, or unhappiness are to be concealed during a job interview. Picture the impression in the following.

> *Christine impatiently thumbed through a magazine waiting for an interview. She had been delayed in traffic, had worried about being late, and now was being kept waiting. She heaved a few sighs, and the receptionist looked at her with a quizzical look. When told to go in, Christine said, "It's about time." As she approached the owner's desk, her facial expression was one of annoyance. She said, "Traffic is such a problem these days. I get so frustrated with it."*

Are you surprised that she wasn't among the final candidates?

A typical emotion associated with job interviews is anxiety. Most interviewers expect an applicant to be nervous. The key is to keep it enough under control in order to think and communicate positively. What might help is to realize that the interviewer is probably nervous, as well. "As silly as it sounds, I'm always uptight at the beginning of an interview. I want the applicants to be impressed by me and my business so I feel the pressure, too," was an interviewer's comment. Another way to relieve anxiety is to use cognitive techniques, discussed in Chapter 1. Thinking, "Just because I'm a little nervous doesn't mean I will do poorly in the interview," and "Even though this is a job interview doesn't make it a 'life or death' manner. I'll just be myself." Right before the interview, a drink of water and the use of deep breathing are soothing strategies.

How well you handle stress and pressure will be of interest in most interviews. To be prepared, have a specific example to describe your success in coping with stress and pressure.

> *ANSWER THIS QUESTION: "HOW DO YOU HANDLE STRESS?"*

SOCIAL SELF.   During an interview this aspect of self will be the most apparent. Both you and the interviewer will create social impressions during this brief interaction. Establishing rapport is necessary; if this doesn't happen, it is unlikely that you will advance to the final stage.

Each of our personalities is unique, and being yourself is imperative. Being hired on the basis of a "false front" is a disservice to both the employer and yourself. Generally, if you are friendly and pleasant and appear to be motivated and interested, most interviewers will be impressed. For some people, one of the hardest tasks is to smile during introductions and, when appropriate, during the interview. Yet, this cordial gesture is all-important.

Because your ability to communicate and interact with others are necessary career skills, the interviewer is likely to either directly ask or probe to determine your abilities. You may even be asked to take a personality inventory because certain characteristics can spell either success or failure for a particular type of job. Rather than be intimidated by an inventory, look upon it as a help for you as much as the employer. Remember job satisfaction? If your personality isn't suited for the duties, you won't be happy.

The social self affects all work relationships, and "people" skills are necessary for successful career development. Among the assets you will want to verbally and nonverbally communicate during an interview are your most positive personality traits and your ability to get along with others.

> *HOW WOULD YOU ANSWER IF AN INTERVIEWER ASKED ABOUT YOUR "PEOPLE" SKILLS?*

BEHAVING IN IMPRESSIVE WAYS

Certain behaviors deserve special attention. Professionalism means being where you are supposed to be with time to spare. Being punctual is an absolute requirement. Being late to a job interview is worse than being late to your own wedding. Guests may wait patiently and not interpret your behavior as rude; interviewers are not likely to be so understanding.

To ensure that you will be punctual, plan to arrive ahead of time. Some suggest as much as fifteen minutes. However, being in the office of the interviewer five minutes before your appointment is fine. Arriving at the site several minutes before that time gives you a chance to freshen up, check your appearance in a restroom, and take a few deep breaths. Don't forget to get rid of gum or any chewable item. To relieve stress, get the following information when the interview is scheduled.

- *Know the day, date, and time of interview.* Getting both the day and the date ensures that no mistake has been made.

- *Know the exact location.* Some companies occupy large buildings or portions of them so ask for details such as floor and room number.

- *Ask about available parking.* You can ask either the interviewer or the receptionist about the best place to park; be sure to bring cash to pay for this, if necessary.

- *Confirm the exact name or names of the interviewer(s).* You may have this information, yet it's good to confirm it.

A good idea is to make a trial run before the interview. At least, drive to the location about the same time of day to see how long it takes. Andrew reported feeling much more confident because a few days before his interview, he had actually gone to the door of the office. "I knew how long it took me to get there, and on the actual day I felt calmer because it was familiar."

Taking extra copies of your résumé with you as well as other supporting documents such as grade transcripts and licenses is advisable. Whether to take anything else to an interview is a choice. Obviously, you will not be taking another person! Having a professional-looking binder with a note pad and a pen is worth considering. You can use it to jot down the points you want to make, such as your assets, as well as a list of questions you want to ask. Referring to these ensures you aren't forgetting anything. As long as you don't read from it or let it detract from the interview, such behavior typically looks professional. Also, interviewers tend to be impressed with applicants who take notes. Prepared written questions show organization skills and assertiveness. Your note taking should not interfere with good eye contact or be distracting. Be prepared, also, for the interviewer to take notes as this is fairly typical.

In certain occupations, taking a **portfolio**, samples of your work, is highly recommended. This is especially appropriate in fields such as art, drafting, and design if your interview is with a person in that specific department or area. Usually, the interviewer will ask to see whatever you have brought; however, if she or he doesn't mention it, be sure that you do. A word of caution is to not be like Tim who spent his entire interview discussing in detail all the finer parts of his drawings. The interviewer was impressed with his work, yet didn't learn much more about Tim.

WHAT ITEMS WOULD YOU TAKE TO AN INTERVIEW?

Once you are in the office, remember you are now making a first impression on everyone you see. Greet the receptionist by name (learned through your research, of course). Some nervous applicants make a mistake of continuing to chat which will probably not be appreciated by a busy person. A better idea is to let the other person take the lead in developing conversation.

Whether to appear busy or simply wait while maintaining open, alert body language is up to you. If any company literature is available, definitely show an interest. You may also choose to review your résumé or interviewing notes. Do appear calm and poised, not like the following.

Alex looked well-groomed. However, his nervous mannerisms in the reception office were being noticed. He chewed a fingernail, tapped his fingers on the arm of the chair, and swung his foot back and forth briskly. "I thought I might have to revive him at any minute," commented the receptionist.

In most companies, the opinions of a receptionist or other staff members do carry weight, and you will want to impress everyone.

Finally, the time has come for you to meet the interviewer. Certain behaviors deserve attention, and practicing them prior to the interview bolsters confidence.

- Smile! Look directly at the person.

- Offer an appropriate greeting such as "hello," "good morning," or "good afternoon" and use the person's name. Use a surname with a title or Ms. or Mr.

- Add quickly to the greeting: "I'm (your name), and I'm here to discuss the (title of job) position with you." This is a good idea in the unlikely event that the person needs a reminder of who you are.

Possibly occurring during or shortly after the greetings is the extremely important handshake. As the applicant, it's better to let the interviewer take the lead. If offered, you respond. Even though it seems so customary and simple, this behavior ranks high among interviewers. "I put a lot of stock in how the person shakes hands," said one employer. Even though you have probably heard it said many times, recommendations about handshakes bear repeating because the first impression is still being created. You can err at one extreme or the other. The overly firm handshake not only can hurt, it leaves one with the impression that the "shaker" is aggressive and overbearing. "It seems as if the person was trying to prove something, and it wasn't positive," was how one interviewer described a handshake. The opposite—a limp, hardly noticeable handshake—leaves a distinctly negative impression.

In a career development class, students actually practice shaking hands. One young man said he thought it was silly until his less-than-positive handshake was noticed by another student. A stereotypic behavior was called to the group's attention. After a male student's handshake to a female came across as less-than-firm, he was asked if this was his typical handshake. He said, "It's how I shake hands with females." He was reminded that he didn't need to differentiate by sex; both males and females are capable and appreciative of assertive handshakes!

> *PRACTICE SHAKING HANDS WITH SEVERAL DIFFERENT PEOPLE AND ASK THEM TO HONESTLY ASSESS HOW YOURS FEELS.*

The interviewer will probably indicate where you are to sit. Be sure you comfortably face the person then wait for her or him to begin the interview. Some superficial conversation may transpire as the person tries to ease the tension of the initial meeting. Even though such chit-chat may feel comfortable, you don't want to be responsible for continuing it too long. Remember, you have a limited time to achieve your goal of giving and receiving valuable information and deciding if this would be a good match.

Other unimpressive qualities and behaviors include poor grooming, lack of enthusiasm, non-demonstration of any past accomplishments, "bad-mouthing" former employers or co-workers, and an inability to explain reasons for leaving past employers (Urban, 1992). Brashness and cockiness are certain turnoffs, as well. Instead, you can choose to be professional and impressive.

SELLING YOURSELF NONVERBALLY

Reviewing the communication suggestions offered in Chapter 2 will help you prepare for the interview. Listening skills are essential both in getting through the interview successfully and in presenting yourself in a positive way. If you come across as an excellent listener, you are well on the way to being a top candidate for any position. You also want to appear poised and professional. Each of the following behaviors will ensure a positive impression.

MAINTAIN THE BEST POSTURE AND BODY POSITION.   Your posture is an indicator of who you are. Being erect and alert while appearing relaxed is the best combination. Interest is shown by leaning slightly forward. Try to sit comfortably with your lower back against the chair back, shoulders back, feet on the floor, and your hands in your lap. Definitely do not cross your arms at any time during the interview. Also, resist any temptation to place your arm on a desk or table in a leaning position.

USE DIRECT EYE CONTACT.   Even though steady eye contact is not the norm in all cultures, it is expected in the American society. This does not mean staring fixedly at the interviewer. When listening, about 75 percent of the time your eyes should be somewhere on the person's face, not necessarily looking directly into the eyes. While talking, the percentage of eye contact is somewhat less, yet at least half the time. If you catch yourself gazing away from the interviewer, just bring your eyes back. Along with the handshake, this is a major factor in the minds of interviewers. "If the applicant does not look at me, he or she will not get hired," was the blunt comment of one employer.

CHANGE FACIAL EXPRESSION.   In a job interview, as in personal conversation, a blank face implies disinterest. Being animated and providing appropriate expressions of interest, curiosity, excitement, pleasure, and even surprise add greatly to the exchange. Employers interpret a great deal from facial expression.

▲ The difference between impressing an interviewer—or not—can be a matter of body language.

"Your face will show whether you are confident and enthusiastic. Facial expression can reveal a sense of vitality, interest, and a high energy level," says Jeanne Baer, a career consultant and training specialist.

> *EVEN THOUGH IT SOUNDS STRANGE, PRACTICE CHANGING FACIAL EXPRESSIONS IN FRONT OF A MIRROR.*

NOD AFFIRMATIVELY.   A moderate number of affirming nods, when appropriate, indicate that you are listening and either agree with or like what you are hearing. Additionally, nods can energize and motivate the interviewer so they are bound to be appreciated. You can overdo these, however. A student after viewing a videotape of a practice interview said it looked as if her head would fall off as she watched herself nod frequently and too vigorously.

USE GESTURES.   Keeping hands in your lap or at your side during the entire interview makes you appear stiff, and your communication style will lack liveliness. Positive communicators utilize a proper number of gestures while resisting the tendency to "talk with their hands," which ends up being annoying. Also, you want to avoid certain gestures such as pointing your finger at the interviewer. Gestures can emphasize and add meaning to verbal comments, and doing so brings life and color to the interview.

AVOID DISTRACTING BEHAVIORS.   Certain habits or nervous behaviors fall into this category, such as tapping fingers on the desk, table, or arm of a chair and fiddling with one's hair or jewelry. Refrain from any movement that indicates undue nervousness or takes the attention of the interviewer away from what you are saying.

> *Tiffany came to the interview with her own notebook and pen. Unfortunately, her preparedness resulted in a problem. Throughout the interview she clicked the top of the pen to the annoyance of the marketing supervisor. "Almost all I remember about the interview is the noise of that pen," he said.*

RESPOND WITH BRIEF COMMENTS OR QUESTIONS.   Remember that you can remain a listener and still make brief comments and ask encouraging questions. For example, after an interviewer describes certain job duties, a comment of, "That sounds interesting," or a question of, "What portion of the time would I spend at the computer?" are quite relevant and demonstrate positive listening.

Selling Yourself Verbally

Even though listening skills are critical during an interview, what is said and how it is said separates successful applicants from the others. An effective interviewer will be sure that you do most of the talking. Occasionally, the meeting goes the other way. "I didn't have a chance to say much of anything," said an applicant after a job interview. "He spent the whole time telling me about the business." The results of these monologue interviews are lack of information about the applicant and, unfortunately, usually a poor impression of the job seeker as well. As the applicant, it's your responsibility to do all that is reasonable to convey what you can do for the employer. In the process, paralanguage, clarity, efficiency, and effective content are key elements.

USE EFFECTIVE PARALANGUAGE.   Variations in the voice itself, called paralanguage, were covered in Chapter 2, and you are encouraged to review that section. During an interview you will want to pay special attention to how your voice sounds to the interviewer. Varying rhythm and inflection can clarify and add interest to what you say. You will want to use moderation in volume, pitch, and speed, and speak distinctly without overly enunciating. You want to be heard and interpreted correctly. Mumbling is bothersome and certainly not conducive to creating a clear message.

> *IF POSSIBLE, CHECK YOUR PARALANGUAGE WITH AN AUDIO OR VIDEO RECORDER.*

BE CLEAR AND EFFICIENT.   Clarity can be achieved by using accurate and specific descriptive words and sentences. Saying that you did a good job is a global comment and not precise; instead, describe exactly what you did that was good. The use of action words, a moderate amount of detail, and adjectives and adverbs to describe activities and behaviors creates clear, interesting messages. Sometimes a person will say one thing and indicate another with body language. If you state that you have a high level of interest in the position, be sure that your nonverbal behaviors don't show disinterest.

Efficiency has to do with saying what you want to say in due time without using distractors and in a concise time framework. "You know" repeated over and over will be a definite annoyance to an interviewer (unless you happen to find one who has the same poor habit). One interviewer said, "If I hear 'and stuff' or 'like' one more time, I may lose it." In this case, listen to the applicant.

> *I really enjoy working with computers...and stuff. Like...uh...learning how to design houses on CAD...and stuff...has been fun. I also am...like...interested in mechanical drafting...and stuff. And...like...I took courses in sociology and psychology...and stuff.*

Do you see why the interviewer was ready to throw up his hands?

Efficiency is also saying what you want to say with just enough detail to be interesting. The most effective responses last less than two minutes. "One of the worst things an applicant can do is talk too much," said Marcia Phelps, Ph.D., an associate director of career services at a large university.

> *"I detest rambling answers. Respond clearly and concisely."*
>
> Ed Rasgorshek, Senior Vice President
> Farm Credit Services of the Midlands
> Omaha, Nebraska

RESPONDING TO QUESTIONS IN THE MOST POSITIVE WAY.   Most of the interview consists of answering questions posed by the interviewer. The way to verbalize in an interview is a little different from the open communication style suggested in Chapter 2. For many responses you will want to sound more sure of yourself than what the use of "I think" conveys. For example, saying, "I think I can offer you a high level of expertise" isn't nearly as powerful as "I'm sure (or confident) that I can." Use "I think" or "I believe" only if you are giving an opinion. Assertiveness is appreciated in the interview. A study showed that an assertive communication style was much more likely to lead to a job offer than either an aggressive or nonassertive style (Gallois, Callan, and McKenzie Palmer, 1992).

A verbalizing behavior to avoid in an interview is any tendency to qualify yourself. **Qualifying** means to use words that limit or discount your abilities. Notice the underlined qualifying words in Aaron's response to his strengths.

> *I enjoy office work. I'm a <u>pretty</u> good typist. I <u>kind of</u> like to talk with people on the phone, and customers are <u>usually</u> satisfied with the way I handle complaints. I <u>only</u> have my Associate's Degree but hope to continue my education. During the past year my jobs were <u>just</u> in construction, but I proved I can work <u>fairly</u> hard.*

Eliminating the qualifying words creates a more assertive and impressive statement.

Definitely avoid any comment that can destroy your chances. Humorous, yet devastating, was a comment in a firefightering interview: "As a child I liked to start fires. I've always had a fascination with fire." Said Mark Munger, a fire department captain, "That's not something we like to hear from a prospective firefighting candidate."

You can prepare by going over all possible questions ahead of time and actually practicing your responses. Excellent job seekers do not go into an interview "cold;" neither do their answers sound rehearsed. Instead, they are in familiar territory and talking about their assets in a confident manner. This section will give typical and not-so-typical, yet possible, questions and recommended answers for your consideration and rehearsal.

> *BEFORE YOU READ THE RECOMMENDED RESPONSES, DECIDE HOW YOU WOULD ANSWER THE FOLLOWING QUESTIONS. AFTER YOU READ THE SUGGESTIONS, NOTE ANY BETTER WAYS TO RESPOND.*

◎   *Tell me about yourself.*

This question is a common opener and one that interviewers may use either as a tension reliever or as a way to elicit information and see how you respond. If you are unprepared, this is a challenging and stressful question. Immediately, one thinks, "What does the person want to know?" Some applicants will even ask, which is not recommended. They usually are told, "Whatever you want to tell me."

The following are *not* desirable answers.

◎   your life story

◎   your weaknesses or liabilities

◎   trivial or uninteresting, nonhelpful information

◎   anything personal

The latter category can be illustrated by listening to Donna's answer. Would this impress the interviewer?

> *Uh…well, I can't really think of anything. Uh…I just got divorced, I have two kids, and I like to bowl. That's about it.*

Because she wasn't prepared, what finally came to her mind would do her no good and possibly some harm. Incidentally, whatever you say, do not end with "That's about it." This implies that you know little about yourself.

Instead of panicking and providing a poor answer, use this as an opportunity to positively present yourself. This is the time to verbalize the assets that are relevant to your interview goal. For a recommended response, select a top asset from each of the following categories and mention it briefly.

◎   experience (either from paid work, volunteer work, or school)

◎   education

◎   personality characteristics, other transferable skills, and goals

Often, an interviewer wants to be told information that isn't in your résumé so the latter category is a good possibility. However, don't hesitate to mention facts from your résumé. Even though the interviewer has probably read it, your response can be an effective review, and it doesn't hurt to be reminded of what you have to offer. Design your response so that you don't tell too much and, instead, leave the interviewer wanting to hear more. Read how Bryan answered the question.

> *For the past three years I've been employed at Raynor Marketing as a sales representative. This past year I was honored as the top salesperson in the firm. My college degree is in marketing. I've had specialized training in professional interactions and client relationships and consider myself to be a positive person who is highly motivated to succeed.*

Notice that he didn't begin with an "uh" or "well," neither of which is necessary. His response was descriptive, yet concise; it set the stage for additional questions. Most importantly, he ended on a very positive note.

    ◈ *Why did you choose this career field?*

Resist a "cliché" or ordinary answer that interviewers hear all too often. For example, a teacher or child development applicant could reply, "I love children." Even though a love for children is certainly a requirement, this response is expected and will not set you apart from all other applicants. "Successful candidates need to convey an appropriate motivation for entering the field of child care. It must truly be for the purpose of helping children and families—not to meet their own needs," cautions Alicia Baillie, a program chair of a child development program. If possible, relay anything in your personal background or experience that is unique, such as Cary's response.

> *When I was in sixth grade, my class visited the local fire station. Because I was so fascinated, I continued to stop there often. In fact, the firefighters considered me a mascot until I was in high school when they decided I was too old to be one. My keen interest plus my desire to help people motivated me to pursue a degree in fire protection technology, and I'm more interested and enthusiastic than ever. I do, however, realize that this career field is much more comprehensive than my sixth grade mind realized.*

Cary also helped himself by showing a reasonable understanding of career realities. Professional truck-driving students, for example, know that their occupation is much more than jumping behind the wheel of an 18-wheeler and driving off into the sunset! If you have chosen a career field wisely, this question is best answered by explaining your decision.

    ◈ *What are your career goals? Where do you want to be in five or ten years?*

If the question is phrased as the latter one, don't worry about the specific five- or ten-year period. Most interviewers just use this as a way to focus on goals. Having some clearly defined goals and being able to articulate these are pluses in your favor. Research about this particular employer will provide insight into its policies and goals, and you want to make your objectives sound compatible. For example, if advancement at a company is rare, a goal of "quickly moving up the ladder" is not in your best interest.

    It may even be necessary to conceal some of your goals. If a company intends to invest time, effort, and money into hiring and training you, the following is a response to avoid: "I want to work for a good company for a few years and then start my own business." If you feel compelled to mention wanting your own business, phrase it as a tentative long-term goal: "I do have aspirations of perhaps owning my own business in the future." Sounding as if you would be there only for the "short-term" or being more focused on "your own thing" than on what the employer needs will diminish your chances for employment.

     ◎ *Why do you want this job?*

This question is easily answered if you have a clear idea of how the job requirements and your abilities and interests match. It's imperative that you make a clear connection between what is needed in the position and your capabilities. Don't be vague or general and respond with, "It sounds like a good job," or "I think I can do a good job for you." State specifically what is good about the job, about yourself, and how the two are linked.

     ◎ *Why do you want to work for this company (or us)?*

This is a little different from the previous question although your research will provide the answer. This is the time to relay positive information about this particular employer. After you have demonstrated admiration for the company, the rest of the response reveals how you can contribute to its positive image. The following is how one applicant fielded this question.

> *This company is a respected leader in the field of architectural design. I'm familiar with past and present projects, and I see why you have earned such an excellent reputation. Because I have developed innovative projects in my present position and strive for excellence in all I do, I'm confident that I could make a significant contribution to your design team.*

Incidentally, if this question isn't asked, be sure that you let the interviewer know that you want to work for this employer. Because this seems so obvious (why else would I be interviewing here?), most applicants don't specifically state this. After I was hired, a member of the interviewing committee said, "A strong point in your favor was that you were the only one among the five finalists who said that you wanted to teach at this college."

     ◎ *Why are you leaving your present position?* or *Why did you leave your last job?*

Ideally, the reason is a positive one or you can make it sound as such. Indicating a desire for more opportunity or even more compensation is a suitable response. You may have not liked some aspect of the job. Without sounding negative or critical of a past employer, you can offer a brief reason for dissatisfaction. If you were laid off or terminated and there's any possibility that this can be discovered (and there usually is), state this. Then, tell what you learned from the experience.

     ◎ *Tell me about your education,* or *How did your education prepare you for this position?* or *Did you get out of your education what you expected?* or *Do your grades reflect your best efforts and your true capabilities?*

Any of these questions about your educational background are designed to find out how you feel about education, in general, and to see if you understand the relevancy of your training. Think about how your education has benefited you and be prepared to discuss this asset.

⊚   *What experiences have you had that qualify you for this position?*

Listen carefully to how this question is phrased. If asked about experiences in general, as in the question here, you can use work, volunteer, and educational experiences to support your qualifications. One or more from each of the categories could make an excellent response. However, you may be asked just about work experiences. Well-qualified candidates have blundered by only responding, "None," or "I haven't had any." Instead, you can answer, "Even though I haven't had paid work experience, I consider my experiences in college (or in a volunteer position) to be valuable work." Then, describe how those experiences have contributed to your ability to perform the job duties.

Another mistake is to avoid mentioning unrelated work experiences. Unless you did poorly in a job, all work experiences demonstrate transferable skills as well as your employability. Likewise, volunteer work, course projects, and activities usually will show leadership, teamwork, ability to get along with others, and dedication, among other assets. On the other hand, few interviewers appreciate applicants who inflate the value of their experiences. Sally had conducted a small research study for a sociology course. Her version of what she had done sounded as if she were ready to move into a researcher's position with no further experience or training. The interviewer was not fooled and certainly was not impressed.

⊚   *What past job did you like best and why?*

This is a golden opportunity to demonstrate enthusiasm. Ideally, the past job and the applied-for position are similar, and your response will emphasize these comparable aspects.

⊚   *What past job did you like least and why?*

If you have not disliked any past job, state this, then briefly describe one that was least enjoyed. Employers understand that most people experience dissatisfaction at least once during their career. If you let the person know that you learned from a less-than-favorable experience, the question is of benefit to you. A cautionary note is not to sound negative about a job or some aspect of it that is similar to the applied-for position.

⊚   *How would you handle this situation? What would you do under these circumstances?* (followed by a scenario)

Situational questions can be quite challenging. Bluffing or acting as if you can do something you aren't capable of is foolish. Admitting that you may need to ask for guidance is much preferred to acting as if you know it all. If you have been trained or had work experience, the best answer is to describe how you would currently deal with the matter. In some situations, there may not be a right or wrong way; instead, the person may be simply interested in your thought process. If the question is related to specific company policy, a good idea is to say that you would follow what is expected.

The field of child care is well-known for asking situational questions. Here's how Mark responded when asked what he would do if three-year-old Stephanie had bitten another child, Joshua.

First, I would check to see if Joshua was hurt and tend to him. Then I would take Stephanie aside. We'd both sit so we were at the same eye level, and I'd talk with her. What I would say would depend upon history. Is this the first time, or does she have a habit of biting? If this was the first time, my message would be that biting is not allowed and suggest some other behaviors to work off frustration or anger. If this had happened before and if a consequence had been established according to the center's policy, I would explain what would happen now. In the past this has worked with other children under my supervision.

Showing knowledge in the subject area required is obviously your best response, and being candid is essential. John learned this the hard way when he tried to bluff his way through a question about overhauling a transmission and was told that he needed to get more training before he would ever be considered. The repair shop didn't want a person to muddle through a job and create more problems along the way!

⊚ *How well do you get along with people?*

You may be tempted to give a to-the-point answer of "Fine." Instead, use **documenting**—giving specific instances to support your response. "Answer with examples of what you have done," advises Tony Reimer, claims superintendent for State Farm Insurance in Rocky Mount, North Carolina. Note the following.

I get along with people very well. In my last position I worked success-fully with several diverse individuals. On evaluations I consistently was given the top rating on ability to get along. I enjoy all types of people.

If you didn't get along with everyone, it's better not to sound as if you did. Most people don't have unblemished records; yet, you don't want to call attention to this or belabor the point.

⊚ *How did you get along with your past employer?*

Hopefully, your answer can be a positive one. If so, provide brief information describing your rapport. If you did not get along, it's best to be honest because this could be revealed by that past employer. Avoid phrases like "personality conflicts," and indicate that you wish the relationship had been better. A cardinal point is to not degrade a former employer, and you certainly don't want to sound as if you are blaming all the problems on someone else. When an applicant told Bob Dinkel that three of his past employers were impossible to work for and unlikable people, there was no doubt that Bob didn't want to take a chance of being the fourth! A simple, "To be honest, we had some difficulty working together. I wish it would have been different; however, I did learn from the experience." If this is the only time you have had problems with an employer, you can state that, as well.

     ⑤ *Describe an ideal job or describe an ideal supervisor.*

If asked the first question, the best answer is to describe the tasks and responsibilities of the position you are discussing. Even though it may not be ideal, if you are spending your time in an interview, it's one you think you would enjoy. Use the research about this position as your guide. The second question is best answered honestly. If the supervisor is totally opposite of the one you would consider ideal, it's better to know as you undoubtedly would be unhappy in this position.

     ⑤ *How would a good friend describe you?*

This is a slightly different way of asking you to describe yourself. A key tip is to use words that would be considered assets for this position. For example, a good friend may say you are "fun, caring, and happy-go-lucky," yet these descriptors aren't necessarily what will most impress a potential employer.

     You may also be asked more specific questions about yourself such as how you handle criticism, make decisions, work under pressure, and follow directions, as well as ones that relate to interactions and people you find difficult. Some employers are interested in what you consider to be your greatest achievement and disappointment thus far. Again, if you have a solid understanding of yourself and think about your responses ahead of time, these questions can be handled with ease.

     ⑤ *What did you like about your past job?*

This question is usually an easy one to answer as long as you enjoyed your work. If possible, indicate satisfaction with responsibilities and tasks similar to the job for which you are applying. If you didn't like your past job, explain briefly the reasons without being critical. "I found I didn't enjoy routine work" is much preferable to "The job was boring" or "The boss never gave me anything interesting to do."

     ⑤ *What didn't you like about your past job?*

This can be more difficult unless what was lacking there is required in the position being discussed. Again, don't sound like a complainer. Instead, explain the mismatch between the required tasks and your personality preferences or a lack of challenge and stimulation. Employers realize that dissatisfaction is certainly possible. Keep your answer brief.

     ⑤ *What are your strengths?*

Assets, assets, assets—having developed a list will solve any question of how to respond. Select your top five or six in the various areas of importance and practice a response that is no longer than a few minutes. Even though your résumé contains the same information or you have already mentioned an asset, repetition of your top strong points is fine.

◎ *What are your weaknesses?* or *In what ways would you like to improve yourself?*

One of the worst answers is to say that you have no weaknesses. Nobody is perfect, and we can all improve in some way. When a student was asked to list his liabilities (weaknesses), he couldn't think of any. One was suggested: inability to recognize any weaknesses!

The preferred answer is to mention a weakness that you are either in the process of strengthening or one that is easily changed. Strengthen your answer by telling what you are doing to change this liability. Avoid naming any that will destroy your chances such as: "I have a drinking problem," "I can't control my temper," or "I have a hard time relating to people." Notice how positive Andrew's response sounds.

> *Being a perfectionist, I've found, isn't necessarily in my best interest. I've read some materials about it and have now developed realistic goals. Instead of perfection, I strive for excellence and find that my efforts produce much better results.*

An interviewer may ask about strengths and weaknesses in the same question. If so, it's better to first touch on a weakness then end with a longer discussion of your strengths.

What if the interviewer doesn't actually ask you about weaknesses? Usually you will also avoid the subject. However, if the weakness is an obvious one that might stand in your way, you are probably wise to bring it up. For example, if you are an older applicant, at some point you might say, "Even though I may be older than the other applicants, I see this as an advantage to an employer. I'm mature, dependable, have a great deal of job experience, and a strong work ethic." If you think you might be perceived as too young, mention energy, ambition, flexibility, and willingness to learn. Anticipating what the interviewer might consider a weakness can enable you to discuss it positively.

◎ *What would satisfy you in a job?*

Knowing yourself well will be appreciated at this point. Having thought about job satisfaction, as covered in Chapter 3, this question will not be a problem. Ideally, your answer will reflect the requirements of the applied-for position. Definitely don't describe factors that aren't possible with this employer.

◎ *What motivates you?*

Candidates decrease their chances by naming only external motivators such as pay and other inducements. Most employers want to hear that applicants are self-motivated by challenge and a desire for excellence. Mentioning that you like to be appreciated for your efforts is fine as well. A high degree of motivation is a true asset, and if you can document instances of high-quality performance as a result of your self-motivation, the response can be of major benefit.

☺ *Aren't you overqualified for this position?*

If your experiences or education or both are perceived as more than the position demands, you will probably be asked this question. You might anticipate that this is in the interviewer's mind and broach the issue, as discussed under the question about weaknesses. It's beneficial to let the person know that you have thought about this and still want the position for what it offers. Mentioning that job satisfaction is more important to you than titles or compensation could turn this potential liability into a definite asset.

☺ *What magazines do you read regularly?* or *Tell me about a book you have read in the past year.*

These are not common questions; yet, not thinking about them ahead of time could lead to an embarrassed silence or a poor answer. Ideally, you could offer something related to your career field; publications that indicate a well-rounded personality are also good to mention. Employers usually don't want candidates to be 100 percent career-oriented. "An outstanding interviewee demonstrates interest and knowledge in several areas. Being informed about other things in the world, as well as the company and the position, is most impressive," says Jeanne Salerno, a director of professional development for a law firm.

☺ *What salary do you expect?*

Not doing your homework may cost you money if you cite a lower amount of pay or could cost you the job if your figure is too high (Lock, 1992). This one question may be one of the most salient reasons to conduct prior research. Knowing the typical salary or range of pay for the position makes this formidable question an easy one. If you do not have this information, you can say that the figure would depend upon a full understanding of the position and other benefits. Also, you can ask, "What is the range of pay for this position?" or state that you are open to a discussion of what would be fair compensation for a person with your background. If a question about salary and benefits is not asked, do not bring up the subject.

☺ *If hired, how long can we expect you to remain with this company?*

This is a "loaded" question, and a recommendation is to refrain from giving any certain length of time. While an employer would doubt that you will remain with the company your entire career life, he or she does want a sense of stability and commitment. Lyn's response is impressive.

Stability and security are goals of mine. I want an interesting and satisfying position that I will be committed to for many years, and your company has several such positions.

☺ *How do you plan to stay up-to-date in this field?*

Keeping abreast of new developments and updating of skills are essential, and you will want to mention several possibilities including further technical training or coursework, reading, and learning from others. Don't make the mistake of just mentioning employer-sponsored training activities. You want to give the impression that you will continue to learn and grow even if you do it at your own expense and on your own time. An interview suggestion from John Buse, president of Precision Machine Co., Inc., is: "Don't say you've done everything and give the impression that there's nothing to learn."

    ◎   *Why should we hire you?*

This is likely to be the most critical question of all and is commonly reserved for the end of the interview. However, be prepared for it at any time, even as a lead-in question. The wording may be slightly different, yet what the interviewer wants to know is what you can do for the business. If the wording of the question includes "over the other applicants," simply disregard that part. Starting out with "Well, I'm not sure I have more to offer than the others" is a poor beginning. Explaining briefly your top several assets as they pertain to this position is the key to your response. Draw from the areas of (1) experience, (2) job-related skills and abilities, (3) education, (4) transferable assets including personality traits, and (5) interests and motivation. Practicing ahead of time is highly recommended although you don't want to sound stilted. Consider Jane's polished response.

> *My work experience has increased the technical skills I learned while earning my business administration degree and given me an opportunity to use many "people" skills. I have demonstrated that I can increase office efficiency and consistently turn out high quality work. I am dependable, positive, friendly, enthusiastic about my career, and very interested in this particular position. I'm confident that I can make a significant contribution to your company.*

If this question is asked toward the end of the interview, you have probably already mentioned some of the assets. That doesn't mean you would want to leave those out. Instead, regard this as a summary of your strengths and repeat the most positive ones. Your prime purpose is to draw a mental picture of how you can benefit the employer. As one business owner put it, "An interviewee should let me know how he or she can solve my problems."

RESPONDING TO ILLEGAL QUESTIONS.   What to do if asked an illegal or questionable question is, in itself, a challenging question. Just as there are inappropriate application questions that could lead to discrimination, several interview inquiries fall into the same category. Generally, if information being sought is not related to the job, the question is inappropriate, if not illegal. These inquiries were covered in Table 4–2 in Chapter 4; be sure to review those before going to an interview.

    Even though most interviewers are well-versed on the legality of questions, some are not. Often, employers don't use the information to discriminate; they are just unaware of the laws. You certainly may ignore the illegality and provide the information. However, because of the nature of the information, this could become an obstacle as in the response: "Yes, I have three children under the age of ten." The interviewer is thinking, "Good chance that this applicant will take plenty of sick leave. That's a definite drawback." Answering could also indicate to a potential employer that you aren't aware of illegalities and will offer anything to get the job.

What is a suitable response to a questionable question? If you think the interviewer is inclined to discriminate, an especially assertive response is appropriate. "I don't see the relevance to the position," or even, "I prefer not to answer questions such as that unless they are specifically related to the position." If you consider it an innocent query, you can ask, "I'm not necessarily opposed to telling you. However, I wonder if it is related to the job duties and responsibilities?" Generally, an interviewer will recognize a mistake and retract the question. Otherwise, the reply will be a clue as to your next step. If relevancy to the position is explained, an excellent reply is, "I appreciate your explaining that to me. I have no physical disabilities that would prevent me from doing those tasks."

If an interviewer persists in asking personal or other illegal questions or doesn't react well to your reluctance to respond, you probably won't be hired. Yet, would you want to work for someone who doesn't abide by fairness and the law? There are far more employers who are objective in their interviewing and hiring methods. You deserve to work for one of those!

ASKING IMPRESSIVE QUESTIONS.   An interview can be ruined by answering "no" when asked, "Do you have any questions?" A cardinal rule of positive interviewing is to have several questions to ask. Not asking anything could suggest disinterest, laziness, or inability to formulate questions. None of these will get you hired. No questions could also indicate nonassertiveness and a lack of curiosity which are both undesirable qualities. A publication written for managers about interviewing offered this tip.

> Do give them a chance to ask questions about the job and the company. If they really want the job, they will have a string of queries. If not, you have to wonder how much they've prepared, and how eager they are to assume the particular position you have in mind (Manager's Legal Bulletin, 1993).

A business owner in a career development class stated, "I learn more about the applicant from the questions asked than the answers given." Is there any doubt how crucial your questions will be? Questions, if they reflect a sincere interest in the business and the position and a desire to contribute, will serve as invaluable assets.

Even though you have done adequate research, there are still questions to ask or information to verify. In fact, the actual research often opens up further possibilities for inquiries. Obviously, if the interviewer has already adequately covered the subject, you could appear to be a poor listener by posing a question. Yet, if you want more clarification, be sure to ask. Following is a list of reasonable topics to explore. Because the time for your questions may be limited, a good idea is to prioritize your list.

- duties and responsibilities of the position

- hours, work schedule, typical day experiences, overtime expectations, if any

- reason position is open

- how employee performance is measured

- advancement possibilities

- opportunities for continued learning, training

- major strengths and growth potential of the company

- present and future company projects, if appropriate

- chain of command, organizational chart

- work environment, equipment, tools

- degree of rapport among personnel

- wellness philosophy and how physical and mental health are encouraged

- materials available from the company

- qualities and skills desired in this position

The last question provides an opportunity for you to sell yourself. If you possess the qualities, affirm this. "That's good to hear because I am a creative person who enjoys being innovative, and I pride myself on being responsible."

> *THINK OF AT LEAST THREE QUESTIONS YOU WOULD WANT TO ASK AT MOST INTERVIEWS.*

Questions are best if they reflect a knowledge base. If an applicant asks, "What does your company do?" the lack of research is obvious. Complimenting the employer in your question is impressive. For example, Ryan said, "I realize that your company was ranked among the top ten national leaders this past year. In what ways do you encourage this degree of excellence?" Kate showed knowledge and offered praise when she stated, "I'm pleased that you strongly encourage wellness. What specific employee programs do you have?"

You may have noticed that salary and benefits are missing from the list of question topics. Even though some employers and career development experts say that it's logical to ask about these, it seems more reasonable to refrain from any salary question and, if necessary, to inquire indirectly about benefits. Above all else, you don't want to sound desperate or as if your interest lies only in what's in this for you. Applicants who give these impressions are usually unsuccessful.

Often, benefits are mentioned by the interviewer when the job and company are described. If they aren't, a simple request for any written material or verbal information about benefits is appropriate. You could even ask about a specific benefit such as child care if this is a strong factor in your deliberations. Benefits are discussed in more detail in Chapter 6.

Regarding salary, if you have researched, you will already know either an exact or approximate figure so there is no reason to ask. Even if you don't know, consider when it would be to your advantage to discuss the subject. At what point would you be in the strongest position to receive the highest offer? Would it be during an initial interview before the employer even knows if you are the first choice? Obviously, your advantage comes after the employer has decided on you. If you like to fish, you probably know that setting the hook comes after the fish has taken the bait! Most people recommend that applicants never ask salary questions. The general opinion is that waiting to discuss salary after an offer has been made "puts you in the driver's seat." Salary negotiation is covered in Chapter 6.

"Until I'm ready to offer you the job, I don't want to be asked about benefits. When I decide to hire you, then it's my turn to impress you."

Doc Chaves, Assistant Vice President
Ameritas Life Insurance Corp.
Lincoln, Nebraska

What you don't say and ask are just as important as what you do. Use the material in KEY STEPS (pages 293–94) to help in the preparatory work necessary for a successful interview. Thoughtful preparation can turn a harrowing interview experience into a pleasant one. A key point is that even with the highest level of preparation, you want to be yourself. Ideally, you can honestly identify with a valid point made by Carolyn Olsen, an instructor of employment techniques: "It's not enough to look good; you must be good."

KEY ADVICE

WHAT IS IMPORTANT IN AN INTERVIEW?

Machine Tool: *"Wear clean clothes and have your hair combed. Be on time; otherwise, make a telephone call and explain."*
John Buse, President, Precision Machine Co., Inc.

Firefighting: *"Interviewees must be prepared to present what they want the interviewer to hear."*
Darrell Eastin, Beatrice, Nebraska, Fire Department Chief

"Individuals need to exhibit energy, enthusiasm, honesty, and a solid work ethic in just a few minutes. If they don't, they'll be in the 'also ran' category."
Mark Munger, Lincoln, Nebraska, Fire Department Captain

Architecture and Drafting: *"It's better to be over-dressed than under-dressed while still being conservative in appearance."*
Lynn Jones, Chairman, Davis Design

Communications: *"My favorite question is: 'If I ran an ad for a position and you think that this is exactly the right job for you, what will the ad say?' I learn so much from the answer."*

Doc Chaves, Assistant Vice President, Ameritas Life Insurance Corp.

Banking: *"I can usually tell when people answer my questions the way they think they **should**. I'd prefer that they be themselves rather than 'on cue.'"*

Ed Rasgorshek, Senior Vice President, Farm Credit Services of the Midlands

Human Resources and Development: *"Be prepared to talk honestly about yourself and let me know why you want to work for **this** company. A professional demeanor is very important."*

Jody Horwitz, Director of Human Resources, Turner Broadcasting System, Inc., Los Angeles

"Be candid and professional. Demonstrate an interest and knowledge in as many areas as possible."

Jeanne Salerno, Director, Professional Development, Kutak Rock Law Firm

Health Care: *"Giving impressions of professionalism and confidence is important."*

Nancy Brown, R.N., Program Manager, State Department of Health

Automotive Technology: *"Arrive on time. Have a résumé there beforehand. Be prepared to answer and ask questions. Appear neatly dressed and clean. Don't wear dirty, greasy clothes that look like you just crawled out from under the car."*

Bob Batt, Owner, Auto Tek Service Center, Inc.

Child Care: *"A successful applicant will be upbeat, positive, and communicate well with good eye contact."*

Sue Collins, Director, KinderCare Learning Center

"Convey what will enable you to succeed with children—compassion, caring, and patience plus a sense of humor and sense of wonder that you can then instill in them."

Alicia Baillie, Program Chair, Child Development

Construction: *"Express yourself clearly and avoid the over-use of common words and slang. Convey a keen desire to be productive and contribute to the company."*

Bob Dinkel, Owner, Accent Fence Company

ENDING THE INTERVIEW

Determining the end of the interview is a responsibility of the interviewer. As the applicant, you want to be careful that you don't take the lead and, perhaps, end the discussion before you have achieved your goal. A career development student emerged from a "mock" job interview after only about five minutes. He had a big smile on his face. "That was quick," he said. "There was a pause so I thanked him for his time and left." The smile left his face when he was told that extremely short interviews usually aren't the most successful ones. "I was just glad to get it over with," he admitted. Be sure you aren't thinking in this way.

On the other extreme, you don't want to continue the interview past an appropriate end. If you know the allotted interview time and are aware of the interviewer's cues, you can be ready for the closing; usually, at the end you will be asking questions. If in doubt, ask if there is time for another one.

If the person does not explain the next step in the process, you are advised to ask. A most stressful situation is waiting for an unknown period of time for word from the employer. "When can I expect to hear from you?" is a polite request for valuable information. You may also ask about calling if you have more questions. Expressing thanks for the time and opportunity and a genuine interest in the position are positive closing remarks.

Evaluating Yourself

Spending time soon after the interview to assess how well you did is time well-spent. Drawing on evaluative material provided to interviewers, check yourself on the following.

- ◉ Did I listen and respond directly to all questions? If I didn't, which questions were troublesome and need more thought and practice?
- ◉ Did I probe for clarification, if necessary?
- ◉ Did I turn negative information into positive?
- ◉ Was the atmosphere relaxed? Did we experience rapport?
- ◉ How did I appear nonverbally?
- ◉ Did I overwhelm or underwhelm the interviewer? (Incidentally, neither extreme is desirable.)
- ◉ Did I demonstrate that I was well informed about the employer and the position?
- ◉ Did I use understandable, appropriate language?
- ◉ Did I ask appropriate questions that didn't sound rehearsed?
- ◉ How do I feel emotionally about the interview?

Review what employees want, presented earlier in this chapter, and ask yourself whether these qualities were evident in what you said and did. Also, check the common mistakes (Table 5–1) and score yourself in KEY STEPS (page 296).

Following Up

Either the same day or the one following, effective job hunters write a letter to the interviewer. Its purpose is to express appreciation for the opportunity to discuss the position and to reiterate what your strengths are in relationship to the opening. You can mention significant points from the interview itself, keeping in mind that you are responsible for matching yourself with the position.

A thank-you note to the receptionist or others who assisted you in some way is also recommended. These written communications show that you are courteous and have a keen interest in the job. A distinct advantage is to get your name registered one more time in the mind of the potential employer. Another possibility is to telephone with additional information; however, this could be an interruption in a busy person's schedule and is recommended only if expediency is necessary. Even though many job seekers are told to follow up, most do not. So this is another chance to set yourself apart in a positive way.

In fact, that is the ultimate purpose of an interview: to set yourself apart from all other applicants. By thoroughly preparing yourself physically and mentally, rehearsing the possible questions that may be asked, and then, if possible, going through a practice or "mock" videotaped interview, you will have done all you can to ensure that this happens.

KEY POINTS

⊚   The interview is the final stage in securing a position.

⊚   Candidates are advised to mentally prepare and know what employers want with the idea that they need to sell themselves physically, mentally, emotionally, and socially. Knowing what is impressive in these areas and what is not is critical.

⊚   Heading the list of impressive behaviors are dependability, ability to get along with others, and professionalism. Several other actions make you a viable candidate.

⊚   Much of the impression you make is based on nonverbal behaviors.

⊚   An interview is designed to glean information; your ability to sell yourself verbally is essential. Thinking about and practicing answers to the multitude of possible questions increases your confidence.

⊚   An interviewer may ask an illegal question, and it's wise to plan a response ahead of time.

⊚   Asking appropriate questions is just as important as responding and will enhance your chances.

⊚   After an interview an honest evaluation and a follow-up with the interviewer are highly recommended.

RECOMMENDED READING

Adams job interview almanac. (1996). Hollbrook, MA: Adams Media Corporation.

Asher, D. (1995). *The foolproof job-search workbook.* Berkeley, CA: Ten Speed Press.

Davis, S. (1996). *Career power.* Boston: Allyn and Bacon (employment guide and audiotape).

Jackson, T. and Buckingham, B. (1993). *Interview express.* New York: Times Books.

Lott, C. S. and Lott, O. C. (1994). *How to land a better job*. Lincolnwood, IL: VGM Career Horizons.

Lowstuter, C. C. and Robertson, D. P. (1992). *In search of the perfect job*. New York: McGraw-Hill, Inc.

Medley, A. (1992). *Sweaty palms: The neglected art of being interviewed*. Berkeley, CA: Ten Speed Press.

Messmer, M. (1995). *Job hunting for dummies*. Foster City, CA: IDG Books Worldwide, Inc.

Morton, P. and Fox, M. R. (1995). *The first job hunt survival guide*. New York: DBM Publishing.

Washington, T. (1995). *Interview power*. Bellevue, WA: Mount Vernon Press.

Yate, M. (1997). *Knock 'em dead 1997*. Holbrook, MA: Adams Media Corporation.

Your Career Path

T he career path begins when a person decides to pursue a certain field of study. Depending upon whether you have been rejected for a particular position, decided not to accept a job, or received an offer, your path has taken various turns. Even though there is a tendency to think of choices as either right or wrong, realize that a decision simply means following a different path. As long as you keep your direction focused on your career goals, you can achieve them via a number of ways.

REJECTION OF AN OFFER

As an applicant, you may be forced to accept and deal with rejection; what if the reverse occurs? After going through the job-search process, you may find yourself not wanting the position. This presents a challenge in that you want to leave a positive impression.

If an offer is given verbally either in person or by telephone, you can respond immediately or tell the person you would like time to consider. If you delay, your response can be either verbal or in writing and you want to be appreciative. Following is a possible verbal response.

> *I appreciate your offer and have given it serious consideration. Even though my regard for your company is*

high, I've decided that the particular position is not what I want. Thank you for your time and interest.

A letter of rejection is brief, sincere, and positive. The beginning paragraph expresses appreciation for the offer and contains a statement declining the position. Giving the precise reason or telling your immediate plans is optional. In another paragraph write positively about the employer, interviewer, or offer and repeat your appreciation for the time and efforts.

NEGOTIATION AND ACCEPTANCE OF AN OFFER

Research before applying or at least before an offer is the key to successful salary negotiation. The primary source of information is the potential employer; ideally, a salary range is provided in an available job description. The next best source is a competitor.

Besides the expected salary, three other areas of information are vital. First, and covered in the next section, are benefits. The second area covers cost-of-living pay increases and the basis and timetable for salary increases. Opportunity for promotion is third.

UNDERSTANDING BENEFITS

Research definitely involves benefits. Preferably, this information would be in writing. Conceivably, benefits can add 30 to 40 percent to one's salary with 36 percent most typical, according to Cindy Siddons, manager, human resources and West Coast benefits, Turner Broadcasting System, Inc., Los Angeles. As such, they should be considered as part of the total package. As one employer remarked, "We pay a slightly lower starting wage, but when you consider our benefits package, we offer an employee much more." Benefits with any employer can include any or all of the areas listed in Table 6–1 and will vary.

> *PRIORITIZE THE BENEFITS. WHICH ARE MOST IMPORTANT TO YOU?*

Benefits may be open to negotiation. For example, some employers don't pay for missed work. You might be able to negotiate so many days with pay. Getting an employer to provide uniforms or pay for cleaning could make a difference in how much money you have available. In large companies, benefits aren't usually negotiable; yet, they may be. "Some companies give higher-level candidates additional benefits such as stock options as part of the hiring negotiation," according to Cindy Siddons, manager, human resources and West Coast benefits, Turner Broadcasting System, Inc., Los Angeles. Besides monetary pluses, benefits can make a difference in morale. Wellness programs and company-sponsored functions have physical, social, and emotional value, as well.

NEGOTIATING SALARY

The other source of invaluable salary information is you. In addition to knowing what the offer is likely to be, you also must know what salary you need.

If the job involves relocation, be sure to take that into consideration and know the geographical differences in cost of living. The bottom line is: If you don't have information about salary, you are in no position to negotiate, and you are at a distinct disadvantage.

Timing in negotiation is critical. Negotiating after an employer has selected you is best. At this point, you have more power than you may ever have. A typical initial reaction to an offer is a feeling of euphoria which can be followed by a quick, "Yes, I'll take it." Enjoy the emotional high while resisting the impulse to accept. Instead, express appreciation, continued genuine interest, and a desire for further discussion. You now have an advantage, and in these cases, it isn't unusual for an offer to be increased. It also shows that you take time to consider important decisions, a positive characteristic.

Negotiation is best done in person; in cases of long distance hiring, the telephone will be necessary. The psychological advantage is in favor of the one sought after—in this case, you! Use this to bolster your confidence while not allowing it to make you appear superior. Keep in mind that offers can be withdrawn.

Your role in the negotiation process is to wait and let the potential employer mention a figure. The experts tend to agree that the one who mentions a dollar amount first loses the most at the last (Bolles, 1996). What if the other person asks about your expectations or requirements? A recommended response is, "I have thought about compensation and have confidence that you will be fair. I'd like to hear what you have in mind." At this point your research will pay off. If the person names the position's maximum amount, and it is near the top of the range, the next step is easy. If the figure is in the middle or lower, you can use your knowledge and leverage to an advantage in your response.

> *I understand how important it is to keep costs low in order to make a profit, and I'm confident that I will help the company do just that. Because of this and the other assets I bring to this position, I believe a salary of $_____ is justified.*

Your figure will be at the top of the range. Be ready to document specific ways you can save and make money for the company so the person can see why you are worth the higher salary. Keep in mind that $2,000 a year difference over several years becomes a significant amount and that most raises are figured on a percentage of the current wage. In fact, $1 an hour difference over a year's time equates to $1,920. Over a 40-year average work life, you would experience a net gain of $76,800 (Barlow, 1994). The next step after your request is up to the employer.

WHAT IS THE MINIMUM SALARY YOU WOULD ACCEPT RIGHT NOW?

Other questions to have answered during this deliberation process have to do with probationary periods, if any, and the all-important salary reviews. If the company has a probationary period, find out its length and purpose. Regarding

T A B L E   6 – 1 ▲ POSSIBLE EMPLOYMENT BENEFITS

Those marked with * are most likely to be offered.

vacation and holidays*	moving expenses
sick leave*	paid parking
personal leave*	child care
professional leave	education and training opportunities*
bereavement leave*	tuition reimbursement
health insurance*	company car or transportation
life insurance*	considerations
accidental death and dismemberment	uniforms and tools
insurance	wellness programs*
disability pay*	health club memberships
retirement and pension plans*	recreational programs
savings plans, stock options, profit	employee assistance programs
sharing programs	outplacement and severance
pretax deduction plans and flexible	counseling
spending accounts	

salary reviews, timing makes a difference. Whether the initial adjustment to salary will be made within 90 days or one year makes a definite difference. Is the raise automatic or based on merit? In some occupations, you will receive an increase regardless of your performance; in others, it's dependent on you. Also, you will want to know the typical increase. It may be set or negotiable. Besides salary and benefits, factors include the following: bonuses, work schedule and hours, required records and reports which might necessitate at-home work, relocation package, social obligations and expectations, community involvement requirements, training programs, advancement and promotion opportunities, expense allowances, and travel requirements/compensation. Take careful notes during the discussion. Before you accept an offer, review all aspects of the job. Because this is a critical decision, you owe it to yourself and the employer to take all the time you need. The exercise in KEY STEPS (page 297) can help prepare you for the negotiation process.

ACCEPTING A POSITION

After verbal agreement, if you are not offered the terms in writing, request this. Again, you are demonstrating that you have a "good head on your shoulders," and neither of you will end up surprised nor disappointed. You may prefer to write a letter of acceptance. This letter expresses appreciation for the offer and enthusiasm about the position. In it, you convey understanding of the terms of the offer including the starting employment date.

During this stage of the process, you will also want to prepare yourself for the first workday. If you don't already know, be sure to ask about orientation activities, dress code, parking, food availability, appropriate ways to address supervisors and other employees, and company policies.

BEGINNING YOUR NEW JOB

The initial days on the job can be exciting, challenging, overwhelming, and frightening, and these feelings can last for some time. Many businesses offer a formal orientation to new employees; however, some just expect you to jump right in!

> *"A challenging aspect of employment for me was the confusion and overwhelming feeling of the first several months. I think it's important that new employees realize that this is normal."*
>
> Lyn Patterson, Human Resources Administrator
> Turner Broadcasting System, Inc.
> Los Angeles, California

Thinking of the entire first year as separate from the rest of the career ladder is a good way to help the work world make sense. You're no longer a student, yet, not really a professional either. Think of this time as a transition stage. Laura Mann, a sales representative for Prentice Hall, summed it up nicely.

> *There is a learning curve with every new job. It seems like the first year you work nonstop and wonder why you ever agreed to take this position. In the second year, things get a lot easier, and you start to enjoy the job more. By the third year, you really start feeling good about your skills and achievements.*

You will be making several first impressions which you will want to be positive. Your appearance is important. The same interview guidelines of appropriateness, cleanliness, and neatness prevail. Part of your preparation for the first day would include finding out what manner of dress is expected. What might have been acceptable elsewhere may not set well with this employer. For example, professors at some universities may be allowed to wear jeans or shorts while other institutions frown upon this. As a new employee, dressing according to the norm or slightly better is advisable. Looking professional in a business setting certainly will be to your advantage.

Communication plays a major role in all aspects of life and takes on even greater dimensions when you are newly hired. Listening intently and reinforcing what you hear by taking notes are highly recommended. You will be receiving so much information, and even with the best memory, you won't have total recall. When you're introduced to someone, write the name along with the title and make a concerted effort to remember the person. Writing directions and explanations will help you and is usually interpreted positively as well.

Another necessary communication behavior is asking questions. If you have concerns about not knowing, realize that lack of knowledge is expected. Not asking any questions is risky and doesn't create a favorable impression.

Acknowledging how much you don't know has a more positive effect than showing how much you know (Holton, 1996). Almost everyone is flattered by being considered a knowledgeable person. When you seek information from a supervisor, co-worker, or secretary, you are, in a sense, elevating him or her.

Every company has its own communication system which needs to be learned as soon as possible. Individual offices may have established procedures for answering telephones and taking messages for one another. You may have your own individual telephone and voice mail. When you use the telephone, be sure to sound professional and friendly. You may have available a fax machine and e-mail as well. Again, check to find out the accepted procedures for the various modes of communication.

A task that you may find disconcerting, yet one that is decidedly beneficial, is reading the company manual or policies. If one is not offered, ask about its availability. You may be expected to read it outside of work hours. Again, ask questions if certain policies are not clear.

For many new employees, setting up a working space is a major early task. Your goal is to create an efficient area. Even though we differ in the degree of neatness we maintain, new employees help themselves by being neat and organized. In most work areas you will have room for some personal touches such as photographs. Avoid any display that is negative, insensitive, and offensive. If you are sharing space with others, be considerate.

Interpersonal relations skills are regarded as essential throughout one's career. When you are new, a demonstration of friendliness and congeniality will be well-received. Logically, other employees would introduce themselves to you. Yet, because long-term employees, surprisingly, don't always know how new you are, they may hesitate to extend an introduction. For example, Mark commented, "I introduced myself to a person I thought was a new employee and was quite embarrassed when he said he had worked here for two years!" If you have a list of employees, you can mark off the name of each one you meet

▲ Being oriented to a new position relieves some of the overwhelming feelings of confusion.

as another way of remembering individuals. "Being friendly is important; however, it's better not to form friendships too quickly either," advises Lois Kemble, an instructor of office technology students. Building relationships in the work place is an ongoing process and is thoroughly covered in Chapter 7.

How much of a friend do you become? Do you socialize outside of work? Are such relationships encouraged? This is a learning experience as companies vary in what is appropriate. Generally, it's best to maintain a balance between your personal and professional life, and in the beginning, to move gradually into work relationships. An open communication style along with an avoidance of profanity and slang are appreciated. Sometimes a problem for new employees is being drawn into petty conflicts or gossip. Even though you may feel that this is a sign of being accepted, it's better to avoid getting involved. Develop professional maturity, which means using good judgment and trying to build positive relationships with everyone you meet.

Learning the "culture of the company" is a good idea, according to Susan Brown, an advertising account executive. A company's unique personality and culture translate into unique sets of rules and **norms**, expected ways of behaving. Knowing the mission and philosophy of the business and paying attention to the ways things are done will make a positive difference. You want to "fit in" before you establish yourself as unique. Observation is essential (Holton, 1996). A new employee may face some teasing. One new firefighter reported that he went through a few weeks of good-natured, "new-person-on-the-block" bantering. "I just laughed and went along with it, and after a few weeks, it was over," he said. "It's a tradition at this station so I knew what to expect."

While enthusiasm is welcomed in most jobs, proceeding with some caution is advisable. Sometimes a person "plunges in" with too much zeal and, in the process, either makes unnecessary errors or gives the impression of wanting to take over. Whatever changes you desire, it is more to your advantage to move gradually. Some new graduates act as if they know everything, which is a good way to create animosity. You will fare better by seeking advice and acknowledging that you have much to learn. Most people are flattered to be perceived as experts. An exception is asking a "lazy question," an unnecessary inquiry made by someone who doesn't attempt to discover an answer through a personal effort, such as reading directions.

Making some mistakes at first is not unusual. When you do, your best course of action is to correct the problem and, when appropriate, to take responsibility for the error. Trying to cover up a problem often makes it worse. Jessica forgot to give her supervisor a message from a client. Instead of admitting it, she said there had been no message. A confrontation ensued which adversely affected customer relations. In order to avoid losing the client, she finally told the true story. Earning back her employer's trust was challenging, and she learned a valuable lesson about honesty and taking responsibility.

During your first year the single most important person is your immediate supervisor. This relationship will be different from any other (Holton, 1996). Suggestions for making this as positive as possible follow.

⑥ Be loyal. No matter how tempted you are, refrain from doing anything that seems disloyal. This includes keeping any negative comments to yourself. Use a personal relationship to vent, not a professional one.

⑥ Learn what is expected of you.

⑥ Be supportive. This includes doing what is asked of you as well as offering more when needed.

⑥ Provide solutions, not problems.

⑥ Do everything you can to help your supervisor perform her or his job well and look good.

⑥ Take responsibility for yourself. Excuse-making or trying to blame the supervisor or a co-worker for a poor performance or a mistake only makes it worse.

In a sense, this relationship is akin to a parent–child one, and you are the child. If you want to succeed in this position, you may have to take more or put up with more than you would from another person. It may seem terribly unfair, yet the reality is that this single person has more control over your future career than anyone else, except you. Building a positive working relationship is absolutely necessary.

In the beginning your willingness to put in extra time in order to learn a new job will be impressive. Even if you don't receive extra compensation, consider it time well spent. Also, you may be asked to do some things that you didn't expect. "In the beginning if I was asked to run get a cup of coffee for my supervisor, I did it," said Matt about his work in a television studio. You will show a keen interest in the work and a desire to learn, and the additional effort will undoubtedly make your job easier in the long run. "During the first years you do what it takes to learn and grow," says Lisa Patterson, senior manager in an accounting firm.

MAINTAINING BALANCE

As much as it's worthwhile to work hard and demonstrate your capabilities and enthusiasm, it's important to be realistic. Like a candle burning at both ends, you can lose the ability to be effective. Most new employees become aware that as long as they are willing to take on all tasks, more will be assigned. At some point you will reach a saturation point. After a few years, Susan became keenly aware of an imbalance. "If you're doing your job as well as you can, and you still feel completely overwhelmed, it's time to let that be known. Otherwise, what can happen is a continual build-up of tasks."

To maintain balance, you can realistically set parameters or boundaries for work. How much is too much needs to be clearly established and then modified if you assume added duties. A good supervisor wants you to perform effectively and will be receptive to knowing when you have more than you can handle. A way to proceed is to request a time to discuss the issue. Then, using the open communication style, you can document your task overload and request what seems realistic. Often, some minor changes can make a major difference. For example, Stephanie was expected to enter data into the computer and keep employment records updated. Because her desk was in a reception area, she was asked questions by people who walked in and often spent a great deal of time either helping them or answering the telephone. After she discussed the problem with her employer, she was given permission to use a small, remote office area. Her productivity increased significantly.

Effective time management can reduce pressure. You may find that coming in early on occasion when things are quiet is well worth your while, or you may shorten your telephone calls. For example, some systems allow you to leave voice mail even when the person is there. While this may seem silly, you might find that it's in your best interest to leave a short, effective message rather than engage in a longer, unnecessary conversation. Time management is covered in more detail in Chapter 8.

Balance also means maintaining a personal life. Getting away will usually make a person much more productive at work. Even though it's common for employees to put in longer than a 40-hour week, do preserve adequate time for pleasure and relaxation. Personal time can serve as a valuable replenisher so, in the long run, your career will benefit.

Keeping Personal Records

Throughout your career, maintaining a personal career file is one of the most practical and worthwhile things you can do. Reasons include a need for documentation or clarification as well as preparation for a change or jobs. Well-organized records make life less stressful. The following are included in a career file.

- all data for an application including job records
- current résumé
- education record including transcripts
- degrees, diplomas, and certificates
- current and past job descriptions

▲ Dilbert reprinted by permission of United Feature Syndicate, Inc.

- salary records
- summary of achievements and honors
- any news clippings or articles about your career, job, or yourself
- your publications and a portfolio of your work
- letters of recommendations from past employers, educators, clients, and others
- names, addresses, and numbers of contacts and past and present references
- all job evaluations and performance reviews
- brochures about seminars and workshops you've attended

When you consider that there's a good chance you will change jobs at least 10 times during your lifetime (Barlow, 1994), keeping a well-organized career file makes sense. Having this information up-to-date and readily available will make the next job search much easier. Sometimes expediency makes a major difference. Just one day before applications closed, David heard of a dream position. Because he had kept a current employment file, he was able to deliver a polished résumé in due time.

MAKING CONTACTS

Networking, significant in the quest to get a job, is essential throughout your career. Relationships that are satisfying help to create a positive professional life. Much of our learning and professional development are dependent upon others. Imagine having to figure out everything by yourself! Instead, from the first day at work, you will undoubtedly ask questions and seek advice, and people will voluntarily offer suggestions and show you how to perform certain tasks. You may even have a **mentor**, a specific person who serves as a guide and role model—who may "take you under his or her wings" and offer to provide help and advice. This may come from an assignment; more often, it just evolves. Effective career designers have several mentors. Cultivating multiple and diverse developmental relationships in order to build a "personal board of directors" is recommended by Professor Linda A. Hill, Ph.D., Harvard Business School (1994). Successful mentoring is usually reciprocal; your willingness to provide help and advice in return solidifies the relationship.

> *THINK OF SOMEONE YOU ADMIRE. FOR WHAT REASONS DO YOU ADMIRE THAT PERSON? IN WHAT WAY COULD THIS INDIVIDUAL SERVE AS A MENTOR?*

Contacts are especially helpful as you advance. Having a number of people who know and appreciate your contributions and who will vouch for your abilities can spell the difference between being promoted or not. If you decide to change jobs, references will be needed; you will be in an enviable position if you can draw from a creditable group of people. You can also find job leads and receive advice from your networking circle made up of anyone you meet professionally during your career.

▲ A mentor can be a tremendous help as you continue to design your career.

> *LIST ALL THE MEMBERS OF YOUR CURRENT NETWORKING CIRCLE.*

You are wise to collect business cards and keep them in a special file. Additionally, you can make file cards with name, title, address, and telephone number plus the circumstances under which you met or by what means you know the person. If the person helps you in any way, be sure to show your appreciation.

People with whom you connect fall into three general categories (Latas, 1993).

1. *Givers*. These are the people who give, give, and give. No matter what you need, they are there. Usually, they seem happy to be of service. In essence, some of their needs are being met by giving to others. Ideally, you will have several of these in your network.
2. *Traders*. As long as they get something in return, they are willing to be of service. You may need to show them how they can benefit. Know that they "keep track," and if you "owe them," they will expect a return favor.
3. *Takers*. Because they are completely preoccupied with getting, these people are of no use to you. Invariably, you will be disappointed if you do ask, so build your network from the other two groups. It's good to realize that even though some of these people may be family members or friends, you'll profit more from a stranger who is a giver or a trader.

One recommended way to build contacts is to serve on committees or teams. In recent years employers have been encouraged to use teaming and to solicit input from employees so you will probably have opportunities to serve both the employer and yourself as a contributor to a group effort. Involvement in company-sponsored activities is another excellent way to make contacts. Many employers encourage participation in volunteer activities. For example, Turner Broadcasting System, Inc., in Los Angeles encourages employees to take part in fund-raisers and community service projects. "These activities give people a chance to get to know each other, to learn to work cooperatively toward a mutual goal, and foster a tremendous feeling that they have contributed," says Lyn Patterson, who has the responsibility for coordinating these projects.

People really do need people! Your contacts will provide advice, support, and actual help throughout your career. A priority of a successful career person is to develop and maintain the most valuable resource of all—a wide network of people.

HANDLING EVALUATIONS

A job review or evaluation is likely to be scheduled. The initial one can occur anytime within the first year; typically, you will have at least one review every year. The most positive attitude is to view this as an opportunity to learn about your performance so that you can continue what is effective and make improvements, if necessary. You may also be encouraged to share your ideas and, in a sense, evaluate the employer. Try to find out ahead of time exactly what is involved in the discussion.

Even though criticism often conjures up negative images, it actually refers to judging both faults and merits. Thus, in essence, a **performance review** is a time for a supervisor to criticize by telling you both the positive and the negative. In this section, you will learn how to positively receive unfavorable criticism. Later in this chapter, how to effectively deliver criticism is covered. Thinking about your reactions ahead of time can be quite useful.

PREPARING YOURSELF FOR CRITICISM

You may be especially sensitive and have a difficult time being criticized. Several emotions are possible. After being told a few ways that performance could be improved,

> Christopher experienced a feeling of hurt,
>
> Keri was frustrated,
>
> Julie felt defensive and angry,
>
> Jim became depressed.

If you know you are apt to react with an unpleasant emotion, take steps to diminish its impact.

> *WHAT EMOTION DO YOU TYPICALLY EXPERIENCE WHEN YOU ARE CRITICIZED? HOW DO YOU REACT?*

To develop a positive way of responding to any criticism, mental preparation or mental realignment is necessary. Rather than see a performance review as an assault on your abilities, view it as an opportunity to improve. Even though we have heard over and over not to take it personally, most of us will. However, *how* you take it personally will make a difference.

> *"We've been conditioned to regard criticism as bad, and we need to learn that it's not the end of the world. A response can be as simple as, 'Thanks. I appreciate knowing that.'"*
>
> Doc Chaves, Assistant Vice President
> Ameritas Life Insurance Corp.
> Lincoln, Nebraska

You can challenge any irrational belief that comes to mind. Think about the thoughts that triggered the hurt, frustration, defensiveness, and depression experienced by the four individuals mentioned previously.

Christopher: The supervisor must not like me as much as she does the others. That's terrible.

Keri: There's nothing I can do to satisfy her so why try?

Julie: I can't believe he would think I can do any better. He's the one who needs to improve!

Jim: I'm just worthless. I'll probably get fired.

The use of cognitive restructuring would help any of these four. Instead of the thoughts they had, a more constructive and realistic one is:

Just because the supervisor is pointing out some ways I can improve doesn't mean I haven't done a good job. I know I have, and this will help me do even better.

The ability to change your thoughts allows you to reframe the entire situation and calm yourself. Calming yourself is also helped by taking a deep breath and either counting slowly to 10 or just remaining silent for several seconds. This will keep you from overreacting.

Avoiding Negative Responses to Criticism

Eliminating ineffective or negative responses can clear the way for ones that work on your behalf. A primary personal purpose of any exchange is to avoid making things worse for yourself, and, if possible, to make them better.

In general, people respond to criticism either aggressively or passively, or a combination of the two. An aggressive method is one of counterattack. Because a person feels wronged, justifiably or not, she or he lashes out. In the work place this will probably get you fired. Passive responses, either verbal or nonverbal, are ones that apologize, acquiesce, or agree. Silence can be perceived as surrender, apathy, or hostility. Some people respond passively while they harbor resentment and then try to get back at the critic later.

A most annoying response is one that denies responsibility. Excuse-making is a far-too-common reaction and seldom achieves positive results. "Yes, but" or "I know I can do better, but" is an irritating response. You are well-advised to leave the word *but* out of the statement. Putting the blame on others or on external circumstances only makes a person appear immature and irresponsible.

RESPONDING POSITIVELY TO CRITICISM

If you want to maintain or increase self-esteem, preserve or improve this relationship, learn, grow, and make the situation better for yourself, positive responses to criticism are the key. Remember "I" statements? Be sure to review this type of assertive language as well as paralanguage and body language. Positive responses use "I" statements. Likewise, your tone of voice and the message transmitted by body position and movements are to be positive and open.

Using a sequence of steps can turn a difficult situation into one of success. What you say depends upon the extent of agreement with the criticism.

AGREEING WITH THE CRITICISM.   Even if the criticism is justified, you may feel defensive and hurt and respond in a way that will make the situation worse for you. Instead, follow these steps using "I" statements.

1. Agree with and acknowledge the criticism using such phrases as "I agree," "I realize," "I know," or "I understand."

2. An optional step (you may not want to tell the reason) is to state the reason briefly being sure you are giving a reason, not an excuse. Do not begin with *but*.

3. State what you plan to do to prevent future occurrences or tell what you think will solve the problem.

Pretend you have been told that one of your weaknesses is punctuality. Instead, of making excuses or trying to blame others or circumstances such as traffic, use the following refreshing response that is likely to produce a positive outcome.

1. I know I've been late several times, and I can understand your concern.

2. (optional) I've had several problems with my car.

3. I'm having my car fixed, and I will be punctual in the future. I realize how important it is.

Dramatically promising that you will *always* be on time is unwise because you might be late in the future.

You can also agree with part of the criticism. The person's interpretation might be all that needs clarifying. For example, if the supervisor says, "You seem to have lost interest in doing a good job," you can respond, "I can see why you would think that because I have been late several times recently. I want to assure you that I haven't lost interest. My being late is due to other factors which I will correct. I realize how important it is." Incidentally, be sure that you know the supervisor's remark is due to your lack of punctuality; otherwise, you may be revealing something the person didn't know!

NOT UNDERSTANDING THE CRITICISM.   Frequently, criticism is vague, and you honestly don't know what the person means. Emotionally, this is difficult to handle because it seems so unfair. A temptation is to defend even if you don't know the person's reason. Definitely, resist this temptation and use the following.

1. State your lack of understanding or confusion with phrases such as "I don't understand why you think that," "I'm confused as to why you think that," or "I don't know why you have that impression."

2. Tell the person what is needed to increase your level of understanding with such phrases as "I'd like you to explain to me why you think that way," "I'd appreciate your telling me what I've done or not done to lead you to think this," or "I would like to have some clarification about this."

Pretend you have been told, "You don't seem to be committed to teamwork," and you don't understand the reason for the comment. You can respond as follows.

1. I don't know why you think I'm not a team player.

2. I'd appreciate your telling me what has caused you to think so.

Notice that you don't explain how you have been a team player. This can be used later, if necessary. At this point, because you don't understand, what is needed is more information. Using "I" statements, you have been open, honest, and polite in letting the person know of your confusion and desire to be enlightened. The critic is now in the responding position. The answer, hopefully, will enable you to respond specifically because you are dealing with concrete, descriptive data.

If, by some chance, the person seems unable to provide you with specific information, you can still guide the conversation in a positive direction. This can be done by polite questions such as: "Can you give me some examples?" "Exactly what has happened?" "Can you describe what I have done?" If you have any idea regarding the reason, you can probe with such questions as: "Is it because I missed the last meeting?" "Are you basing this on my disagreement with the team at our last meeting?" Be careful about this, however, as you may be telling something the person doesn't know and adding "fuel to the fire."

If the person still doesn't provide you with the needed data, the best you can do is express continued confusion and lack of agreement with the interpretation by saying, "I am committed to working with the team and still would like to understand why you think I'm not. If there is something I can change, I'm willing to do it. However, without specifics, there's nothing more I can do." See if you can respond positively by completing the KEY STEPS activity (page 298).

NOT AGREEING WITH THE CRITICISM.   Emotionally, the most difficult situation is one in which you disagree with the criticism. You know what led to the person's interpretation, yet you don't agree with it. A positive response is still in your best interest. Give yourself a few seconds to compose yourself then use the following steps.

1. State your disagreement politely, yet firmly. Avoid a quick "I disagree." Instead in a calm, modulated voice, say, "I don't see it the way you do," or "I don't agree," or "It seems we don't agree."

2. If appropriate, use precise descriptive language to tell what happened and what you experienced that would lead to a different interpretation. Another option is to simply state your disagreement and wait for the other person to speak. A future discussion is a possibility to suggest, or you can acknowledge that two people can disagree, and move on.

Pretend that your supervisor is talking with you about concerns regarding your interactions with a co-worker.

SUPERVISOR: *There have been two incidents between you and Michelle in which you seemed to lose your patience. The first occurred two weeks ago when you were showing her how to use the new word processing program. Then yesterday I overheard her say to you, "I wish you would give me more of your time because I don't understand it yet," and you replied, "I think I've given you plenty of my time."*

YOUR RESPONSE: *I don't think I have been impatient with Michelle, and I'd like to explain to you what happened both times. After you asked me to demonstrate the new software, I did so. Then I spent a couple of hours during work time and an hour after work guiding her through the basics. I suggested that she read the manual and continue to practice on her own. I don't think she did that because yesterday she asked me several basic questions which I had already covered that are also in the first chapter of the manual. What you heard was a request for help after I had already answered questions three different times. By that time I may have sounded frustrated; however, I think I have shown a great deal of patience. I would be glad to discuss this further with both you and Michelle in order to clarify the situation.*

This type of response takes longer and requires more effort than a quick denial of the supervisor's version of the situation. Yet, just responding that you have been patient or, even worse, lashing out at Michelle would likely make the situation worse.

If you are completely caught off guard by criticism that seems unfair, especially if your feeling is one of anger, it's best to delay a response. You can simply state your surprise and confusion, be sure that you understand the criticism, then state, "I would like to think about this and then discuss it with you." Backing up for a while to compose ourselves rather than quickly reacting allows for far more constructive responses.

You may receive both a verbal and a written performance review. You then may have an opportunity to respond in writing to the evaluation and can express agreement, lack of understanding, or disagreement. Be sure that your written words show the same openness and positiveness as your spoken ones!

Positive responses to criticism are built on honesty and sensibility and aren't difficult to learn. They lead to enhanced self-esteem and a feeling of

▲ When two people can positively give and receive criticism, both they and the employer benefit.

being in control. A formal review is quite likely to include some criticism, and a good idea is to plan your reaction. During a workday, criticism is also going to occur. You can expect it from co-workers, subordinates, and customers or clients. Remaining in charge of your emotions, being able to exhibit a calm exterior, and using positive responses will move relationships in positive directions.

Discussing Salary Increases

A formal review usually includes an increase in salary. If no set amount has been established, you will want to have salary information and an idea of what you think is fair. This depends upon the range of salary for employees of your same tenure either in the same company or in others. Have documentation of reasons why an increase is justified.

Perhaps you will work for an employer where formal reviews are not given and salary increase times are not established. It may or may not come as a surprise that some employers will avoid giving salary raises as long as they can. Then it's up to you. If six months have passed and a salary increase has never been addressed, you are justified in initiating a discussion about this. Of course you may wait longer if you want; bringing up an increase before a six-month time isn't advisable.

Asking for a raise isn't easy. In his book *Sharkproof* (1993), Harvey Mackay describes it as more traumatic than wearing a bathing suit to the beach after a long winter of hot fudge sundaes! He offers several good pieces of advice.

- Request a raise based on your performance, not on a personal crisis or need.
- Know what you're worth and what is possible.
- Don't threaten to leave; this is a sign of weakness.
- Be prepared with documentation of your fine work.
- After clearly defining what you have done for the business, tell what you intend to do in the future. A good idea is to present your goals in writing.
- Pick the most opportune time in terms of your performance, the economic condition of the company, and the employer's state of being.
- Know what you will do if no raise is forthcoming.

If there is to be no increase, the reasons should be explained, and you can benefit from hearing what they are. If the employer contends that lack of profit doesn't permit a raise, you can suggest other benefits in lieu of money. For example, Jason was given three days of vacation with pay. After six months if he was still as productive, he was guaranteed a raise. You may need to be assertive and ask for reasons and ways to justify an increase in the future. You and the employer are involved in a give-and-take proposition, and you are entitled to a fair wage in return for your contributions. Always be sure that you are giving as much as you are taking.

If you receive a raise, strongly consider investing it in your future. Commonly, young people live for the moment and neglect a golden opportunity to make their money grow. For example, a 25-year-old who sets aside $2,000 annually for 10 years and then stops will have more assets at age 55 than a person who invests $2,000 in an IRA every year for 20 years but doesn't start investing until the age of 35 (Switzer, 1996). If your company offers a tax-deferred investment program, you are especially fortunate. Otherwise, find other sound ways to ensure a financially sound future.

> WHAT, IF ANYTHING, ARE YOU DOING TO INVEST IN YOUR FINANCIAL FUTURE? WHAT CAN YOU DO?

CONTINUING TO LEARN

A common assumption is that after graduation from college and entry into the career field, formal learning is over. Most people realize that they will learn on the job yet often fail to recognize the need for other learning experiences.

Do you recall that a common interview question has to do with how you plan to keep abreast of changes in your field? Anyone committed to "staying current" will need to actively seek information and then cultivate new skills. Ideally, your employer will be committed to helping in this endeavor, and education and training will be among your benefits. Often, employees are encouraged to attend conferences, workshops, and other training sessions by receiving paid leave and, in some cases, even having registrations and other expenses paid by the employer. This still can mean some hardship on your part as you put in extra time preparing to be gone and then play "catch-up" when you return. Yet, taking advantage of these experiences is highly advisable. "Advancement or promotion will depend a great deal on how good one becomes. Willingness to give up free time to attend classes is the only way to stay current and be promoted," says Bob Batt, who started his own business and now offers automotive fleet and aftermarket training through a community college program.

What if the employer doesn't provide or pay for learning and training opportunities? The clear answer is to learn and train on your own time at your own expense. You can read professional and trade publications as well as take classes and attend conferences and training sessions even if it takes personal time, effort, and money. Similar to your efforts in getting a job, you can research and even visit other employers in your career field. Check KEY STEPS (page 299) to motivate yourself.

The benefits are many. Primarily, you develop into a more valuable employee by learning more, upgrading skills, strengthening self-esteem, and increasing self-efficacy. Learning experiences are usually rejuvenating. You can also make contacts and keep informed about other employers. Janet attended a regional conference and later reported, "I didn't learn as much as I had hoped, yet I met several interesting people. In fact, I just called one of them as we have decided to relocate to his area. He gave me several job leads!"

According to Dave Sonenberg, director of career counseling and placement at Southeast Community College, anyone who wants to advance keeps an eye on the future and does whatever is needed to become more marketable. He says, "Just knowing that improvement is important gives you an edge. People throughout their career life who increase and enhance their skills become winners."

KEY ADVICE

WHAT WILL MAXIMIZE CAREER SUCCESS?

Medical Laboratory Technology: *"Be interested in learning more at every chance."*
  Janis Bible, program chair

Environmental Laboratory Technology: *"Continuing education, perhaps working towards a higher degree, helps one advance."*
  Don Mumm, program chair

Microcomputer Technology: *"After entering into a microcomputer career, a person must be constantly reading and learning to remain current in an ever-constantly changing field."*
  Linda Bettinger, program chair

Child Development: *"Continued professional growth is a necessity."*
  Alicia Baillie, program chair

Nursing: *"Continue to improve work skills through workshops and all other opportunities."*
  Virginia Hess, program chair

Office Technology: *"Keep up-to-date in your field; continue your education formally and informally."*

   Jo Ann Frazell, program chair

Machine Tool Technology: *"In this profession we are in a continuous explosion of new technology which mandates retraining to remain technically competent. Additional education also opens the door to new opportunities."*

   Millard Carnes, program chair

Surgical Technology: *"Keeping your skills current and updating your knowledge is a real asset to advancement in the field."*

   Ruth Walsh, program chair

Drafting Technology: *"Continuing education is becoming more and more essential with technological advances. More education and training can open new doors of career opportunity."*

   Dan Masters, program chair

A definite quality that separates those who succeed from those who don't is commitment to continued learning and training. Count yourself fortunate if your employer encourages and supports such efforts. If this isn't the case, your taking the initiative to fulfill your potential will be rewarded in a variety of ways. Lifelong learners are invariably the career winners.

ADVANCING IN YOUR CAREER

Do your career goals include promotions and advancement? Most people possess the American dream of upward mobility. Yet, advancement isn't for everyone. Some individuals aren't capable of the higher level skills required for that position. Others would not be happy in that particular job. I remember discussing with my department chairperson whether to apply for his position when he retired because it was the next step on the ladder for me. He said, "I think you could do a very good job, but I don't think you'd like it. You love teaching, and that's not what I do." After a discussion of exactly what he did, which was certainly not to my liking, the decision was made.

Some companies will expect you to be promotable. In these cases, those incapable of advancing will be the first to be let go. Also, you may have to accept a promotion into a position you don't want in order to get to where you do want. Other times you may move into a **lateral position**, one that is at the same level as the present job. What is necessary is to determine whether your final goal is where you want to be and what you want to do.

Personal success and satisfaction need to be defined by you. This may mean that moving up may not mean moving forward. For example, you may need to get different types of experience in order to be promotable. Ed Rasgorshek, a senior vice president in the credit industry, told of leaving the company for a few years in order to get direct lending experience in a bank.

"I needed a diverse background to get where I wanted to be. I went to a new employer for a few years to get different experiences, then returned." Career advancement is similar to climbing on a jungle gym; as long as you keep your eye on your objective, your movement can be in various directions (Weddle, 1994).

> *ARE YOU INTERESTED IN ADVANCEMENT? TO WHAT LEVEL?*

TAKING ACTION

If you want to advance, planning becomes significant. You start by choosing employment where promotional opportunities exist. Then, certain behaviors enhance your chances.

- Perform as well as you can in your present position.
- Do more than what is expected of you whether this means additional time spent, more work completed, or greater displays of effort.
- Document your accomplishments.
- Display professionalism in your everyday actions and by becoming involved in career organizations. In all circumstances, demonstrate a high degree of ethics.
- Keep your résumé and other records updated.
- Observe those above you. If possible, use job shadowing to see what the job entails.
- Research as carefully as you did when you chose this career field. Learn as much as you can about all aspects of the company and the upper positions. For example, for what reasons are people promoted?
- Prepare yourself to initiate a discussion of advancement possibilities if the company has no set timetable and if promotions haven't been mentioned.

In all situations, the use of open, positive communication skills is likely to produce the best results. Jerry Baxter, Lejeune Steel Company, Minneapolis, credits dependability and "people" skills for his amazing advancement from an hourly welding job to plant manager of a large company. "I've always believed that problems are nothing but a wake-up call for creativity," he said.

> *"A promotable employee has demonstrated a history of performance, a positive attitude, the willingness to 'go the extra mile' without complaining, and does more thinking about the 'good of the group' rather than of him or herself."*
>
> David R. Hanna, Assistant Vice-President (retired)
> New York Life Insurance Company
> Cleveland, Ohio

MAKING RELOCATION DECISIONS

Even though you could be asked to relocate without a promotion, the two usually go hand-in-hand. Perhaps one option clarifies the other as you could be offered a higher level position you don't especially want, yet be moved to the perfect geographic location.

For some people, relocation isn't really a choice. "I knew that in order to move 'up the ladder,' I would have to move geographically, as well, and accepted that as part of life," said my brother Dave. He and his family relocated six times in sixteen years as he moved up the ranks to become one of five regional managers and an assistant vice-president for New York Life Insurance Company. "The last tenure was the longest. The 13 years before I retired I spent in one location," he recalled.

In most instances, the decision is somewhat complicated. Along with several other career decisions, whether to relocate requires a thoughtful process. A major obstacle is fear of the unknown which leads a person to immediately turn down a relocation opportunity. As one who has lived in four different parts of the country and moved numerous times, I'm amazed by the reluctance of individuals to even consider living elsewhere. While some areas are less than desirable, almost all sites have unique advantages so try not to limit yourself because of fear.

You can gather helpful information from a chamber of commerce or a special office that provides material to potential citizens and from other company employees who live there, especially those who have relocated. Most employers will provide you with a firsthand look at the new location, and if you have a significant other, he or she is usually included in the visit, too. You will want to know the anticipated length of your tenure there and whether or not you could expect to return to your present location. If expenses are higher in the new location, will the company pay a cost-of-living differential, or will the salary be higher enough to compensate? Any decision carries with it a concern about whether it's right or wrong. A good idea is to challenge the concept of rightness or wrongness. In all probability, if you relocate, you will have wonderful and not-so-wonderful experiences just as you would have if you didn't move. One definite benefit of relocation is the opportunity to experience newness and to broaden your life experiences.

FOSTERING LEADERSHIP SKILLS

Advancement usually means becoming a leader. Generally, **leadership** includes taking responsibility and being in a position to direct, guide, and influence others. Depending upon the specific leadership position, an individual may be expected to perform different roles.

TYPES OF LEADERSHIP ROLES.   Think of an example of a leader of any group of which you have been a part. Did the person emphasize completion of tasks—getting things done? If so, she or he would be considered an **instrumental leader**. This type of leader concentrates on performance and would be apt to reward or punish employees based on how much they accomplished and the quality of their performance. You may prefer this role both as a follower and as a leader. The instrumental leader would probably have a personality type on the Myers-Briggs Type Indicator that prefers facts, takes care of details, and likes efficient standard operating procedures (sensing), chooses to analyze the facts and apply logic to decision making (thinking), and likes to bring about closure in an orderly, organized way (judging).

Advantages of this personality type include the ability to be productive, meet deadlines, be objective, and complete tasks in an organized fashion. As a leader, you would likely earn respect from others, yet be considered distant from them. Instrumental leaders expect others to complete tasks efficiently. Some disadvantages of instrumental leadership are of being perceived as cold and unfeeling and of ignoring people's concerns in the interest of task completion.

The other type is the **expressive leader** who emphasizes collective well-being. Tasks are considered less important than getting along with people, being supportive, and maintaining harmony. The personality preferences usually found in expressive leaders are intuition (capable of visualizing many ideas and preferring flexible policies and different ways of doing things), feeling (considers personal feelings and values in decision making), and perceiving (is open, tentative, and spontaneous).

If you favor this type, others will probably feel warm and affectionate toward you as long as you maintain fairness. This is sometimes hard for expressive leaders to do even though they want to be fair. Ideas are welcomed by an expressive leader, and the environment is likely to be friendly and personal. A disadvantage is that expressive leaders can have difficulty getting tasks accomplished. Productivity may be slowed in the interest of harmony and the desire to listen to everyone's ideas.

Perhaps the ideal type would be a blend of the two. Whether the style is instrumental or expressive would depend upon the circumstances. For example, the president of a manufacturing firm hosted a breakfast for his supervisors at which time he solicited ideas for an upcoming project. He praised their cooperative efforts. At the end of the meeting he announced the upcoming schedule, made sure everyone understood their assignments, and told them the completion date. He said, "I sincerely appreciate your efforts so far, and I expect the same caliber of work from you. The success of this venture depends upon all of us."

WHICH TYPE OF LEADER STYLE DO YOU FAVOR?

CHARACTERISTICS OF EFFECTIVE LEADERS.   Being an effective leader goes far beyond successful job performance. Those who succeed are likely to be intelligent, creative, objective, enthusiastic, optimistic, energetic, self-confident, have good judgment, and persevere (Bittel, 1984). The book *The 7 Habits of Highly Effective People* (Covey, 1989) provides insight into behaviors that promote leadership.

1. Anticipate problems; don't just react.

2. Continually sharpen your skills; don't be completely satisfied with the way you do something now.

3. Have a vision so you know what needs to be accomplished to get to where you want to be.

4. Manage your time well so your life is well managed.

5. Work well with others and draw on their energies.

6. Seek first to understand, then to be understood.

7. Think win/win. Get rid of the idea that in any situation one person wins; when one comes out as a winner, the other loses.

An outstanding leader is an excellent communicator. Being able to give clear instructions is primary. The use of the open style of verbalizing encourages exchange and creates a positive communication climate. Listening demands equal attention. Most business executives spend a larger portion of their workdays listening rather than talking or writing. Unfortunately, listening is often a neglected tool even among managers (Kurtz, 1991). Active listening, discussed in Chapter 2, helps a leader develop a full understanding of another person's situation, concern, or point of view. As you manage others and deal with customer or client concerns, you will want to listen closely as a means of solving problems and building rapport.

As a leader, planning and organizational skills are needed in contrast to the lower levels where the "doing" part of work is instrumental. In most businesses time equates to money made or lost. Poor planners or those who are disorganized waste precious time and end up losing money for the business.

Perhaps more challenging is what Doc Chaves, assistant vice-president of corporate communications in a large insurance firm, calls the vision issue. "A leader has to be able to assess the task at hand while seeing the total picture; she or he has to always be looking for better ways to accomplish what is to be done." Anthony Robbins (1991), a national leader in peak performance, says that great leaders are not realistic by most people's standards because they have a vision and are undaunted by the fact that something has never been done before. He thinks of excellent leaders as extremely optimistic individuals who, if anything, overestimate what they can accomplish.

> *"Above all, a leader needs to provide vision—the ability to scan the horizon, envision what is over the next hill, and translate the vision into an imagined reality for those one is leading."*
>
> Patricia K. Knaub, Ph.D., Dean
> College of Human Environmental Sciences
> Oklahoma State University
> Stillwater, Oklahoma

Perhaps one of the most difficult functions of a new leader is in delegation of responsibilities and tasks. To **delegate** means to commit powers or functions to another. "If you don't delegate, you won't have the time to do your job. Delegation means to give clear directions, then let them 'run with the ball.' Also important is to know when to check how they are doing and make adjustments, if necessary," explains Lisa Patterson, a senior manager at a major accounting firm.

A leader determines who can best do the job or who is available and then makes assignments. For most people, the most difficult aspect of delegating is to let go. "I have a hard time thinking that anyone can do it as well as I can with all my experience so I tend to step in and either do the job or at least help a lot," said Mark soon after his promotion. According to Susan Brown, advertising account executive, "An excellent supervisor is available for help yet gives you autonomy. Not being able to delegate means spending too much time and energy involved in the business of those at a lower level."

A major benefit of delegating is that you are setting the stage for your own further advancement while you help others. Grooming subordinates and allowing them to learn and grow teaches them to do your job so it is easier for you to progress.

What if tasks aren't completed or someone does the job poorly? Then another invaluable skill is needed. Anyone placed in a leadership position must be able to give criticism. This can be extremely difficult for certain personality types. "They put me into a supervisor role because I was good at my job. It was a horrible experience because when people didn't perform, I just couldn't tell them," said Sharon, an individual who scored a very strong feeling preference on the Myers-Briggs Type Indicator. In spite of your personality type, you can learn effective ways to deliver criticism.

Delivering criticism in a positive way is an art. An effective beginning is a positive comment about the person. Then, with the use of "I" statements, undesirable behaviors or practices are specifically described. Beginning a sentence with the word *you* is definitely to be avoided. Note the following.

> *James, I'm impressed with your creative ideas, and I'm eager to put them into practice. I do have a concern about your ability to meet a deadline. The report you were assigned to write was due yesterday, and I still don't have it. I'd like to know the reason.*

This method of openly verbalizing the concern or displeasure is likely to elicit a desired response. Practice your delivery (see KEY STEPS, page 300).

As necessary as giving criticism and advice is the habit of praising. If you want an emotionally healthy and productive work place, appreciation and recognition of employees and their accomplishments are vital (Strasser and Sena, 1992). You have probably heard the advice, "Catch them doing something good." Positive comments from a leader can be strongly motivating. Human beings have a need to be recognized which can range from a sincere compliment to formal public recognition. Everyone, as well as the business, benefits from a positive work place.

IF YOU HAVE SUPERVISED, CAN YOU RECALL PRAISING AN EMPLOYEE? IN THE WORK PLACE, WHEN WAS THE LAST TIME YOU WERE RECOGNIZED?

Leaders are expected to get along with everyone and to meet the challenge of building teamwork and positive relationships among their subordinates. The information in Chapter 7 about personality temperament types at work can reveal how to deal with differences in a positive way. As a leader, you can use this knowledge to assign tasks and to help develop an appreciation of one another's strengths. "As a manager, one of the most interesting challenges has been to mesh different personalities into a solid team. From the quiet, laid-back type to the caustic, obnoxious one, each can find a way to get the job done with your understanding and encouragement," says Ed Rasgorshek, a senior vice president in the lending industry.

Outstanding leaders possess empowering beliefs, and they teach others to tap their full capabilities (Robbins, 1991). Becoming an effective leader at work requires more than you might have anticipated. Even though advancement has many benefits, you will also need to work hard, keep abreast of anything related to the career field, and continually strive to develop and improve your leadership style. Assess your leadership capabilities in KEY STEPS (page 300).

> *WHAT LEADERSHIP CHARACTERISTICS DO YOU POSSESS? IF YOU ARE LACKING, IT'S POSSIBLE TO DEVELOP MOST OF THEM.*

CHANGING CAREERS AND JOBS

While you may feel as if you're the only one contemplating or making a career change, you're definitely not alone. According to the Career Center on America Online, 40 million Americans—nearly one third of adult workers—are in career transition. The average person can expect to have three different careers during a lifetime (Bolles, 1996). People leave jobs daily and over their career life change jobs about seven times (Lindgren, 1996). Years ago an individual most likely started with and stayed with not only the same career but also the same employer. The career world is simply not like that anymore.

Dissatisfaction stemming from a poor choice is a common reason for a career change. As Marci explained, "For years I didn't understand why I hated to go to work. After attending a conference, I realized that my personality type and the career field were completely incompatible." At earlier stages of life, most people aren't aware of what they really want out of life. Betty Knapp of Apple Valley, Minnesota, had a nursing career, then changed to real estate. Today she is a multimillion-dollar sales producer in the Twin Cities area. "I decided I wanted to make more money so I found a career that I enjoy where higher incomes are possible." The opposite course could be taken. Connie Hanna Gengenbach, who was a marketing merchandising manager for a large home building corporation in San Jose, California, returned to teaching. She explained, "Even though the marketing position had satisfying elements and the pay was lucrative, I missed the deep feeling of satisfaction from challenging the minds of children and being a positive influence in their lives."

Most of us experience a change in needs over time. You may be familiar with the **hierarchy of needs** (Maslow, 1968). The theory is that human beings are motivated to satisfy their needs on one of five levels: (1) physiological, (2) safety, (3) love and belongingness, (4) self-esteem, and (5) self-actualization. Conceivably, as lower needs are met, higher ones become dominant, and a present career or position may not offer what is needed. To reach self-actualization, the highest level, humans work to achieve their full potential and make a meaningful contribution to the world. Self-actualizers desire more meaning from life which could demand a change in career or position.

Well ahead of the average of three in a lifetime, Sally Beck, a college placement specialist, reflected on her careers.

> *About six or seven actual career changes is a fair assessment of my professional life, most for personal or professional growth. I've loved several while a few weren't so pleasant; yet, I've learned and grown from each and would do it all over again.*

Whatever is your reason for a change, you will again want to do thorough research on yourself and the career possibilities. Earlier chapters plus other books can be quite helpful. The book *What Color Is Your Parachute?* (Bolles, 1996) focuses on career changes. You will want to include an assessment of what areas were unsatisfying so that you choose differently the next time.

More commonly, people change jobs as a result of what can be called "pushes" or "pulls." When dissatisfied with a present position, a person feels pushed to look elsewhere. Individuals who were asked why they opted to change their career or a job within that field responded as follows.

- ◎ "I wasn't challenged."
- ◎ "Whatever I did went seemingly unnoticed."
- ◎ "I found out that it just wasn't 'me.'"
- ◎ "I was burned out. The stress was unbelievable."
- ◎ "My supervisor was overly demanding, and it didn't look as it things would change in the near future."
- ◎ "It was a dead-end job."
- ◎ "At first I was willing to work for less than I deserved. However, that got old after some time."
- ◎ "There wasn't flexibility or support for family time."
- ◎ "Just earning money wasn't enough. I wanted to make more of a difference in life."

As you can see, some of these situations would not have developed if the person had been knowledgeable before accepting a job.

> *IF YOU HAVE BEEN DISSATISFIED WITH A JOB, DO YOU KNOW WHY?*

While it's a good idea to always be open for better opportunities, you will want to carefully examine reasons for dissatisfaction. Is it just a temporary problem? What would it take to make the job satisfying and is this feasible? The best course of action is to have a frank discussion with your supervisor about your concerns. Too many job changes can become a liability, and you may leave one job only to find the same hardships in another. Nevertheless, if you truly decide that the current situation is unacceptable and not likely to change, a search is advisable, preferably while you still hold a job.

A few things will be different from the same job-search strategies discussed earlier. Depending upon the demands of your present job, it may be best to use an employment agency. When interviewing, it is imperative to remain professional and positive when discussing why you are leaving your present job, and unless you have informed the current employer of your intentions, be sure to ask potential ones not to contact anyone in your work place at this time.

A change of jobs could be precipitated by a "pull," an attractive offer. You may be satisfied and be contacted either directly by another employer or by search firms, commonly called **headhunters**. This is flattering, yet you don't want to be led into making an unwise decision. Careful research, logical decision making, and honesty with whomever has contacted you are of utmost importance. Because you may want a future contact with this person, sound advice is to "burn no bridges."

Another "pull" is a desire to live in a new place where you can find employment. Government offices and chambers of commerce will have data showing unemployment rates and types of employment available. You could be like one young woman who said, "I've always wanted to live in Phoenix so I just went there to look for a job. I've been here ten years and still love it."

More education could be attractive. Ryan Turner left a good job as a financial analyst to pursue an advanced degree at Harvard. "I wasn't in a career path I wanted, and I can now explore and assess other opportunities," he explains. Additional education can be a definite benefit in all career fields.

▲ A career change means researching and making contacts again.

When you decide to change jobs, professionalism is essential. Typically, you will schedule an appointment with your immediate supervisor to inform him or her of the upcoming change. The person may try to persuade you to stay. If this doesn't happen or if you decide you still want to leave even after the persuasion attempt, one matter to discuss is the length of time between your resignation announcement and your last day, what is called **notice**. The usual minimum amount is two weeks; however, if you can stay longer, offer to do so. Either at that time or shortly thereafter, submit a written resignation letter. Being willing to help train your replacement is a positive action. Employers expect people to leave jobs, and a good supervisor will not take your resignation personally. Being professional and gracious will instill a positive impression that will be beneficial in the present and perhaps the future, too.

No job is totally secure. An employer may **downsize**, which entails laying off workers. Other names have been given to this practice such as organizational readjustment or "right-sizing." An article in a free newspaper in Belfast, Northern Ireland, reported that a shoe manufacturing plant was going to "make 1400 people redundant." However phrased, the effects are the same—people lose their jobs. Mergers between companies also lead to reduction in employees.

You may be one of those affected, and you have a right to know why. Generally, being laid off has nothing to do with job performance. Just as you can be involved in an accident only because you are in a particular place at a certain time, downsizing or a merger can impact on you. Depending upon the employer, you may be given **severance pay**, an amount of money as compensation, and you could be aided in a job search.

Even if you are given no compensation or help, your future is helped by controlling your frustration and maintaining both a professional attitude and behavior. It can help to realize that because downsizing is so common, unemployment doesn't have the stigma of the past. Coping with stress, covered in Chapter 8, will be beneficial to anyone going through a career transition.

A more difficult situation is being fired, sometimes called **termination**. Different reasons could account for this; however, it usually means that an employee hasn't done a satisfactory job. "Whenever I fired anyone, it meant that the person was either incapable of performing the tasks or not willing to make the effort. People were not terminated after a first instance; warnings were always given," said David Hanna, a retired regional office manager.

"Incompetence or absenteeism are two major reasons for termination."

David R. Hanna, Assistant Vice-President (retired)
New York Life Insurance Company
Cleveland, Ohio

Termination can come as a total surprise. A challenge is to remain calm and under control as you would only hurt yourself more by being hostile. After the initial shock, you can accede to the firing and leave without even knowing the reason. A better choice and certainly your right is to find out all you can. Then you can either ask for another chance with an assurance that you will improve, or, if you feel you have been unjustly treated, you can take legal action. A professional association or trade union probably has resources, or you can hire your own attorney. The use of open communication is again recommended. Notice the difference in the following two responses.

> *Closed.* Nobody could work for you. You've been unfair with me and everyone else since the beginning. You never have liked me. You can take this job, and....

> *Open.* I understand why you took this action although I would have appreciated more feedback about this problem. As for me, I've learned from the experience and am determined to do much better in my next job.

The open style may be more difficult, especially in an intense emotional situation, yet it's much more effective. Put yourself in the place of the employer. Would you provide a positive recommendation for the person who used the open communication style? Most employers would at least be as positive as possible. How about the one who was closed? Not a chance!

Leaving even the worst situation in a positive way can make a definite difference. As in all of life's crises, the more you can learn, the better. Being fired can be needed motivation. "I remember being fired from my second job because I was late so often. I learned the hard way the importance of punctuality and never let it stand in my way again," said the president of a large construction company. He is the classic example of someone who weaved a new pattern into the fabric of life when the bottom fell out of his.

Beginning a new career or job is akin to starting over although you do so with more maturity and experience. Change can be frightening, and the old, familiar life seems so safe: "I really hate what I'm doing, but this isn't a good time to make a change. I'll do it next year" or "I'm too old to start over. I can just 'hang on' until retirement." Yet, in a survey of its members, the American Association of Retired Persons found that only one in five said their quest for a new career ended unhappily (Lewis, 1996b). Consider the impact of career satisfaction and nudge yourself out of that comfort zone toward fulfillment of self.

OWNING YOUR OWN BUSINESS

You may always have had aspirations of owning a business, or the desire may evolve later. Business ownership is not easy and, in some ways, not as desirable as one might think. "I want to own my own shop so that nobody can tell me what to do," said a young automotive technology student. He was surprised when a business owner told him that he would have even more people telling him what to do. Customers or clients typically take priority over the owner's time and personal desires. This section will cover only the basics of entrepreneurship. Further research, then weighing the pros and cons are wise investments.

What's required? Unless you plan to have a one-person business, you must possess the leadership qualities described earlier in this chapter. In addition, you will either have to have a "head for business" or be able to hire someone who does. So many creative, innovative visionaries fail because the boring book work doesn't get done well.

Offering a needed product or service of high quality is stressed by Louis and Jerre Garcia, retired successful retail business owners. According to them, a customer can always find a cheaper price so quality, service, and interpersonal skills are essential. Betty Knapp, a top realtor and relocation specialist for Burnet Realty in Minneapolis, says, "To excel, make the present client believe he or she is the focus of your full attention and be sure to provide the finest service."

> *"A successful business owner recognizes a regular customer. Using the person's name and knowing what he or she wants truly makes a difference."*
>
> Louis Garcia, retired business owner
> Wainae, Hawaii

Persistence is also necessary. Typically, a new business owner has to face many pitfalls and endure frustrating and depressing situations. Being determined and tenacious can bring you through adverse times such as facing the reality that owning your own business usually means that you put in more time and effort than your employees, and they get paid before you do. You may have more flexibility, yet successful entrepreneurs work far more than the standard number of hours. Even aside from actual work on the job is a common occurrence of "living your work," which means you don't walk away

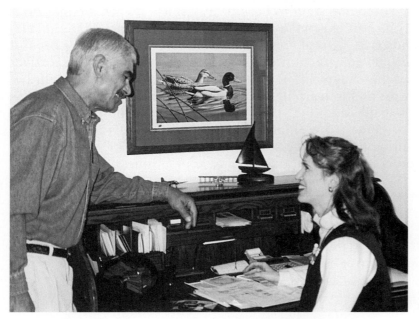

▲ Opportunity for a successful business is increased by rapport between owner and office manager.

from it when the workday ends. Ryan, a young man who had an opportunity to take over his parents' business, showed keen awareness when he declined the offer and said, "I don't want to own something that owns me."

> *"Even though I love owning my own business, I realized from the beginning that there would be demands, either from customers or myself, for me to take care of business outside of regular business hours. You don't just leave work and go home."*
>
> Bob Dinkel, Owner
> Accent Fence Company
> Lincoln, Nebraska

Another surprise to many would-be business owners is the amount of paperwork required by the government along with what is needed to keep proper records. Then there is the shock of realizing that making a profit isn't easy. Too often, people forget about **overhead**, all the expenses involved in running a business. Employees might not realize that employers pay out much more for them than just wages, including worker's compensation insurance and the employer's share of social security. "A major mistake of many new owners is committing too much money too soon. Some will spend far too much to rent or buy an office or building or to buy fancy new equipment. Even extensive advertising can 'eat away' at profit," says Bob Dinkel, a business owner since 1980. Conferring with an accountant and an attorney before starting a business is an excellent idea. Use KEY STEPS (page 299).

If you decide you really want to become a business owner, a major decision is whether to buy an existing business or start your own. Many factors enter into this choice. A helpful free resource is SCORE, Service Corps of Retired Executives, an organization composed of retired business executives (listed at the end of this chapter). The group provides advice and help in drawing up business plans and in learning how to run a profitable enterprise. "It's important to be sensible and analytical and not allow emotion to override your logic when it comes to making decisions," according to Jeanne Baer, owner of a consulting business she started herself. "You also want to know what your passion is and incorporate that into your business. It's essential to do what you love."

In spite of the difficulties, having your own business provides many benefits such as the following.

- ⊚ potential for reaping a substantial profit
- ⊚ the pride and joy of being responsible for a successful venture, which leads to an increase in self-esteem
- ⊚ enhanced self-efficacy
- ⊚ feelings of power and influence

- ⊚ rewards that come from making a contribution
- ⊚ flexibility to do as much as you want and, in some instances, when you want to do it

Whether you decide to buy an existing business or begin your own, you are likely to encounter skepticism. According to Ted Milner, who started his own employment agency, others will attempt to destroy your dream. "Courage is the most important ingredient. My advice is to go for it 100 percent!" Going for it 100 percent is excellent advice after you have explored carefully all aspects of business ownership and decided that "doing your own thing" is worth the necessary sacrifices.

Ending Your Career

The end of a career seems so far away for most people that few begin to actively plan for retirement until it is almost upon them. Yet, the best advice is to begin years before you think your career will end. For example, a $2,000 contribution into an IRA at an annual percentage yield of 6 percent will grow to $361,887 over 30 years (Switzer, 1996).

Generally, those who do not plan find themselves financially handicapped. Women are especially at risk in that they have a 60 percent chance of being poor in old age (Perkins, 1992). Only 30 percent of American women, ages 25 to 64, save for retirement, according to a 1993 Merrill Lynch survey. Rather than plan, women, more than men, are more likely to retire in response to life events, such as illness of a loved one, frequently before they are financially ready (Szinovacz and Washo, 1992). Regardless of your sex, the best course of action is to save and invest on your own in addition to any employer retirement plan.

People also fail to plan for a rewarding retirement. Not having a positive reason to get out of bed in the morning is almost certain to lead to feelings of worthlessness and depression. A recommendation is to examine the reasons you chose your career field. Can you find satisfaction for similar reasons during retirement? Paul had led an active professional life serving people—as a college chaplain then as a minister of visitation. After retirement, he volunteered to continue to work in social service agencies and at a hospital. "The only difference is I don't get paid, but I didn't get that much money even when I was working," he said with a twinkle in his eye.

A retirement advantage is having more discretionary time to pursue hobbies and other interests. According to David Hanna, "The best part is an obvious one—not having to go to work each day. The freedom from career responsibilities and the flexibility in making your own schedule offer a laid-back lifestyle that is extremely enjoyable." Retirement that lacks meaning and purpose isn't as pleasant. "I love gardening and reading, and I enjoy taking trips, but after a while, I decided I missed making a difference. Now I'm tutoring young children, and it has filled the void," reported a 70-year-old woman. Other possibilities lie in organizations that could benefit from your help. Whether you are a member or serve as a volunteer for a nonprofit group, you can continue to make a positive difference in the world throughout your life.

> *IF YOU WERE TO RETIRE TOMORROW, WHAT WOULD YOU DO?*

Assessing the benefits and drawbacks of retirement is recommended as such knowledge can help one decide when and if to retire. "Not being in the mainstream and feeling somewhat isolated from the career world has been somewhat bothersome," reports Dave Hanna. Obviously, if your financial situation is such that you would suffer from loss of income, retirement will be much less enjoyable. Retirement, like all the stages of a career, requires planning and adjustment. After a successful career you deserve the finest retirement. Remaining actively and purposefully involved in the world can make this time of life as successful and rewarding as the preceding stages.

KEY POINTS

- Rejecting a job offer is to be done in a professional way.

- A critical part of a career is being able to negotiate your compensation package. Analyzing benefits and researching salary ranges are parts of the preparation. Making sure you are getting what you are worth will make a major difference. Acceptance of an offer should include details in writing.

- Beginning a new job will be challenging. Knowing what to expect and having an idea of what to do makes this easier.

- Early in your career it may be difficult to maintain a balance between your professional and personal life. Learning how will benefit you throughout your career life.

- Keeping accurate and detailed records related to career will save you time and alleviate stress.

- Continuing to network is highly recommended.

- Most jobs include a formal evaluation. Avoiding negative responses to any criticism and learning how to respond positively will further your career. You will be at an advantage if you are prepared to discuss salary increases. You may initiate the subject either then or at another time.

- One of the best ways to enhance your career is to continue to learn and update your skills.

- Advancement throughout your career involves taking steps to ensure that this will happen and making wise promotion decisions including relocation.

- Leadership skills are essential for upward mobility. Using an appropriate role and developing characteristics of an effective leader make this possible.

⑤   Changing careers and jobs isn't unusual. Either because of a "push" or a "pull," you may find yourself in transition. Even if you don't want a change, you may be let go because of downsizing, mergers, or termination. Learning how to accept this and move on is important.

⑤   If you want to buy or start your own business, a positive course of action is to examine exactly what this involves and weigh advantages and disadvantages. Resources are available to help new business owners.

⑤   At some time you will probably end your career by retiring. Planning for this in advance makes the transition much more positive. Part of this involves understanding the drawbacks and the benefits and then doing all you can to ensure a positive retirement experience.

RECOMMENDED READING

Bolles, R. N. (1996). *What color is your parachute?* Berkeley, CA: Ten Speed Press.

Brim, G. (1992). *Ambition: How we manage success and failure throughout our lives.* New York: Basic Books.

Covey, S. R. (1989). *The 7 habits of highly effective people.* New York: Simon & Schuster.

DuBrin, A. J. (1992). *Your own worst enemy: How to overcome career self-sabotage.* New York: Amacom.

Gorman, T. (1996). *Multipreneuring.* New York: Simon & Schuster.

Heldman, M. L. (1988). *When words hurt: How to keep criticism from undermining your self-esteem.*

Mackay, H. (1993). *Sharkproof.* New York: HarperCollins.

Strasser, S. and Sena, J. (1992). *Work is not a four letter word.* Homewood, IL: Business One.

Weddle, P. D. (1994). *Career fitness.* New York: Cadell & Davies.

RESOURCES

Service Corps of Retired Executives (SCORE)
1129 20th Streeet, NW, Suite 410
Washington, DC 20036
1-800-358-5855 (local groups provide free business counseling)

CHAPTER SEVEN

Relationships in the Work Environment

During a career you have choices in the quantity and quality of your relationships. Most of us haven't received formal training in relationships; instead, we have just been expected to know what to do. Yet, positive relationships don't just happen! Because interpersonal relations can be taught, you may be able to improve your skills as you design your career. If so, seize the opportunity to enhance your success potential.

PROMOTING POSITIVE RELATIONS

Employees are more valued if they add to a productive, positive work environment. The ability to relate well with others pays off. "People, including others outside your immediate area, will help you achieve your goals if you get along well with them," says Mitch Hall, divisional vice president of financial analysis and reporting, Domino's Pizza, Inc. Relationships with support staff, such as secretaries and administrative assistants, are instrumental. Actually, anyone with whom you work can contribute to your success, and you will experience more happiness and satisfaction at work if you enjoy the interactions.

> *"Highest on the list of employable qualities are interpersonal skills—the ability to interact with and relate to all kinds of people is absolutely essential."*
>
> Marcia Phelps, Ph.D., Associate Director
> Career Services, University of Nebraska
> Lincoln, Nebraska

WHAT DO YOU THINK WILL PROMOTE POSITIVE WORK RELATIONS?

After reading this chapter, check your own behaviors in KEY STEPS (pages 301–2).

REALISTIC EXPECTATIONS

Expecting a relationship to be 100 percent harmonious and believing that people will always act as you want are unrealistic ideas. Nobody is perfect, and we are all humanly limited. Having unrealistic ideas about a co-worker, supervisor, or customer leads to frustration and disappointment. In fact, congenial relationships are more likely when people are clear about expectations. Consider this scenario.

> *When Scott started his job with an engineering firm, he wasn't properly oriented. The second day on the job, he left a great deal of work for the secretary to do by the next day. The next morning he was given a cool reception and later told by his supervisor that he was expecting too much. Who was to blame?*

Ideally, his orientation would have included realistic expectations. Otherwise, he needed to ask questions and request guidelines. In many companies who does what, how much, and other such pieces of information are handled casually or not at all.

Employers may be unrealistic. If you feel overworked and overwhelmed, steps can be taken. One is to be honest about your work habits and productivity. Could you make some changes to improve the situation? After that, be observant and talk with your co-workers. Do they share your feelings? At this point it would be easy to let this dissolve into a "mutual griping society," yet your best course of action is to remain positive. If you decide that the expectations are unrealistic, a final step is to make an appointment with your supervisor. Later in the chapter you will learn ways to resolve issues.

HAVE YOU EVER WORKED FOR SOMEONE WHO HAD UNREALISTIC EXPECTATIONS? IF SO, WHAT WERE THEY AND WHAT DID YOU DO?

POSITIVENESS AND FRIENDLINESS

In the work place your ability to maintain a positive attitude will make a vital difference. If you have ever been surrounded by people who give off an aura of "gloom and doom," you probably realize how difficult it is to remain positive.

On the other hand, if you are cheerful and look on the bright side of life, you will undoubtedly infect others. This doesn't mean that you must wear a constant smile and never utter a less-than-positive word. Seeing the pleasant in the middle of the unpleasant is greatly appreciated. "No matter what kind of a day she is having, you can almost always count on Patti for a smile and a kind word. She is like a ray of sunshine on a cloudy day" is how a staff person at our college has been described. One of the most empowering assets to possess is a positive attitude.

Friendliness is a positive behavior. While individuals are friendly in their own unique ways, greeting others with a smile is expected in the work place. Especially affirming is to use the person's name. Sincerity is important. Nancy told of a co-worker who greeted her and everyone else with the exact same words each time their paths crossed. "Hello and how are you today?" began to sound hollow after a while. Another friendly behavior is to express interest in other people by asking questions about their vacation plans, hobbies, and family. As long as you don't go beyond sensible inquiries, most people will appreciate your interest. Generally, if people inquire about your holiday, they would like to tell about theirs. Be sure to ask!

> *CAN YOU BE TOO FRIENDLY IN THE WORK PLACE? THINK OF SOME CONDITIONS OR SITUATIONS WHEN THIS MIGHT BE SO.*

You may find yourself working for an employer with definite policies about **fraternizing**, a term used to mean socializing with others from your work place. Generally, co-workers are not restricted from social activities with each other outside of work. However, you may be discouraged from dating or becoming seriously involved with a co-worker, and there may be rules regarding socializing with supervisors. Obviously, you will want to become aware of

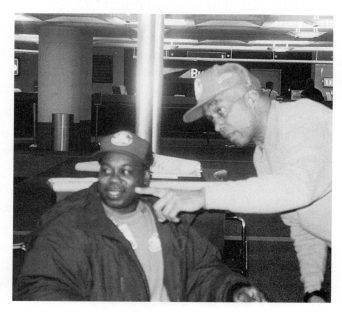

▲ A positive attitude and friendliness create a congenial work environment.

any such policies. Beyond that, maintaining a healthy balance in degree of involvement is beneficial.

A balance of time is also worthy of attention. Spending too much time being friendly as opposed to getting your work done can occur. You may not realize how much productivity is lost while you and co-workers visit about your weekends. Succeeding in a career and maintaining friendly relationships are both feasible as long as you know where the fine line of time and energy lies.

SENSITIVITY AND UNDERSTANDING

Having an awareness or sense of the perceptions of others and being able to discern the world from their perspectives is **sensitivity**. The ability to feel with others, **empathy**, is desirable, but not essential in the work place. The stage is set for sensitivity when employees and supervisors are aware of each other's responsibilities, capabilities, and even limitations. Co-workers who take the time to get to know one another and then are sensitive create a more positive working environment.

Of particular help is to use your knowledge of personality preferences. Individuals with an intuition preference who usually like to do several things at a time can become impatient with the strong sensors who need to focus their attention and who like to complete one task before beginning another. Those with a judging preference want matters settled sooner than the perceivers do and are usually more traditionally organized. Feelers and thinkers who don't understand each other will "rub each other the wrong way." Sensitivity enables us to accept that people have their own preferred modes of thinking and behaving.

Even more enlightening is to understand temperament type, which is made up of two preferences (Keirsey and Bates, 1984). If your preference for taking in information (second letter of your type) is sensing (S), link it with your fourth preference, either judging (J) or perceiving (P). If your second letter is intuitive (N), join it with the third one, either thinking (T) or feeling (F). In understanding temperament type and other combinations in the work place, an especially useful book is *Type Talk at Work* (Kroeger and Thuesen, 1992). See which one of the following temperament types sounds like you.

> SJ (sensing–judging) is orderly, dependable, realistic; understands and conserves institutional values; expects others to be realistic; can be critical of mistakes more easily than he or she will praise expected duties; strives to belong and contribute; prizes harmony and service.

> SP (sensing–perceiving) is flexible and open-minded; willing to take risks; highly negotiable; can be perceived as indecisive; hungers for freedom and action; best at verbal planning and short-range projects.

> NF (intuitive–feeling) is empathetic and highly responsive to interpersonal transactions; keeps in close contact with others; sees possibilities; searches for meaning and authenticity; gives and needs verbal and nonverbal praise and affirmation.

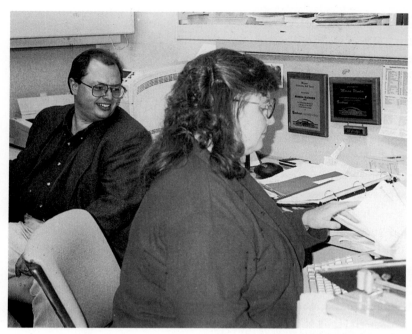

▲ How she can operate in such a mess is hard for a person with a judging personality preference to understand.

NT (intuitive–thinking) is responsive to new ideas; hungers for competency and knowledge; works well with ideas and concepts; is not always aware of others' feelings; likes to start projects but may not follow through; focuses on possibilities and nonpersonal analysis.

> *FIND THE STRENGTHS AND WEAKNESSES IN EACH TEMPERAMENT TYPE. THINK OF SITUATIONS IN WHICH THIS KNOWLEDGE WOULD BE USEFUL.*

Sensitivity can also be demonstrated in crisis situations. When Raoul's son was ill, his supervisor showed concern and understanding when he made out the monthly schedule of assigned projects. "You can catch up later," he told Raoul.

SUPPORTIVENESS

Sensitivity sets the stage for helpful actions that show understanding and caring—**supportiveness**. Raoul received several comments and notes from co-workers, and a few took over some of his duties.

Opportunities abound to show support in the work place. Even little actions can mean a lot. After learning of a co-worker's diagnosis of cancer, Sally suggested that they get together soon to talk. Because Sally had recovered from the same disease, she could be especially supportive. Ted sent a cheerful balloon to the hospital room of his supervisor's daughter. Patti, who had received some training in family counseling, spent some lunch hours with Alicia who was going through a divorce. Just showing in some way that you care and are thinking about a person in crisis can do wonders.

In addition to being supportive to those with whom you work, the same behaviors toward customers, clients, or patients may be appropriate. Several personal experiences with health-care employees before and after cancer surgery underscored the major impact they have on patients.

- The nurse at the University of Illinois Medical Center in Chicago gave me a reassuring smile and said, "Don't worry. We see many patients with these tumors, and we know exactly what we're doing!" (This was such a relief after being told that mine was a rare cancer.)

- The world-renown specialist muttered to himself and to the medical students who were observing the scan of my eye, "Melanoma, melanoma—doesn't look like it, but I don't know what else it could be. Hmmm." (Knowing about melanoma cancer, my stress level was at an all-time high. I thought, "Doesn't he know that I can hear?")

- The young radiologist at Mayo Clinic chatted in a friendly fashion. "You're from Nebraska? I've never been there. What is it like?" Before the scans, she calmly explained to me what she was doing and what would happen. (I thought that she was wise beyond her years and seemed to be aware of the psychological studies that show that stress is lessened when people know what to expect.)

- The last thing I remember as I was being wheeled into surgery at Mayo Clinic was the confident voice of the surgical aide who had brought me there. "Wow, we have the 'A team' doing this surgery!" (My response was a sincere, "Thanks for telling me." I felt supported and positive.)

- The young resident said a brief hello from behind a desk and looked at what appeared to be my medical records. I was there for a postoperative visit with the surgeon. For 10 long minutes he didn't look at me or say anything except an occasional "Hmmm" as he read and cracked his knuckles! (Another stressful situation in which behaviors of a specialist heightened the tension.)

- One of the most positive, dearest, and supportive persons I have ever met is Wolfgang Kuss at Midwest Eye Laboratory in Minneapolis. I call him my eye designer. When I first had an artificial eye made, I felt uncomfortable to say the least. Wolfgang, who had fled East Germany before the Iron Curtain, immediately set both my husband and me at ease. We laughed and felt more positive than we had for some time. (His attitude made all the difference in the world. I continue to look forward to my checkups with Wolfgang.)

- This story is somewhat humorous now, but at the time nothing about the situation was funny. During a uterine scan a few years after my cancer surgery, the radiology technician was unsmiling and unfriendly. The only thing she said during the 15-minute ordeal was a question: "Did anyone ever tell you that you have two uteruses? It sure looks strange." Then she left the examining room and didn't return for another 15 minutes. I lay there fighting terror, knowing that I didn't have two uteruses but wondering what she was seeing. (A case of poor judgment and an uncalled-for comment. The ending was happy as what she saw was nothing strange.)

> **WHAT WERE THE SUPPORTIVE AND NONSUPPORTIVE BEHAVIORS IN EACH OF THESE ACTUAL SITUATIONS?**

If your job involves people in stressful circumstances, be aware that what you say and don't say and how you behave will make the situation better or worse. An enlightening study demonstrated that patients who had been treated in a warm and sympathetic manner asked for half as much painkilling medication as another group. Also, those who had enjoyed a warm doctor–patient relationship were discharged from the hospital an average of 2.7 days sooner than others (Benson, 1987). Positive, supportive interactions are significant to those in need. In building the best possible relationships, you will be sensitive to and aware of opportunities to be supportive to everyone with whom you connect throughout your career.

> **WHAT HAVE YOU EVER DONE AT WORK OR IN SCHOOL TO SHOW SUPPORTIVENESS?**

COOPERATION AND COLLABORATION

Acting or working willingly and agreeably with another person is **cooperation,** an essential element in success. Cooperation is evident in your attitude and actions. Anyone who refuses to be cooperative will hurt both relationships at work and career success. Being cooperative could mean that you

▲ Being supportive to a co-worker makes a positive difference.

won't be able to do something exactly the way you want or that your way will not necessarily prevail. Yet, the rewards of cooperation generally outweigh temporary frustrations.

In the process known as **collaboration**, all participants contribute ideas or efforts to solve a problem or produce an end result. It's necessary to be receptive and nonthreatening. The open communication style of verbalizing and active, receptive listening can make the difference between a constructive or a destructive climate. Also important is the use of body language. Picture the following meeting.

> *Trish felt uncomfortable when Bill began to talk. "You all know that nothing will ever come of our work here unless we are all in total agreement," he said as he pointed his finger directly at the other group members. Trish had good reason to think that "total agreement" meant agreeing with Bill's ideas.*

> *WHAT COMMUNICATION ERRORS DID BILL MAKE? DO YOU AGREE WITH TRISH'S ASSESSMENT?*

Negotiation skills are well worth cultivating because in almost every group situation, **conflict**—which means disagreement—is inevitable. Actually, having a difference of opinion is positive as long as it's handled well. A major obstacle is the tendency to think that our being right is essential. Once you realize that conflict is not a matter of who's right or wrong and is simply a difference in thinking, the stage is set for artful negotiation. A suggested format for resolution of an issue or topic follows.

1. *Define and describe the issue or problem and the common goal.* Clarity is essential. The discussion continues until all members agree on the specific issue to be resolved and the goal to be achieved. Putting them into writing is a good idea.

2. *Brainstorm to generate all possible solutions.* Creativity and openness are essential ingredients at this stage. The key to brainstorming success is: All ideas, no matter how ridiculous, are accepted, and no judging comments are allowed.

3. *Evaluate each possible idea or solution.* Each member has the right to eliminate an idea if it is completely unacceptable. For other reasons the possibilities are narrowed to about two or three.

4. *Decide on the best solution at the time.* A vote, either verbal or written, selects one solution.

5. *Agree to test the agreed-upon solution and meet again to evaluate.* This step is especially valuable. When a solution is treated as tentative, consensus is easier to gain. A date for evaluation is established at this time. Morale can be destroyed if this follow-through is not done. If at the agreed-upon time, the solution isn't working acceptably, the process begins again.

During the evaluative stage, a positive communicator will use certain questions and phrases that express openness and encourage everyone's participation.

- ⊚ I understand your reasoning, and I'd like to hear how you would go about it.
- ⊚ How would you put that plan into effect?
- ⊚ I liked your first idea; however, I have a few reservations about....
- ⊚ Another possibility that ties in with your idea is....
- ⊚ Another approach might be to....
- ⊚ I agree. Have you also considered....
- ⊚ I think that's an excellent suggestion, and I'd like to add to it.
- ⊚ What do you think about....

Knowledge of personality preferences and temperaments can be put to good use in resolution efforts. Notice what each of the following temperament types contributes to a group directed to find ways to increase productivity.

NF: I have several ideas to share. I think it's important that we try to avoid downsizing as that would seriously impact on people's personal lives.

NT: Looking at that idea logically, I doubt if it will work. However, I have another possibility.

SJ: That sounds practical to me. I'm ready to decide.

SP: I'm certainly willing to compromise. I would, however, like to make sure that all ideas have been thoroughly discussed.

Differences in personality can lead to some problems in collaborative efforts; yet, the encouragement of diversity will typically yield the best results. Using the negotiation steps, open communication, and the strengths of different personalities help ensure that shared goals are achieved, and everybody wins.

▲ Teamwork is essential in all types of work.

CONSIDERATION AND HELPFULNESS

Being thoughtful and courteous are appreciated behaviors. A considerate person does not assume that a co-worker or supervisor is available at all times. A technique called **approachability checking** can be especially useful. Whether you are in the same personal space or contacting the person by telephone, asking if the person is busy or if this is a good time to talk is highly recommended. A simple, "Do you have a few minutes right now?" is polite and sets the stage for a positive exchange. Incidentally, don't ask for a few minutes if you really want a half hour.

Related to asking about approachability is to be available. Said a supervisor, "When I walk up to an assistant's desk and it's obvious that he or she is involved in a personal phone call, the worst thing the person can do is continue to talk; yet, it happens all too often." Be sure that you have your priorities in order and are available to others at work.

You will have numerous occasions to be helpful. Sometimes it may be only a matter of letting someone with a smaller job use a copy machine ahead of you. Other times you may fill in for another employee or assist with his or her duties. Keeping a proper perspective is imperative as being overly helpful can lead to feeling overwhelmed. Leigh was a secretary in a large firm. She frequently took on extra work and tried to help by taking on tasks assigned to others. One day she exploded to her immediate supervisor and was amazed to realize how resentful she felt about the additional load she had so cheerfully assumed.

If you're considerate, you will also avoid irritating behaviors. In a small office area that housed several desks, Jeff had his radio tuned to a loud rock-and-roll station. His choice of music was not shared by everyone. Ruth spent several minutes at a time making personal phone calls. To make matters worse, she rarely answered the telephone letting it ring until someone else answered it. Spending your employer's time on personal matters can be a definite detriment to your career.

> *WHAT IN THE WORK PLACE WOULD OR DOES IRRITATE YOU?*

What is irritating to one person may not be to another. An informal survey yielded some interesting answers to the question of annoyances identified in Table 7–1.

With career experience in both banking and education, Richard Ross, a college dean, described the attitude of "I don't ever make mistakes" as especially bothersome. "Everyone makes mistakes," he said. Relating positively to others means that you are keenly aware of what would typically be offensive or annoying and then try to avoid those behaviors.

Consideration is extremely important when you relate to customers or clients. Being a positive representative of an employer isn't always easy and requires patience, determination, and an understanding of human behavior. For example, most people do not like to wait for long periods of time so the best employees do all they can to serve customers efficiently. At times, waiting

T A B L E   7 – 1 ▲ IRRITANTS IN THE WORK PLACE

People who:

- gossip
- are late
- leave early
- don't look at me when I speak
- don't return my greeting
- talk too much or too loudly
- don't talk
- lie
- won't take responsibility
- blame others

- use too much profanity
- are overly opinionated
- think they know it all
- believe that they work harder than others
- complain too much
- don't respond to messages
- take much longer breaks than others
- ask too many personal questions
- wear too much cologne

is unavoidable; in these cases, a considerate employee would be aware of who was there first or, if necessary, ask. Apologies for delays are also in order.

The impression you make on another can be damaged by modern technological devices. For example, do you recall telephoning a business then being put "on hold" even if you weren't asked if you wanted to be? Even if permission is given, you can create a positive impression by keeping the time short or checking back with the person at short intervals.

Effective telephone skills are essential if you want to avoid offending those who call. The following deserve attention.

- Sound friendly and professional. Tone of voice will create a definite impression.

- Speak slowly and distinctly enough to be understood. This is especially necessary when you are leaving a message. Have you ever had to rewind a message several times because the person seemed to be going 80 miles per hour when giving a return phone number?

- Use approachability checking.

- Avoid irritating noises such as clicking your tongue.

- If you have another call, keep that conversation short in order to get back to the initial caller.

- If the telephone rings when waiting on a customer, don't completely forget about the person you were helping.

Other customer relations tips include greeting people with a friendly smile, listening attentively to their requests or complaints, handling complaints in an accommodating and cheerful manner, and treating the customer or client as if your roles were reversed. Remember how it feels to be on the other end of the telephone line or on the other side of a desk or counter. Being rude or condescending wouldn't be appreciated by you; neither are these behaviors pleasing to anyone else.

"*Courteous behavior on the part of each employee is crucial in maintaining positive customer relations.*"

Bob Dinkel, Owner
Accent Fence Company
Lincoln, Nebraska

Customer relations can be challenging, yet the rewards are well worth it. Even if you are not monetarily rewarded, you can give yourself a well-deserved "pat on the back" for being considerate and for probably preserving your job. Because customer relations are considered the "bottom line" by business owners, employees who turn customers away or even create negative impressions are usually fired. Customers and clients don't care if the employee is an honors college graduate from a prestigious university. If they are not treated with understanding and respect, they will take their business elsewhere (Gibbs, 1995). You can prove to be an invaluable employee if you excel in customer relations.

Consideration means that you won't engage in **gossiping**, defined as idle talk. What makes it troublesome is when the gossip is based on rumor or innuendo that is potentially hurtful or damaging to somebody. Conceivably, idle talk can be harmless; generally, it is not. When asked to advise people just starting their career, Lori Hall, director of education and community programs for the American Heart Association, said, "Be friendly to everyone and avoid gossiping like the plague. It's a waste of time, you'll never get ahead that way, and it could come back to 'haunt' you." People who gossip are typically

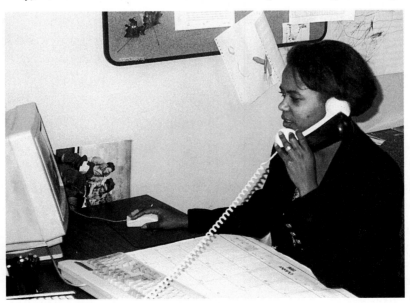

▲ Effective and positive telephone skills are needed in the work world.

regarded by others as petty and even unethical. Essentially, you are hampering your chances for success.

Good questions to ask yourself are what good comes of it and why do I want to gossip? You might put yourself in the place of the subject of the gossip. How would you feel? Even with the best intentions, gossip may be hard to avoid because the practice is common. You do, however, have choices. If particular people or groups are prone to gossip, you can avoid them, or you can be like Cindy who said assertively to three co-workers:

> *Whether it's true or not, I feel uncomfortable discussing her personal life, and I'd like for us to talk about something else.*

If this honest disclosure of feelings brings about a negative reaction, that person is probably not worth your time anyway.

TEAMWORK

In most jobs, teamwork is expected, and your contribution is vital to the total effort. Lazy workers are looked down upon by co-workers and supervisors, and an inefficient team member sets up obstacles to task completion. While you are at work, your responsibility is to the job at hand. Tammy worked in a law office as a clerk and word processing specialist. When the attorneys were gone, she used her time to read magazines and even polish her fingernails. "The work can wait" was her attitude. She was surprised when another employee told her how offensive her behavior was. Be sure not to cheat your employer and, in the long run, yourself by just getting by.

A common occurrence in most businesses is for employees to believe that their work is more demanding and stressful than anyone else's. Picture this scenario: Kent, Roberto, and Anh are on their break in the cafeteria having a conversation.

> KENT: I'm so busy I can't stand it. All the quarterly reports I have to do are really getting to me.

> ROBERTO: Just be glad you don't have to fill all the orders that are coming in right now. I probably won't even have time to take a break later.

> ANH: You think you guys have it rough. If I have to field one more irate phone call, I think I'll find an easier job.

As they're busily trying to "one-up" each other with a worse story, another employee walks by the cafeteria and thinks, "I don't see how those three have time to take a break. They evidently don't have nearly as much work to do as I do!" Acknowledging others' workloads would be a refreshing change from this scene. Less griping, refraining from a "poor-me" profile, more receptive listening, and recognition of the contributions of others will create a much more positive work environment.

▲ It's best to avoid judging others based on your own style.

PRAISE

Appropriate affirmations can create a warm atmosphere and be rewarding to all involved. **Positive strokes** are verbal and nonverbal behaviors given in reference to another that feel good to the receiver. The work place provides countless opportunities to give positive strokes. Some ideas follow.

- Compliment someone on personality, efforts, and, as more commonly done, appearance.
- Congratulate people for accomplishments and awards.
- Thank all those who help you.
- Simply tell someone you enjoy working with him or her.

Because of fear of misinterpretation, employees may hesitate to give their supervisors a positive stroke. Remember that they, too, are human, and if you are sincere, the stroke will most likely be appreciated.

Praise is a verbal positive stroke and, if given sincerely, generally brings about a favorable reaction. Even if the recipient doesn't respond, he or she probably enjoyed the feeling. Praise has been recognized as a powerful motivator and one that is the most inexpensive. In a study of morale-building factors, employees rated full appreciation of their work higher than good pay (Kovach, 1980). The most positive work environments are those in which sincere praise abounds. Supervisors can enhance relationships with their employees by providing praise and recognition. In addition, leaders at work improve morale by showing respect to everyone, being honest, soliciting input, and being encouraging. Reassurance and encouragement are motivational tonics and are bound to improve working relationships.

APPRECIATION OF DIVERSITY

Rather than fear what is new and different, a successful career person is open to what is novel. Today's work world is a mosaic composed of various ethnic, racial, religious, and age groups. The mixture provides opportunities to learn and expand your horizons. During a seminar, two employees spoke of the benefits of daily interactions.

> JAN: I had no opportunity to know any African-Americans in my small rural-based community. I'm so glad this job has given me the experience of working with Bob, who is really great. It's been fun and enlightening.

> KEN: Ever since the Persian Gulf War I harbored resentment toward anyone who came from the Middle East. However, after working with Najat, I've realized that all groups have wonderful people. I don't stereotype any longer.

Even if your impression of a person is positive, it's better to resist a tendency to stereoytpe. One person or even a small number does not represent an entire group. In fact, you will probably find more diversity within an ethnic or racial category than between two different groups.

In recent years most employers have made an effort to emphasize multiculturalism. Even if yours does not, what is enjoyable is to seek out and learn as much as you can about a particular person including the cultural uniquenesses. Except for some educational institutions, the work place offers more possibilities for diverse interactions than you will find anywhere. "I didn't realize how much fun people over the age of 50 can be until I worked with a couple of them," reported Greg. "I enjoy being with them as much as my own age group."

Your career will also benefit from an appreciation of diversity. Lack of tolerance is a major handicap. According to Mark Munger, a captain in a fire department, "A psychological profile and targeted questions during the interview quite successfully identify any applicant who is biased in any way. That person's chances of being hired are 'slim to none.'" If a person does get hired as a firefighter and then demonstrates prejudice, he or she is subject to serious discipline.

> *"The fire department is extremely intolerant of bigotry and intolerance."*
>
> Mark Munger, Captain
> Lincoln Fire Department
> Lincoln, Nebraska

Diversity contributes to a more successful and satisfying career. Variations of human beings interacting together are as appealing as multicolored gardens of different sizes and shapes of flowers. The splendor of diversity provides opportunities for expansion of self.

MANAGING CONFLICT EFFECTIVELY

Despite your best attempts to maintain positive relationships, disagreement will occur. Earlier in this chapter negotiation skills were emphasized. This section focuses on interpersonal conflict outside of a formalized group setting.

CHOICES IN CONFLICT SITUATIONS

A beginning point in effective conflict management is to recognize alternative courses of action. Instead of being a reactor, you can be the actor and decide how to behave. Human beings create or construct their own reality by their actions and interactions. Because a situation evolves entirely as a result of the behaviors of those involved, you, as a participant, have the power to determine the course of the interaction.

One possibility is to ignore an irritation. Most work environments have at least one annoying person, and even those who aren't disagreeable will occasionally rub you the wrong way. You can simply disregard the behavior. Because you are not at the mercy of another person's behavior, another choice is to act positively regardless of his or her actions. "I'm glad you called my attention to that," was Pat's reply to an antagonistic comment about an error she had made in a report. Even though the person had no business being critical, Pat chose to defuse a potentially volatile situation. She even topped it off with a smile!

At other times, avoiding or defusing isn't advisable, and resolving the conflict may be in your best interests. In most businesses, there is a "chain of command" and either stated or unstated norms for handling disagreements. Regardless, conflict can be poorly managed unless certain obstacles are eliminated.

OBSTACLES TO ELIMINATE

A major barrier is unwillingness to take responsibility in a conflict situation. "The devil made me do it" syndrome makes resolution extremely difficult, if not impossible. Who or what else besides the devil gets blamed when things are difficult? The list is seemingly endless: other people, the employer, the weather, and even the time of the month! Comments typical of lack of responsibility are "It's not my fault," "He or she is just impossible," "Nobody can get along with her," "If only...," "I can't help it," and "There's nothing I can do about it." Ironically, when people perceive themselves responsible or at fault and recognize self-errors, conflict is easier to resolve. Isn't it less difficult to change yourself than it is to change another person? Shouldering your share of responsibility for the problem and the solution-finding process is empowering.

Intention can become another obstacle. Human beings feel good when they are right. Some even act as if being right is essential so their intention in any conflict situation is to convince another person to accept their point of view. When both parties are working hard to win, resolution is impossible. Another intention is self-protection which can be taken to extremes. In resolving issues, self-disclosure is beneficial. If a primary goal is to shield the self, a person is likely to reveal little. In addition, he or she may appear quite defensive.

Related to intentions are **conflict styles**, the ways people handle disagreement. Two are especially likely to interfere with resolution. A familiar one is the competitive style in which a person uses aggression to defeat what is perceived as an opponent or adversary. The intent is to win or get one's way. The other is an avoidant style. A person seeks to evade a conflict situation. He or she may be upset yet will avoid any confrontation. Avoiders use a tactic called **gunnysacking**—legitimate grievances and irritants are suppressed or "stuffed" into an imaginary gunnysack. This can go on for a long time until the gunnysacker has a bagful of concerns. People who do this can damage their own health, and as the resentment builds up, relationships inevitably suffer. The gunnysack image is intended to illustrate what can happen when the sack gets too full. The bag bursts, and often, the avoider becomes aggressive. To empty your gunnysack, use the exercise in KEY STEPS (page 303).

Perhaps you have heard of passive-aggressives who combine the two. For some time the person utilizes the avoidant style, and all seems fine. Then, and often over the smallest thing, the style changes to a hurtful antagonistic one. Or, the person uses covert and manipulative behaviors to get even. Obviously, these styles prevent positive management of conflict.

CHARACTERISTICS OF EFFECTIVE CONFLICT MANAGERS

Conflict is more easily resolved if the people involved possess certain characteristics. If you want to become more capable in the area of conflict management, the following qualities will help.

SELF-ESTEEM.   With high self-esteem, you have an advantage. Individuals with lower levels of self-esteem are easily threatened. In times of disagreement, they may come off as tough and abrasive in an attempt to defend the self. Others who feel inadequate may refrain from being involved in resolution of conflict even though they have legitimate concerns and points of view. People who feel good about themselves don't see conflict as a personal war, and with self-worth not at risk, they expend their energies in resolving the problem.

ASSERTIVENESS.   A hallmark of positive conflict management is assertive behavior. According to a corporate vice-president, opinions of nonassertive individuals are either unheard or overlooked while aggression brings about negative reactions. Assertiveness is revealed in body language and in the way ideas are expressed. The open style of verbalization is assertive language.

OPTIMISM.   The optimists of the world enter a conflict situation the way they do other realms of their lives—with the belief that this issue can be resolved. An optimist with a open mind is committed to an attitude of wanting everybody to win. "Negaholics," on the other hand, dampen the spirits of those involved. Optimists are usually adept at coming up with alternatives, and in a conflict situation, the ability to see numerous options is beneficial. When things are seemingly "bogged down," the person with an optimistic attitude can bolster spirits and restore a sense of enthusiasm.

INTERNAL LOCUS OF CONTROL.   When people are responsible for their behavior, conflict is easier to handle. Conflict resolution can be severely sidetracked if participants spend their time finding fault and affixing blame. Those with an internal locus of control prefer to use their time and energy in solutions.

Individuals who "are in the driver's seat of their own lives" set the stage for conflict resolution because they want to do so. They aren't limited by feelings of "We *have to* settle this," "This *needs* to be solved," or "We *should* discuss the matter." Those forcing thoughts stifle enthusiasm and lead to a rather dour communication climate.

An internal locus of control also means that others do not control your thoughts or behaviors. You can choose to be civil even though another is being rude, and because you aren't reacting, you have the power to lead the resolution process. Being in charge of yourself is also necessary in order to possess another invaluable characteristic: the ability to manage emotions. Instead of thinking, "She made me so mad when she left her work for me to finish," you can choose whether you want to be angry or not. If you use thought-changing and other relaxing techniques, you can remain calm even when it might be easier to erupt. On the other hand, emotional management means that you can convey feelings during conflict so you can let the other person know of your disappointment or frustration in appropriate ways. Most people have difficulty finding the proper balance of emotionality during conflict so don't be dismayed if your management doesn't always go well. Keep in mind that you can call a time-out if your emotions are getting the best of you.

FLEXIBILITY.   "My mind is made up, and that's it," she said with a nod of her head and a self-satisfied look. This happened during the first five minutes of what developed into a serious confrontation. Her lack of flexibility was frustrating to the other two participants. Instead of priding yourself on having your mind set, realize that flexibility is sorely needed in positive conflict management. Being able to see the other's perspective can quickly change a deadlock into resolution. Changing your mind is a sign of thinking power and strength, not a sign of weakness. If you want to become skilled at conflict resolution, practice flexing your brain frequently!

SENSE OF HUMOR.   During a disagreement the appropriate use of a positive sense of humor can defuse the situation. Be sure that any humor is not at the expense of someone else. Ideally, the humor is related to yourself. When Senator Bob Kerrey of Nebraska was initially running for Congress, a loud critical voice from the audience said, "I don't know why I should vote for you. During one whole year when you were governor, I don't remember anything you did except entertain that actress, Debra Winger." Kerrey smiled and replied, "I know what you mean. Sometimes I don't remember much else about that year either!" The crowd broke into laughter, including the critic, and what could have been an adversarial situation didn't materialize.

UNDERSTANDING.   Correctly comprehending the other's point of view is invaluable and is much more possible when you understand personality differences. A quick review of temperament types, described earlier in the chapter, can reveal how individuals can think, feel, and act so differently. A chapter called "Conflict Resolution" in the book *Type Talk at Work* (Kroeger and Thuesen, 1992) is well worth your attention. According to the authors, different personality types define conflict differently and approach conflict management with diverse ideas and behaviors; disagreeable situations tend to magnify differences and bring out the worst. No type excels at handling conflict, and knowing the strengths and weaknesses of yourself and others increases understanding.

Empathy, which is a deep level of understanding, can enable you to accept behavior that would ordinarily bother you. "I remember what it was like when I was going through a divorce," said Beth, "so I'm able to understand and empathize with him even when his mood seems irritable." Understanding everyone's perspective sets the stage for successful conflict resolution.

Conflict Management Skills

A **collaborative style** is one in which individuals seek mutually satisfying solutions by being assertive and cooperative. Making use of this style and open communication techniques, a discussion can lead to a positive settlement. A key word in turning disagreement into resolution is "yes." As much as possible, use this magic word as it is a powerful tool in disarming the other side (Ury, 1993). "Yes, you have a point there," "Yes, I agree with you," and "Yes, that's right" create a positive communication climate necessary to resolve conflict.

A necessary ingredient in the resolution process is a common shared meaning. If you were asked, "True or false? It's better to withdraw from a discussion rather than fight," your answer would depend upon how you define certain words, especially *fight*. Those who conceptualize fighting as hurtful, threatening behaviors would probably respond with true. Others who see fighting as a potentially fair way of handling conflict would answer false. Countless examples of different meanings are possible. Jason was told that he wasn't being productive, and he thought he was. He and the other person had different ideas of productivity. At any time during a discussion, checking whether or not meanings are shared or disparate is highly recommended.

> *"In order to understand each other, what is often necessary is to translate English into English. The key component is listening."*
>
> Doc Chaves, Assistant Vice-President
> Ameritas Life Insurance Corp.
> Lincoln, Nebraska

Especially beneficial is for the participants to agree on what is wanted from a discussion. Establishing a shared meaning initially promotes a collaborative atmosphere. From there it's a matter of proceeding in a positive way.

A technique called fair fighting can produce positive results. Incidentally, **fighting** is simply defined as a way of resolving disagreement. Unfair fighting, the type with which most of us are familiar, is definitely to be avoided. **Fair fighting** consists of behaviors that aim to resolve conflict in an amicable way.

Setting the stage involves selecting the best time, place, and conditions for resolving the issue. Most important is to wait until you have calmed down before you have a discussion. Even the finest management skills can be forgotten in the wake of anger. Even though most of us prefer to settle disagreements quickly, a waiting period is usually preferable.

The following are criteria of fair fighting.

- *Winning–losing.* Getting rid of the win–lose notion is necessary. If one person wins, the relationship loses. The focus is on resolving the issue; when resolution occurs, everyone wins.

- *Involvement.* Perhaps you have had a discussion which was more of a monologue than a dialogue. When you fight fairly, all individuals are involved in the exchange. Verbalizing and listening are shared behaviors.

- *Communication.* Open communication is to be used. "I" statements, not "you" statements, coupled with active, receptive listening and a high level of disclosure of key elements of the issue, are essential. A review of dimensions of awareness, described in Chapter 2, would be helpful. An important one to share is each person's desired outcome. Also, making use of ways to give and receive criticism from Chapter 6 can create a much more positive communication environment.

- *Injury.* Be careful to direct criticism to behaviors, to avoid personal attacks, and to maintain consideration for the feelings of others.

- *Directness.* Remaining focused in the present and on the subject at hand is difficult, yet vital to a fair fight. If a new topic is presented, the issue gets sidetracked. You can agree to discuss other topics at a later time and get back to the matter at hand.

- *Specificity.* Clarity, not vagueness, is needed. The first clarification involves the issue. What exactly is to be discussed? After the conversation begins, people may interpret words and behaviors differently. In fact, most of the problems in the work place are caused by dissimilarity between what one person intended to mean and another's perception (Van Oosting, 1992). Achieving shared meanings is everyone's responsibility.

- *Responsibility.* All parties are to take a share of the responsibility for the disagreement itself and the process required to resolve it.

- *Feelings.* Depending upon the nature of the relationship and the situation, you may want to share emotions. What may appear to be anger could actually be hurt or disappointment. When people honestly reveal what they are feeling, confusion disappears, and a positive connection can occur. Yet, feelings can interfere with discussions so managing emotions is necessary.

☺ *Humor.* As strange as it seems, if in some way, positive humor creeps into the discussion, the mood of both will probably lighten. Any use of sarcasm or nasty humor is to be avoided.

A "spoonful of sugar" doesn't hurt. The use of sincere affirmations during discussions can make a major difference. Kelly was frustrated with an immediate supervisor and found herself saying things she knew she would regret later. The supervisor said, "I consider you to be a good thinker, and I'm sure we can get this resolved." Kelly found herself becoming calmer as she realized that the supervisor would listen to her ideas. Even when you disagree with others, acknowledging their strengths is usually quite beneficial.

What about an issue between you and a supervisor? The same criteria can certainly be applied. You don't want to come off as a complainer who doesn't offer any alternatives. If perceived mistreatment has come from the supervisor, you can address this specifically using open communication. It is advisable to document the discussion and, depending upon the situation, make sure that the particulars and the final resolution are agreed upon in writing. Company policies may address the exact procedures to be followed. Fair fighting isn't easy and requires more time and effort than just erupting. Yet, your career development will be enhanced each time you resolve issues fairly.

DEALING WITH DIFFICULT PEOPLE

Who is a difficult person? "No matter what I do or say, nothing makes any difference because I work for the most difficult person in the world," "She's just impossible," "Nobody could get along with him" are descriptions of difficult people. This person may be an irritable co-worker, a passive-aggressive supervisor, or a hostile client.

You might put this into a different perspective by asking, "Am I ever a difficult person?" Truthfully, we all can be difficult at times. However, a difficult person makes a habit of it and, as such, creates major challenges in work relationships.

TYPES OF DIFFICULT PEOPLE

Seven patterns of difficult behavior have been identified in the book *Coping with Difficult People* (Bramson, 1988).

☺ *Hostile-aggressives:* People who try to bully and overwhelm others.

☺ *Complainers:* Individuals who gripe incessantly but do not act to improve their situation.

☺ *Silent and unresponsive:* People who respond as little as possible so aren't helpful.

☺ *Super-agreeables:* People who are reasonable but who either don't produce or act differently when not in your presence.

⊚ *Negativists:* Pessimists whose favorite reaction is, "No, that won't work."

⊚ *Know-it-all experts:* People who seem to think that they know much more than you do on every subject.

⊚ *Indecisives:* Individuals who don't seem to be able to make up their minds and stall all decisions, as well as perfectionists who don't complete tasks.

CAN YOU ADD ANY DIFFICULT TYPES TO THE LIST?

Incidentally, if you see yourself in any of the categories, do what you can to change those behaviors.

DEALING WITH A DIFFICULT PERSON

Being aware of difficult behaviors is helpful. Yet, learning indispensable coping skills allows you to handle your career in spite of a difficult person. If possible, avoiding the difficult person is probably the best solution. This may not be realistic; however, you can try to decrease contact time. As much as he tried, Chad found it extremely difficult to get along with Todd, who operated the copy center in the large investment firm. "As often as I can, I have someone else take and pick up my work from the copy center," he said. "It's just not worth the stress."

Understanding the difficult person's perspective is useful. Is there a reason for the annoying behaviors? Most people aren't naturally nasty, and if you can figure out the underlying causes, your reactions will likely be less negative. Empathy can be especially helpful.

A beneficial strategy is to resist attributing a person's behavior to a permanent flaw of character. We usually realize that our own temperamental ways, annoying behaviors, or angry outbursts are situational; yet, someone else is "just that way." After Gary tells a crude joke that demeans women, you might think, "Gary is sexist and rude." Yet, he may consider the joke just humorous or be reacting to a feeling of anxiety regarding assertive women. You can use "I" statements and verbalize your objection to the comment or behavior and keep the door open for positive change. Usually, reasons for difficult behavior are more complicated than we might think, yet over time can be remedied.

Putting into practice what you know about personality preferences helps. For example, I used to become quite frustrated with a staff member who absolutely would not leave the matter at hand. "Don't bother me right now. I'm busy with this," was a common reply to my request for help. Initially, this seemed a sign of rudeness and inflexibility. Then, I realized that the individual had a strong sensing preference and that being interrupted and then sidetracked would be especially bothersome. I now wait patiently until I have full attention. It's not uncommon to be uncomfortable with a preference opposite from ours even though it could be useful behavior for us.

Both cognitive and behavioral techniques can alleviate the stress of a difficult person. Remember that other people do not control you and aren't able to make you feel, think, or do anything. Cognitive restructuring can then be used. "Just because she was short tempered (and usually is) doesn't mean it's going to ruin my day" changes the reality. Behaviorally, you can make a change as well. Interestingly, whenever one person in a relationship changes, the interaction will also change. For example, kindness in the face of animosity is a powerful behavior. **Reciprocity**—experiencing a similar feeling—can change a person's behavior. Think of a person for whom you felt no particular liking or disliking. If this individual showed a genuine liking for you, it was probably hard to not reciprocate or feel similarly toward her or him. With a difficult person, you can try to indicate regard even if you are forced to fake it for a while. The results may be amazing.

When confronted with a difficult person, positive communication skills, especially the open style of verbalizing and receptive listening, are powerful tools. Difficult people usually want to express their opinions and grievances, and you can alter a stressful interaction just by listening. Check how you deal with difficulty and conflict with an exercise in KEY STEPS (page 304).

COPING WITH A DIFFICULT BOSS.   If the difficult person is your supervisor or boss, you have an even greater challenge. How to recognize, understand, and cope with a difficult boss is covered in the book *Coping with Difficult Bosses* (Bramson, 1992). You may work for an individual who values control more than people. One employee said, "All of us have just learned to conceal things from her. Attitudes and behaviors that are controlling destroy communication and trust." Unfortunately, a difficult supervisor can be so threatening that an employee just decides to quit. Instead, you may want to try to change the situation. Above all else, it's not advisable to just gripe to other employees as this can be hazardous to your career well-being. Instead, try the following.

- Decide what the boss or supervisor does or does not do that is annoying or frustrating.

- Evaluate your actions, reactions, and interactions with the person. Could a change in your behavior be helpful?

- Determine your specific wants and goals and think about how to communicate those.

- Use a costs versus benefits analysis to decide exactly whether and what to discuss with a boss.

- If appropriate, involve others in a discussion with the supervisor.

- Carefully follow the suggestions in the fair fighting section in this chapter. The way you communicate will make a definite difference.

- Be prepared in case bringing this to the person's attention results in reprimand or termination.

HAVE YOU EVER HAD A DIFFICULT BOSS? WHAT MADE THE PERSON DIF-FICULT? HOW DID YOU HANDLE IT?

Regardless of the behavior of anyone else, you can utilize positive relationship skills. Doing so will greatly increase the chances of turning a difficult person into a pleasant one. In the process you will have enhanced a relationship and the potential for your career success.

FORGIVING AND MOVING ON

One of the most disturbing situations in the work environment is to have a confrontation with someone or an interaction with a difficult person that seemingly never ends. Unfortunately, some people seem to lack the capacity to let go. They carry a grudge and make it obvious that they are still angry. Teresa was hurt and upset when she was seemingly criticized at a staff meeting by Steve, another supervisor. Even though he attempted to explain his position, Teresa refused to listen. Two years later she is still snubbing Steve and making remarks about him to other employees. Who is really being hurt?

Grudge bearers damage themselves as much as they do others. If you are such a person, consider the negative consequences. Harboring grudges, resentments, and other bitter feelings requires energy and ends up diminishing self-esteem. The inability to forgive can lead to increased blood pressure, loss of sleep, and other problems. The person who forgives is released from anger and resentment and freed from any psychological hold the injurer may have had (Enright, Santos, and Al-Mabuk, 1989).

Thinking of forgiveness as simply letting go of the past may make it more acceptable. To "forgive and forget" isn't necessary; you can forgive without forgetting. Erasing a wrongdoing from memory is unrealistic and usually impossible. Forgiving doesn't mean that an injury is condoned or even pardoned. If you have truly been ill-treated, you can still put it behind you. What can help is to realize that people can agree to disagree and then to separate the issue from the person. Too often, people like Teresa seem to think if someone doesn't see it the way they do, that person is unlikable. To continue with a petty, "let's-get-even" attitude is immature and will be a major obstacle in your career development.

Those who can forgive are strong people. They usually have high self-esteem and are able to forgive imperfections in themselves, as well as in others. When you err, do you forgive yourself? If you have, then you can also extend forgiveness to others. You may not resume the same type of relationship you once had, yet you can be civil and get along in the work place. To do less is a disservice to your employer as well as to yourself.

DO YOU HAVE A GRUDGE? IS THERE SOMEONE YOU HAVEN'T FORGIVEN? CHALLENGE YOURSELF TO DO SO AND MOVE ON WITH YOUR LIFE.

As you design your career, realize that relationships will play a major role. Whether interactions and relationships are positive is largely your choice. To a great extent, the caliber of work relationships will determine both your career satisfaction and your degree of success.

KEY POINTS

- Career development is keenly influenced by interactions and relationships.

- In order to promote the most positive relations with employers, supervisors, and co-workers as well as clients, customers, or patients, certain thoughts and actions are necessary. These include:
  - ▲ realistic expectations
  - ▲ positiveness and friendliness
  - ▲ sensitivity and understanding
  - ▲ supportiveness
  - ▲ cooperation and collaboration
  - ▲ consideration and helpfulness
  - ▲ avoidance of irritating behaviors
  - ▲ teamwork
  - ▲ praise
  - ▲ appreciation of diversity

- The ability to manage conflict effectively will be a major asset throughout one's career life.

- In order to resolve conflict, it helps to recognize your choices and to eliminate obstacles such as lack of responsibility, an intention to win, and use of the competitive and avoidant conflict styles.

- Specific personal characteristics are useful in conflict resolution.

- Conflict management skills can be learned. Open communication and other fair fighting techniques pave the way to satisfying work relations.

- Dealing with difficult people, including a difficult boss, is challenging; yet, people have choices and can learn to cope.

- Resentments and ill feelings in the work place are harmful. Those who can forgive and move on beyond disputes possess an invaluable asset.

RECOMMENDED READING

Alessandra, T. and Hunsaker, P. (1993). *Communicating at work*. New York: Simon & Schuster.

Bolton, R. and Bolton, D. G. (1996). *People styles at work: Making bad relationships good and good relationships better*. New York: Amacom.

Bramson, R. M. (1988). *Coping with difficult people*. Garden City, NY: Anchor Press/Doubleday.

Bramson, R. M. (1992). *Coping with difficult bosses*. New York: Carol Publishing Group.

Bright, D. (1988). *Criticism in your life: How to give it—how to take it—how to make it work for you*. New York: Master Media.

Hanna, S. L. (1995). *Person to person: Positive relationships don't just happen*. Englewood Cliffs, NJ: Prentice Hall.

Keating, C. J. (1984). *Dealing with difficult people*. Ramsey, NJ: Paulist Press.

Kroeger, O. and Thuesen, J. M. (1992). *Type talk at work*. New York: Delacorte Press.

Scott, G. G. (1990). *Resolving conflict with others and within yourself*. Oakland, CA: New Harbinger Publications.

Ury, W. (1993). *Getting past no: Negotiating your way from confrontation to cooperation*. New York: Bantam Books.

CHAPTER EIGHT

Challenges in the Work Place

C hallenges are inevitable in the world of work. This chapter identifies predictable and unexpected tribulations and, most importantly, suggests ways to deal with them.

DISCRIMINATION

Being treated unfairly is frustrating and challenging. **Discrimination** is making a distinction in favor of or against someone on the basis of the group, class, or category to which she or he belongs. When such a distinction is made in the work place, an injustice has occurred.

SOURCES OF DISCRIMINATION

Even though discrimination in employment is illegal, it still exists, and you may experience it when you apply for a job. Experiments conducted by the Urban Institute involved individuals who, except for ethnicity and race, were well-matched. When they applied for advertised positions, in most cases non-Hispanic, white applicants were treated more favorably than either African Americans or Hispanics (Sundstrom, 1994). In a comparison of the black and white candidates who were the same on all hiring qualifications, the white person advanced farther through the process than his or her black counterpart in one out of five cases. The authors of the report concluded that job discrimination is widespread (Turner, Fix, and Struyk, 1991).

Racial and ethnic discrimination received more publicity in the past; yet, other types of discrimination based on sex, age, sexual orientation, disabilities, physical appearance, or any perceived difference occur. For example, being extremely overweight is a major handicap in many career fields. Even though an employer is unlikely to admit it, trim, physically fit candidates generally enjoy an advantage. A study revealed that overweight people, especially women, are extremely susceptible to job discrimination. Often, the people who discriminated weren't aware of their biases (Ianzito, 1995).

Even an incorrect perception can be an obstacle. Marcus explained, "I'm a heterosexual male with some effeminate mannerisms. Even though I can't prove it, I'm certain that's why I wasn't in a final pool of applicants." Gays and lesbians generally suffer even more discrimination if they reveal their sexual orientation.

After being employed, you may be a victim of discrimination. Privileges and promotions can be unfairly awarded. Past discriminatory practices have contributed to a generally segregated hierarchy of power. In the early 1990s only 6 percent of management positions and 2 percent of upper management positions in 94 large corporations were held by white women or by African Americans, Latinos, or Asian Americans (Hatchett, 1994). A female employee told of an incident: "The manager told me I was doing a great job but that a younger man who had a wife and five children needed my job more than I did. He said I was to be laid off. After I threatened to bring charges, he transferred me to another department." Conditions have improved, yet much remains to be done to ensure equality for all.

HAVE YOU EVER BEEN A VICTIM OF DISCRIMINATION? WHAT DID YOU DO?

HANDLING DISCRIMINATION

What can be done? Because being perceived as defensive lessens the chance to be hired, you are best served by adopting an optimistic attitude and assuming that an employer is not going to discriminate. You can accept your uniqueness and use it to your advantage.

A potential deterrent can be explained or camouflaged. A young woman who stammered decided to mention this at the beginning of the interview. "Interestingly, because I revealed it initially, I had less difficulty during the discussion," she said. Another candidate wore a long-sleeved blouse so that a tattoo was invisible during a job interview. "I'm certainly not ashamed of it, yet as a practical measure, I realize that not everyone approves of tattoos." An experiment by John T. Molloy, described in his newspaper column (1995), used six people who were interviewed at least three times for jobs. Their various looks ranged from no attempt to disguise a disability to doing everything they could to camouflage it. They were more successful when the disability was not as evident.

You may not be able or want to cover up a uniqueness. If so, you can still present yourself positively. Susan Dunn spoke candidly about limitations resulting from cerebral palsy. "I haven't suffered from overt discrimination; yet, I'm confined in applying for positions because of somewhat limited finances and dependence on public transportation. I accept this and go from there." Her attitude and determination to overcome the challenges make others forget that she has any disability, and she doesn't allow circumstances to interfere with her career.

If you don't land a position, assess the situation rationally. Unsuccessful applicants may soothe disappointments by rationalizing or blaming. "I didn't get that job because I'm a woman (or a man)," "It's because they're giving all the jobs to minorities," or "They just won't hire minorities" are obvious scapegoating thoughts that become further obstacles.

If you honestly believe that you have been a victim of discrimination in the hiring process, you can contact the Equal Employment Opportunity Commission office and learn your options. The laws are both preventive and punitive. The 1964 Civil Rights Act and its later amendments make it unlawful for an employer to refuse to hire, to discharge, or to discriminate against an individual based on race, color, religion, sex, or national origin. The federal Equal Employment Opportunity Commission (EEOC), which was created to enforce the act, investigates complaints, seeks conciliation, and files discrimination suits. "Discrimination based on outmoded stereotypes continues to exist. Ignoring it won't make it 'go away,'" says Ruthe Parker, supervisor of computer aided design, Interface Data Systems, Phoenix, Arizona.

The Americans with Disabilities Act (ADA) makes it illegal for employers with more than 15 workers to discriminate against people with physical or mental impairments if they are qualified to perform the essential functions of a position. Reasonable accommodations are to be made unless the change would result in an undue hardship on the business or a direct health/safety threat to any employee. For example, a person adept in using sign language assisted in a job interview for Jill who is deaf. A disabled person can request accommodations that are necessary to perform a job. Knowing your rights is essential, and if you have a little-known disability or one that isn't readily apparent, you may need to be more assertive.

> "The employment of qualified persons with disabilities is an opportunity to include *people who can make valuable contributions*."
>
> Lyn Patterson, Human Resources Administrator
> Turner Broadcasting System, Inc.
> Los Angeles, California

In addition to these protective legal acts, another preventive program is affirmative action. In the early 1960s the administration of President John F. Kennedy defined **affirmative action** as efforts by employers to find qualified minorities (Macionis, 1996). The policies successfully opened doors that had been closed to racial and ethnic minorities as well as women. Affirmative action programs vary yet have one common theme: to encourage employment of diverse groups of people while eliminating past discriminatory practices. "Our goal is to have a work force that represents the population. Affirmative action removes barriers and gives all people a chance to fairly compete. All applicants must be qualified to be considered," states Pat Kant, employment manager for the City of Lincoln, Nebraska.

A controversy over affirmative action stems from a perception of reverse discrimination. Becoming well-educated in this area is important. Many people do not know that quota systems are not necessarily a part of affirmative action programs. In fact, the U.S. courts have rejected rigid quota systems (Macionis, 1996). Some programs will use screening criteria to overcome discrimination against people of color or women. In these cases, a white man could be affected. While this is unfortunate, it is beneficial to keep in mind that he is being hurt in only one area of life and only as an exception to his group while racial and ethnic minorities and women usually suffer because their entire groups have been and still are subordinated (Feagin and Feagin, 1996).

Accurate information can make a difference. A few years ago the word had spread among students in a fire protection technology program that the city fire department was helping minorities by boosting their entrance-test scores. After checking it out, they learned that the rumor was false. Deputy Chief Dean Staberg contends that all candidates who are hired must possess very high qualifications and test scores. "A minority status is not enough to get a firefighting position."

Ideally, in the future this society and others will no longer require a system for righting past wrongs or formal programs that bring about a diverse work place. Then we will all benefit. "I have been stigmatized because of perceptions that I got my job on the basis of my minority status, and this is difficult to handle because I know I was highly qualified," said a Native American. According to Jose J. Soto, an affirmative action/equity officer, "At least 90 percent of affirmative action is at the front end of the hiring process—in targeting people who have been excluded and in encouraging and recruiting applicants from all groups. Any preferential treatment is minimal and is not what the programs are about. Having a diverse work place is valued, and this is made possible through affirmative action."

"Affirmative action does not guarantee that any one type of person, a minority or a female, will get a particular job. It does guarantee, however, that everyone will have an equal opportunity to compete for available jobs."

Jose J. Soto, Affirmative Action/Equity Officer
Southeast Community College
Lincoln, Nebraska

GIVE REASONS FOR AND AGAINST AFFIRMATIVE ACTION. SEEK TO GET ACCURATE INFORMATION ABOUT THIS TIMELY ISSUE.

How can you go about handling discrimination after being hired? Most companies have written policies regarding discrimination which include a description of the procedures to follow if you feel you have been wrongfully treated. You can also talk to a supervisor or owner about the matter. The company may have an equal opportunity specialist or someone in the human resources area to provide advice. Another possibility is an employees' association. If you aren't satisfied with the help you receive in-house, the Equal Employment Opportunity Commission is a valuable resource. Legal action is a possibility; however, exploring all options carefully before making a decision is in your best interest.

Equity issues will continue to exist for some time. Erasing past injustices takes time and effort. Laws are in place to prevent, protect, and redress injustices. Changing attitudes and behaviors typically takes longer. During your career life you can contribute to the worthy goal of equality by challenging discrimination.

SEXUAL HARASSMENT

Often thought of as a form of discrimination, **sexual harassment** was given a formal legal definition by the Equal Employment Opportunity Commission in 1980 (Fitzgerald, 1992). Harassment behaviors are unwelcome sexual advances, requests for sexual favors, and other verbal or physical conduct of a sexual nature. Sexual harassment is present when submission or rejection of such behaviors is made a term or condition of employment; is used in employment decisions; or creates an intimidating, hostile, or offensive working environment. The conduct may be verbal or physical and may also include the circulation of sexually explicit photographs or literature.

At least 50 percent of women and a smaller percentage of men have been harassed on the job or campus. Even though most harassers are men, it's important to realize that *most men are not harassers* (Bravo and Cassedy, 1992). To avoid being a harasser, assume that off-color jokes, sexual innuendos, and advances are not welcomed, realize that a "no" means just that, and honestly assess how you would feel if you or someone you cared for became a victim of harassment.

As with other forms of discrimination, a business is likely to have written policies about sexual harassment. If not, you can educate yourself and be

▲ Dilbert reprinted by permission of United Feature Syndicate, Inc.

assertive if confronted with sexually explicit or implicit behavior. The Affirmative Action/Equity Office at Southeast Community College recommends the following actions.

- ⊚ *Object!* Let the harasser know that the behavior is offensive and unwelcomed and that it must stop. No response is usually interpreted as approval. If you do not want to confront the person, be sure to communicate with a supervisor or staff person.

- ⊚ *Document!* Keep a record of incidents including date, time, specific behaviors, your reactions, and outcome.

- ⊚ *Talk!* Let a third party know of the harassment.

- ⊚ *Report!* If the behavior continues, you are better off reporting it to an appropriate authority.

The work world of today is much different than that in the past. Most employers are intolerant of sexual harassment and have provided safeguards and resources to eliminate unethical behaviors.

FAMILY ISSUES

How do people manage both career and family? In the past, the question wasn't revelent because traditional family roles called for only one wage earner. The other person, usually the woman, took care of the family and the house. Those days for most people are gone. The proportion of women in the labor force is approaching that of men (Lindsey, 1997). Many men today want a balance between career and family, and all loving parents want quality care for their children. Fortunately, most employers are aware of this and believe in the value of family.

Rather than accept an either-or principle of work or family, as was typical of women in the past, it's better to learn what is possible. As Melanie stated, "I used to think that when I had a child, I would 'put my career on hold,' and I was willing to sacrifice. Now I've decided that there are several alternatives and that it doesn't have to be one or the other." Highly recommended is for dual-career parents to develop what is called a shared or egalitarian marriage in which roles are flexible and household and child-care responsibilities are fairly shared.

> *WHAT ARE SOME WAYS PARENTS CAN DEAL WITH WORK AND FAMILY ISSUES? WHAT CAN EMPLOYERS DO TO HELP?*

In order to have a baby, time must be provided. Maternity leave has been common for several years while paternity leave is relatively new. In the past, whether to grant a leave and what type of leave employees received were completely up to the particular company. Only recently did the United States join other industrialized countries and adopt a national family-leave policy. The Family and Medical Leave Act, which took effect in 1993, stipulates that in companies with 50 or more employees, a person can take up to three months of unpaid leave for births, adoptions, and family emergencies. Even with its limitations, the law is a milestone in recognizing the value of family.

In other ways employers make provisions which include:

- permanent part-time employment with benefits
- job sharing in which two workers split a single full-time job
- at-home work whereby an employee can complete certain tasks at home especially with a computer
- flextime that allows employees to choose within limits when they arrive and leave work

One example of flextime is for a company to specify an eight-hour workday, then leave it up to employees to decide whether they start at 8:00 A.M. or 9:00 A.M. Another is allowing employees to work four 10-hour days a week. A survey by Hewitt Associates, reported in the March 1996 issue of *Personnel Journal*, showed that 67 percent of more than 1,000 employers offer some kind of flexible scheduling arrangements, an increase of 13 percent since 1990. Flextime was most common, followed by part-time employment then job sharing.

Employers and government can cooperate in helping parents find quality child care. A good example is the Child Development Venture program in Lincoln, Nebraska. According to Lynn Murray, coordinator, the program matches employed parents with quality care providers and makes available educational programs and encouragement. "We work to empower parents," she says.

Generally, a family faces a dual challenge of high costs and limited accessibility to quality care. A promising trend is for employers to provide a child-care benefit either financially or physically. Ideally, a child-care facility is available at the place of employment or in near proximity. This relieves parental anxiety and allows parent–child interaction during the day. Even though the situation is better, much remains to be done. Calling it a "stalled revolution," the reality is that employers still demand a full day with 110 percent effort with little or no help with day care (Smolowe, 1996).

Education and a change in thinking broaden possibilities. Often, a female will say she must stay home with a child. Males typically don't feel they *have* to stay home although they might prefer to do so. If staying home is a person's free choice and it is affordable, being a full-time parent may be the best course of action–for either sex. However, career interruptions do handicap people; in actuality, such suspensions of employment partly account for the gender gap in earnings because women, far more than men, "put their careers on the back burner."

The good news is that career development doesn't have to suffer if you become a parent. Research supports that children who receive quality child care suffer little, if any, from parental employment (Hamburg, 1992). The key is to provide the most positive experience for a child while you are in the work place. Then, as in the case of Rosa, a restructuring of thought is beneficial. "By working and parenting, I'm delivering a powerful message to my children that life can be as full and satisfying as we are willing to make it. None of us is suffering; in fact, our lives are enriched." If family and child care are a priority for you, find an employer who shares these values and makes an effort to provide what you need.

A related, contrasting challenge is **addiction to work** (Conroy, 1995). Referred to as "workaholism" in the late 1960s, it is a compulsive, single-minded dedication to a job to the exclusion of almost everything else. Obviously, addiction to work and a happy family life are not compatible. Even if an addict wants to contribute to family life, he or she is too exhausted physically and mentally to do so.

What is especially difficult about this type of addiction is that society smiles on hard work, and businesses are likely to promote the addictive behaviors. The drive to excel is instilled in most human beings during childhood. Excellence is rewarded, and addictive work behaviors are reinforced. Initially, addicts may believe they are just doing what is necessary and then they find themselves dissatisfied unless they are doing more. They begin to feel panicky or depressed when they aren't working.

Prevention is the best way to escape from becoming a work addict. That doesn't mean you won't devote time and effort to your career. A person who passionately loves work, is satisfied with achievement, and works toward goals is not necessarily an addict; nor is the individual who works overtime periodically or puts forth extra energy when necessary an example of this compulsion. "The flexible time scheduling that I love about my job can also be challenging during the peak sales times when I may work 60 to 70 hours a week." says Laura Mann, a sales representative for Prentice Hall. As long as you

▲ Quality day care is beneficial to children and helps parents pursue careers.

differentiate between what is necessary at times and an addiction to work, you can design a successful career. Balance is the key. Overdoing your work and jeopardizing health or personal relationships is at-risk behavior. If your own conscious efforts to restore balance to your life don't make a difference, counseling is recommended. Amazingly, when your personal and professional lives are in harmony with each other, the quality of both is higher. Sacrificing one for the other is unnecessary.

TIME MANAGEMENT

Too much to do in too little time is a common challenge for almost everyone who pursues a career. To add to the dilemma, you may find yourself in a job where support resources are lacking. "I love my work, yet I struggle with the feeling that I can never get everything done. The work load is high, and there is a lack of technology/resources/money to do the job right. I still don't have a PC on my desk, and we just cut staff," reports Lori Hall, who is responsible for education and community programs for the American Heart Association. To compound the problem for some people, chronic procrastination will magnify the pressures. Learning to manage time effectively is one of the greatest challenges in the work place.

"I didn't (or don't) have time" has probably been said by everyone at one time or another. When I remind students that they really did have time to complete a paper or study for an exam, I can get indignant protests. There just wasn't *any* time, some say. How much time do we literally have? The answer is that each of us has 24 hours in every daylong period, which is 8,760 hours each year. In reality, we do have time; we just may not have time left over. "We always have time if we but use it aright (sic)," said the German poet and dramatist Johann Wolfgang Goethe, who died in 1832. This is still true today.

When we persist in thinking that we don't have time, it really does seem to be nonexistent. Kelly insisted that she wanted to exercise regularly, but she just didn't have time. After a suggestion from a friend, she decided to awaken 20 minutes earlier and use that time to exercise. She found time that had actually always been there. Another fallacy in thought is, "I'll do that when I have more time." The reality is that we will never have more time available than we have right now.

> DO YOU EVER SAY, "I DON'T HAVE TIME?" IF SO, CHALLENGE THE THOUGHT!

FINDING TIME

How does one find time to manage? A constructive action is to keep track of exactly how your time is being spent. After accounting for a full 24-hour period, Angela said, "I was amazed at how much time I spent on the telephone!" Use the activity in KEY STEPS (pages 305–6) to enlighten yourself.

You will probably find small segments of time that can be saved and used differently. At work can you spend a few less minutes at lunch or on break? Can you consolidate trips from one part of the building to another? Is it possible to shorten your telephone conversations? At home can you give up a television program? How much time are you actually using for pleasure? Even though enjoyment is necessary, you may be indulging yourself more than you realize. Cutting out just 30 minutes of spent time a day gains you about 183 hours within a year!

Even consciously increasing your rate of speed can save precious time. At work, Rick often walked to different parts of a large building. "I doubled my walking speed, saved several minutes each trip, and, in the process, probably did something good for my health." In other activities, without realizing it, you may be taking longer than necessary. Becoming aware of this and then deciding that you can easily increase your speed are precious time savers.

THINK OF ROUTINES IN THE WORKDAY. HOW COULD TIME BE CUT?

ELIMINATING TIME WASTERS

Do you spend time looking for misplaced items such as papers? Because these searches can add up to hours of time, we help ourselves by being more careful about where things are placed. Taking precious time to organize a desk and file cabinet and then making sure to put items away can increase the amount of time you have later. Your own personality may be responsible for wasting time. Each of the preferences identified on the Myers-Briggs Type Indicator has its own potential drawback.

E (extraversion): Because energy is drawn from human interactions, those with a strong extraverted preference may spend far too much time connecting with others. Just walking from one area to another may take twice as long as the person stops to chat along the way. Also, the individual may be easily distracted by the activities of others.

I (introversion): Living in an inner world and relishing introspective activities may result in time passing with no observable accomplishments. If a task involves interacting with large numbers of people, one with a strong introverted preference is likely to delay initiating the necessary activity.

S (sensing): The strong sensor can become immersed in details and needless facts and figures and let a great deal of time go by. Because strong sensors usually prefer to do one thing at a time, they may plod along and take longer to complete a series of tasks.

N (intuition): Endless possibilities are usually in the mind of a person with a definite intuitive preference. Having imagination and vision is an asset; however, mulling over endless ideas can become overly time-consuming.

T (thinking): Deep analysis is not usually done quickly. Strong thinkers weigh facts objectively and then apply reason to their decisions. These behaviors take time.

F (feeling): Because they want to take into consideration personal feelings and values and make everyone happy, people with strong feeling preferences may have a hard time making a decision. Time goes by while a "feeler" agonizes over any choice that might upset another person. Also, individuals with definite feeling preferences have a hard time saying "no" to the requests of others.

J (judgment): Planning and closure are fundamental to those with definite judging preferences. While these people are usually well-organized and skilled in scheduling, they may spend more time than necessary figuring out how to accomplish a task and not enough time actually doing it. Because they are mindful of time, it's possible that the judgers will fret more about its passage and create more stress for themselves.

P (perception): "Going with the flow" has its advantages; yet, a strong perceiver is typically a procrastinator. Planning is more of a challenge, and scheduling is much less likely to occur. Being laid back can mean that time passes, and when a deadline is on the horizon, these people are in trouble. Strong perceivers tend to also be unorganized and usually have difficulty locating needed items.

Being aware of potential pitfalls that stem from personality preferences allows you to use your weaker preference when that's in your best interest.

> *THINKING OF YOUR OWN PERSONALITY PREFERENCES, WHAT TIME WASTERS CAN YOU IDENTIFY IN YOURSELF?*

Another aspect of personality, perfectionism, can be a handicap. Listen to the woes of Paula.

> *It takes me forever to get started on a project because I want everything around me to be neat and in place. Then I worry about each word I write or lay-out design I'm working on. On top of that, I'm concerned about how I look so it takes me so long to get ready for work and then twice as long as others during the day to stay looking professional. Time goes by, and I feel as if I've accomplished nothing.*

A perfectionist is an expert time waster and is bound to be frustrated because no matter how hard he or she tries and regardless of the amount of time spent, perfection is impossible.

DEFEATING PROCRASTINATION

The habit of procrastinating or **chronic procrastination** is a formidable enemy of constructive time management. Putting tasks off once in a while for positive reasons is no cause for alarm and can even be in your best interest. However, if procrastination keeps you from getting what you want and increases stress, any effort to rid yourself of it is time well-spent. If you honestly want to complete a task, putting it off postpones the happiness that comes from achievement and creates undue stress during the interim.

Procrastination eventually saps motivation. Lack of accomplishment leads to a feeling of "What's the use?"

REASONS FOR PROCRASTINATING.   Identifying the reasons for chronic procrastination can be beneficial. Then you can find other ways to satisfy your needs or decide whether the reason is worth the costs.

⊚   *Is the task unpleasant or seemingly overwhelming?* Certainly if you don't want to do something or feel defeated before you begin, you are likely to postpone any action. What can be done? Breaking any activity into smaller segments can make it simpler and more palatable. You can also evaluate unpleasant tasks. For example, reorganizing a file drawer isn't usually a delightful task. Ask: (1) How important is this? (2) How bad will it be if I don't do it? (3) What are the rewards? You can then decide if it's worth your effort.

⊚   *Is procrastination used as an excuse for a poor performance?* "Well, I know if I had started on that project earlier, I could have done a great job" or "I could have made thousands of dollars more in sales if I had spent more time" could be true statements, or they might be wishful thinking. Rather than play the "if only" game, start earlier and spend the time needed to be successful and see if your thoughts are verified. If procrastination isn't the main cause of lack of success, you have learned a valuable lesson.

⊚   *Is procrastination a safeguard against lower self-esteem?* If you have a tendency to evaluate your self-worth on the basis of a single project or completion of a task and are fearful of your capabilities, you may delay rather than risk failure. Perfectionism poses a problem because those who think an imperfect performance will diminish self-esteem will probably opt to do nothing. "I didn't get it done" may be a cover-up for "I was afraid it wouldn't be good enough." Rather than measure yourself by a "narrow yardstick," restructure your thinking into realistic standards of achievement and realize that self-esteem is not dependent upon one particular performance.

⊚   *Is procrastination a way to gain sympathy?* Donna played the "poor me" game to explain why things didn't get done. "I want to be a good mother and take the kids to the zoo, but too many other things always come up. As a single mother, all the responsibilities are on my shoulders, and having to work every day doesn't leave any time for pleasure or just time to myself." Finally after numerous pleas for sympathy, a friend told her she was tired of hearing all the tales of woe. Donna then maturely took a look at herself and decided to make some changes.

Check your behavior in this regard. If you have a pattern of procrastination, do something about it *now*!

EFFECTIVELY MANAGING TIME

What else can be helpful? Several tips are offered by experts in the time management field. You can select the ones that work for you.

MAKE USE OF SELF-KNOWLEDGE.   Are you more energetic in the morning, afternoon, evening, or late at night? Unless you are getting adequate rest, this answer may not be obvious. "I'm just not a morning person. Of course my going to bed at 1:00 or 2:00 A.M. may explain that!" said Jennifer laughingly. With enough rest, you will feel more energetic at all hours yet still have more productive times of day. Tackling the most difficult tasks during this time makes sense.

If you have several tasks, which one do you undertake first? If you are energized by doing the easiest ones, that's the best choice. Conversely, you might opt to begin with the least pleasant or difficult ones in order to get them out of the way. For example, in writing this chapter I chose to tackle the subjects that would require more research or were the most challenging first. With each completed difficult portion, I knew I was getting closer to the easy part. Whatever motivates you the most is the best choice for you.

What physical environment works best? You may require a quiet atmosphere with few distractions or be more productive in the middle of noise and activity. What skills can you utilize to increase your productivity? For example, can you save time by typing a memo rather than handwriting it? What tasks are time-consuming for you? If you are slow at some tasks and speedier at others, you may be able to do some trading. For example, whenever there is a collating-of-papers job, I either ask or get someone else to do it while I, in turn, am willing to perform a task in return. Knowledge of self means understanding facets of your personality and learning to modify the way you behave if a different mode is likely to be more time effective.

USE PLANNING AND SCHEDULING TO YOUR ADVANTAGE.   You may be well-organized and an excellent planner. If so, you have probably already discovered what method works best and if it's effective, you may skim this part! If you are lacking in this area, read on.

* *Decide whether to develop a schedule that is macro (bigger picture and longer span of time) or micro (more focused over a shorter time frame).* You can also create a schedule for both. For example, you may want to look at what you want to accomplish during a month (macro) or decide to focus on one day at a time (micro). Often, people opt to maintain a weekly schedule.

* *Categorize what you want to do.* Especially helpful is to prioritize. You may have a category of "must do" activities such as meeting with your supervisor or paying a bill. Other activities could be classified as either moderately important or unnecessary, but nice. Once you have the lists, you can select appropriate days and times. Other ways to categorize are by types of activities,

goals, or subject. For example, I have an ongoing list of tasks under such headings as family, textbook, teaching, paperwork of life (insurance, taxes, and the like), and household.

⊚ *Schedule enjoyment and pleasure.* Whatever category system you use, make sure you have time for fun. In our busy lives it's common to make lists. About two thirds of students in my classes say they make lists. Most, however, fall by the wayside when they are then asked, "How many of you put pleasurable activities on your list?" A common belief is that we will enjoy ourselves when our lists are completed. My husband saved me from this when he stated a truism: "Sharon, your list will never be completed so adding pleasurable activities to the list is a 'must.'" Besides a chunk of time for pleasure, carve out smaller segments for just relaxing or what can be called "down time." Such time is usually invigorating and increases productivity levels.

⊚ *Plan efficiently.* If you take time to plan, you can often save both energy and time. Either the night before or early in the day, time spent looking ahead can reap benefits. As an owner of a contracting company, my husband has a variety of tasks each day. When he plans efficiently, he can stop at the bank on the way to an appointment with a prospective customer, then check on a crew on his way back to a supplier to order materials. Without planning he would criss-cross the city several times a day unnecessarily using up a great deal of time. Even if you don't travel, you can plan ways to conserve time. Can one meeting with two people take the place of two meetings with each one individually? Todd decided to more efficiently contact his staff of 15 by using voice mail before business hours instead of waiting and calling each one. "When we converse on the phone, it takes at least twice as much time as leaving a message does. While talking personally is a good idea, there are times when it's better to be more expedient." Thinking ahead and planning will help make you a more effective time manager.

⊚ *Be realistic and flexible.* A major problem stems from planning to accomplish too much. Having a reasonable perspective on task completion alleviates frustration and stress. If you find that you have done what you planned and have time left over, you can always do more. Realism does not have to be a deterrent! Then, no matter how well you plan and schedule, unexpected events, interruptions, and distractions will occur. Being flexible and even scheduling a percentage of available time for such occurrences are definitely recommended. Then if they don't happen, you will have that wonderful extra time.

⊚ *Learn to say "no."* Being assertive means you say "yes" and agree to take on your reasonable share, and it also means that you decline. Saying "no" may be your most challenging interpersonal task. Yet, if you continue to accept more than your share, you will find that time is not available for your own goals and tasks.

⑥   *Reward yourself.* We typically forget to give ourselves a pat on the back for completion of tasks. Instead we lament what didn't get done. Emphasizing our lack of accomplishment creates the illusion that our time management efforts didn't work. Consequently, people tend to "throw in the towel" and resort to former patterns of inefficient behavior. You can solve this dilemma by focusing on and giving yourself credit for all you did accomplish.

⑥   *Allow for inefficient periods.* In the quest to become an expert time manager, you can become overzealous and then be bitterly disappointed when you fall behind or suffer from unproductive periods. As difficult as it may be, you are better off accepting the fact that you will likely stumble at times. Whether it's related to your mood, biological clock, or stems from no apparent cause, the attitude that this, too, will pass and tomorrow will be a better day can get you through the most inefficient times.

WHEN ARE YOU MOST ENERGETIC AND EFFICIENT?

People who are effective time managers avoid much of the predictable job stress. In order to both succeed and enjoy the process, learning and using time management methods that work for you are essential during all stages of your career.

BURNOUT

Ron, a computer analyst, groaned as the alarm clock sounded. He had slept poorly and had awakened with a throbbing in his head that he was sure would worsen as the day progressed. He was still recovering from a cold that had plagued him for weeks. He barely talked to his wife before she left for work, and he became increasingly depressed as he drove through the city to his office. He thought about the new program he was to develop and how he had postponed working on it. "I just can't concentrate," he said aloud. "I don't seem to have the ability I once had." Later at work, he responded abruptly to a co-worker's question and snapped at one of the secretaries. "What's wrong with me?" he asked himself.

Ron is the victim of **burnout**—a state of mental, emotional, social, and physical exhaustion characterized by a lack of interest and enthusiasm for one's job. Burnout occurs when work loses its meaning, and the costs outweigh the rewards. It is most likely to be experienced by people who need and want to feel useful and important (Leatz and Stolar, 1993).

An imbalance between investment in a job and the outcomes or rewards will contribute to burnout. Julio related a common tale: "I put in long hours and work as hard as I can, and it never seems to be enough. I don't get recognition except with a paycheck, and I'm not experiencing personal satisfaction right now either." Other contributors, identified in a study of health-care providers, were inadequate communication among staff and administration; unrealistic expectations from administration, patients, and other staff members;

and conflicts with and lack of support from co-workers (Riordan and Saltzer, 1992). In a study of teachers, burnout was related to emotional exhaustion and lack of personal accomplishment (Nagy and Nagy, 1992).

SYMPTOMS AND EFFECTS OF BURNOUT

Signs of burnout can include having inflexible points of view, being indecisive, and harboring a negative, defeatist attitude. People who are suffering from burnout begin to doubt their abilities and are quick to find fault in others. Emotionally, a burnout victim can feel depressed, helpless, hopeless, and frustrated; the physical effects include fatigue and lack of energy (Leatz and Stolar, 1993). Social exchanges are marked by irritability and hostility, or they may be almost nonexistent as burnout victims tend to isolate themselves.

An employee with burnout may be chronically late or miss work frequently, withdraw from others, and accomplish little. *Sluggish* is a good word to describe burnout victims like Ron. A common symptom is a general malaise, a feeling of tedium that doesn't have one apparent cause (Leatz and Stolar, 1993). The victim typically doesn't understand what is happening, and this leads to extreme frustration with oneself, others, and the work place itself. Then the burnout becomes more extreme.

Adverse effects reach beyond the work place. White-collar husbands under increased distress at work were less likely to respond with humor, enthusiasm, or positiveness to wives or to try to bring humor into their lives. Both partners agreed that conversations were less intimate and enjoyable (Krokoff, 1991). Because burnout is dreadful, knowing how to prevent or remedy it is crucial.

> *HAVE YOU EVER SUFFERED FROM BURNOUT? DID YOU KNOW WHAT IT WAS?*

OVERCOMING BURNOUT

Burnout can be prevented by employing stress-management techniques that are covered later in this chapter. Sometimes, burnout occurs despite one's best efforts to deal with stressors. Then it's best to recognize that you have symptoms of burnout, know that you can reverse your condition, and take steps to counteract it. A questionnaire in KEY STEPS (page 307) can be useful. By the way, student burnout is also possible!

Seeing burnout as surmountable may be difficult while you are experiencing it. During a burnout period, lowering your expectations is advisable because the reality is that you won't accomplish as much as you usually do. If poor time management is involved, take steps to improve in this regard. Use positive self-talk, cognitive restructuring, and self-reward for achievement. What you think influences how you feel and act. Realistically, burnout isn't a permanent condition. A positive thought is: "Just because I'm not enthusiastic about my career right now doesn't mean this is the way it will always be."

Social support from co-workers and supervisors can be quite beneficial in lessening job-related tension. A study showed that communication, increased participation in decision making, and social support were related to reducing burnout (Miller et al., 1990). Being frank with those around you is necessary as your behavior could easily be misinterpreted. In order to receive support, you may need to explain burnout and ask for help. As with most problems, it helps to realize that you are not alone in your thoughts and feelings. Because burnout is so common, you will probably discover that others also are experiencing or have experienced it. Using an Employee Assistance Program (EAP), if available, is an excellent idea.

Advocates of "mental health days" believe that staying away from work a day or so, when appropriate, is a way of preventing or overcoming burnout. Companies and organizations that realize the costs of employee stress have instituted types of personal leave for purposes such as this. If you have an opportunity to take a day or two off, consider this a wise career investment. Control over burnout is up to you.

STRESS

Underlying all challenges at work and responsible for intensifying any hardships is **stress** which, according to Hans Selye (1974), the "father of stress research," is the nonspecific response of the body to any demand made upon it. When you perceive any demand to adjust, you experience stress. Stress has been studied for years, and one fact is clear: Stress cannot be avoided. **Stressors,** the conditions that cause stress, are numerous and never ending. Instead of life being a bowl of cherries, one could say that life is a bowl of stressors!

Stress from your personal life almost always affects work performance. What is called **home-to-work stress contagion** means that stressors at home

▲ An understanding co-worker can help cope with burnout.

are typically brought into the work place. A recent study by the World Health Organization showed that more than two out of three workers consider stress to be their primary health concern and believe that work-related stress is a direct cause of their health-related problems (Seaward, 1995). Knowing that both one's personal and professional lives are fraught with stress, common interview questions are "How well do you handle stress and pressure?" and "How do you cope with stress?" This section will explore effects, sources, and, most importantly, coping strategies.

EFFECTS OF STRESS

Stress that is either not handled or mishandled is related to numerous physical and psychological problems. For years it has been obvious that stress may be the greatest single contributor to illness in the industrialized world (Eliot and Breo, 1984). Even though stress doesn't *cause* a disease, it is a major contributor to serious conditions such as cardiovascular problems; cancer, lung and stomach ailments; and diabetes. It aggravates any health problem. Chronic stress may lead to illnesses like heart disease (Moyers, 1993). A Swedish study contained an alarming statistic: Workers with serious work-related problems and job stress were five times as likely to develop colon cancer (*Time*, 1993). Conditions such as headaches, digestive disturbances, and poor sexual performance can have a stress link. How can stress be involved in such diverse physical conditions? Under stress, the heart, lungs, and nervous system plus other bodily functions work harder. Most importantly, stress appears to weaken immune systems so we are susceptible to all health problems (Morris, 1993; Moyers, 1993).

The other three areas of self can also suffer. Mismanaged stress contributes to relationship or social problems, emotional distress, and severe mental challenges. Stress leads to irritability, and a "stressed-out" person easily becomes a difficult person. Family life suffers as well. Violence is more likely when high levels of stress are present. Stress is directly related to anxiety, frustration, anger, depression, and lack of concentration and clear thinking.

In the work environment stress takes a heavy toll. Lost productivity, absenteeism, and higher company medical expenses typically have a stress connection. Current estimates indicate that job stress costs employers more than $200 billion per year in absenteeism, tardiness, burnout, lower productivity, high turnover, workers' compensation, and rising health-care premiums (Seaward, 1995).

HEALTHY STRESS

Even with its potentially high costs, stress is not always negative. A certain amount of stress can be motivating and healthful. Equate stress to the strings on a violin. If they are stretched tightly, the tone of the violin is sharp; too loose and the sound is flat and lifeless. Either way beautiful music is an impossibility. The key is to adjust the strings to a desirable degree of tightness. Similarly, individuals can benefit from knowing how much and what type of stress is good for them. Each person is different. For example, you may be one who feels quite relaxed sitting in a boat all day fishing. Another person would be bored and actually experience stress engaging in the same activity. Stress that is good for you is called **eustress**. One's attitude about an experience is what determines whether the stress is a eustress or not (Selye, 1978). All human beings need some stress in order to flourish. "Stress is the spice of life. Who would enjoy a life of no runs, no hits, no errors?" wrote Hans Selye (1974) in one of the first books about stress.

How do you know when your level of stress is unhealthy? There will be clues. Are you experiencing frequent headaches, stomach distress, minor aches and pains, muscle tension, or fatigue for no apparent reason? Do you feel uneasy, tense, or irritable? Are you having difficulty sleeping or concentrating? Even apathy may be a sign. Your body will send signals. Learning about stress, what is an optimal level for you, and how to handle it in a positive way is a "must" in terms of a healthy self and career success.

SOURCES OF STRESS

Most of us have long lists of stressors. Some deny that they have stress; this means they are either unaware of what stress actually is or they try to ignore its existence.

> *WHAT ARE THE STRESSORS IN YOUR LIFE?*

Stress has a myriad of sources which researchers have uncovered. One of the earliest studies (Holmes and Rahe, 1967) identified major changes and their ranking. The top stressful events then were (1) death of spouse, (2) divorce, (3) marital separation, (4) jail term, and (5) death of close family member. When students are asked how they might avoid the top three, they quickly see that not getting married would seem to do it! Among the top 20 of the life event stressors specifically related to career were:

- being fired at work (#8)
- retirement (#10)
- business readjustment (#15)
- change to a different line of work (#18)

Others were outstanding personal achievement, trouble with one's boss, and change in work hours or conditions.

> *THE LIFE-CHANGE STUDY WAS PUBLISHED IN 1967. CAN YOU THINK OF OTHER CAREER-RELATED STRESSORS TODAY?*

A current work stressor is the high demand placed on most employees. Even though a person has always been expected to perform, the parameters were generally set, and an eight-hour manageable day was the norm. According to Doc Chaves, assistant vice president of Ameritas Life Insurance Corp., "Today we're all trying to do more with less which puts more work on everyone." And from Jody Horwitz, director of human resources, Turner

Broadcasting System, Inc., Los Angeles: "In our multi-task oriented and fast-paced environment, a person is often asked to go beyond traditional, narrowly defined job duties and cross over into many different areas. One individual can have a tremendously large range of responsibility."

How does one cope with the inordinate amount of pressure characteristic of most positions? Obviously, the time management suggestions presented earlier and the stress coping tips that will be covered are quite helpful. Other ideas came from interviews with employers and business owners.

Doc Chaves, Ameritas Life Insurance Corp.:

"If you feel overwhelmed, first do an honest self-assessment and try to relieve the load. Then check with peers. Are they, too, feeling too much pressure? If several of you are experiencing high stress levels, a good idea is to discuss this with your supervisor."

Jeanne Baer, Creative Training Solutions:

"Take a hard look at what you want out of life, keeping in mind that it's important to take care of your physical and mental health. Individuals must set some limits and realize that too much pressure damages quality. Communicate your concerns to someone who can change the situation."

In the early stages of any job, overwhelming feelings of confusion and frustration are to be expected. After a reasonable time, however, what is expected of you and what is realistic will need to be in equilibrium if you are going to experience career success. Expressing what is realistic is necessary.

A potent stressor in today's work world comes from concerns about or the actuality of being let go as companies readjust themselves. Today's employee has no guarantee of absolute stability. Unlike yesteryear when a person believed that unless he or she faltered, the job was secure, downsizing can affect anybody at any stage of career. "I knew it was happening to others. After giving 22 years to this company, I just never thought it would be me," said Robert. Because this type of termination is so common, help is now provided by various groups. Experience Unlimited is a support group for unemployed and underemployed professionals that is offered through public employment services. Said one participant:

Being let go is a shock to the system. Where do you go? What do you do? When you're out of a job, you feel lost and hurt. I don't know what I would have done without Experience Unlimited and its encouragement and helpfulness.

Cathleen Plager works through Job Service of Nebraska to coordinate a group that emphasizes education, networking, and support. She advises any professional in transition to check with the government Job Service in your geographic area to see if such a support group exists. And if it doesn't, you can start one!

Rather than live in fear of being let go, you are advised to do your job as well as possible, update yourself continuously, and have some contingency plans. Most people find that it's not the end of the world to lose a job and, once the initial shock is over, are in a position to profit from the experience.

An interesting aspect of life changes is that both negative and positive events are stressful. The common ingredient is the prompting of some type of coping or adaptive behavior. When too many events happen in succession, the strain may produce unhealthy effects. During your career life, you are bound to have rewarding experiences as well as some setbacks. Knowing that either type will increase your stress level can encourage you to cope effectively.

Another study (Lazarus, 1981) dealt with minor irritants, or the hassles of everyday life. Viewed as ongoing stressors, these are often left unattended because they occur so often and are seemingly routine. Jan was annoyed by a tiny squeak every day as she drove to work. She kept telling herself that some day she would get it fixed. That some day never seemed to come until she realized that her irritation at work and at home might be related to the annoyance she experienced each day. Just one day at work can be filled with such stressors. The little annoyances and frustrations that continually plague us may add up to more stress than life's major events have (Lazarus, 1981).

> *WHAT EVERYDAY HASSLES BOTHER YOU? WHAT ARE YOU DOING ABOUT THEM? IF YOU ARE DOING "NOTHING," THE ACCUMULATION OF STRESS MAY BE HARMFUL.*

Stressors are either external or internal. **External stressors** are those that come from outside of self. Other people, events beyond your control, and the environment deliver daily doses of stress. Can you name some? **Internal stressors** are those we create. Irrational thoughts, unrealistic expectations, inability to express emotions, and unnecessary worry fall into this category. When thinking about stress at work, it's helpful to divide the stressors into these two categories. Generally, you have little or no control over the external ones and almost total control over the self-created ones. When you feel the tension mounting, ask yourself:

- Are my thoughts rational? Am I thinking logically?
- How realistic are my expectations about myself, about others, and about my work?
- Am I constructively expressing what I feel? Do I have positive outlets for frustration and anger? Am I dealing adequately with my emotions?
- Am I a "worry-wart?" Do I fret and worry needlessly?

Do you see how you could be creating more stress for yourself? Focus on the areas that are especially troublesome and change your behaviors.

Worry, one of the internal stressors, is quite common. A study showed that college students worried during much of each day. Academic success was the most common reason with social relationships, health, finances, and career also mentioned (Vasey and Borkovec, 1992). **Worry** is a feeling of unease or tension. It is typically needless and involves fretting. People have a hard time differentiating between worries and concerns. The difference lies in your ability to do something about potential disasters. Concern leads to action while worry arises from feelings of powerlessness. People who worry usually do not act; they simply fret and multiply the stress they already have.

Certain myths perpetuate one's tendency to worry (Goulding and Goulding, 1989).

- Worrying keeps your worries from coming true.

- Other people make you worry.

- Events make you worry.

- If you love or care, you worry.

- If you are human, you worry.

Concern about people and events is normal, and some situations bring about tension. The key is to not allow worry to take over. Worriers manufacture and magnify stress in their lives. If worrying is one of your traits, make a concerted effort to eliminate as much of it as possible.

Sorting out real concerns from the mass of imaginative and insignificant worries is a worthy activity. Ninety percent of what we worry about never happens (Buscaglia, 1992). Two practical books, *Not to Worry!* (Goulding and Goulding, 1989) and *Why Women Worry and How to Stop* (Handly and Handly, 1990) describe methods that can free you from unnecessary anxiety and reduce the impact of this internal stressor. Some quick tips are:

- Change "what if" to "so what if." For example, change a thought of, "Oh, what if I don't get this job?" to "So what if I don't get this job?" This isn't intended to promote a don't-care attitude but to allow you to put things in proper perspective.

- Set aside 30 minutes to really worry and refuse to do so at other times.

- Keep a worry journal so that the thoughts are put on paper. Usually, you will then reduce the amount of time you dwell on the issue.

- Definitely *act* on your worry if possible.

- Use a thought-stopping technique. Say to yourself firmly, "Quit (or stop) thinking this way!"

Remember that worry will not prevent problems; instead, it robs the present of potential joy.

Other internal stressors come from overloading yourself, having unrealistic goals, taking on too much, negative self-talk, neglecting your physical health, and even living a boring life. The list goes on and on. An awareness of the sources can enable you to analyze, possibly decrease the numbers, and reduce the impact of stressors.

Taking Charge of Stress

Perhaps, you are one of the fortunate people who already has what is called **psychological hardiness** (Kobasa, 1979). In a classic study of middle- and upper-level executives who had experienced high degrees of stressful life events, the differences between those who became ill and those who did not were noted. Those who stayed well shared the following personality characteristics of hardiness.

- a strong commitment to self and various areas of life

- a sense of meaningfulness or purpose

- the attitude that change is challenging and vigorous

- an internal locus of control

Having an internal locus of control is extremely beneficial for many reasons, including sound physical health. David Felten, M.D., Ph.D., has identified lack of control in any situation as a factor in a diminished immune system (Moyers, 1993). If the descriptors of hardiness don't sound like you, consider what you can do to become hardier!

When faced with a stressor, you can choose to deal with the problem or issue, negotiate or compromise to resolve conflict, or stay away from stressful people and situations. Regardless of whether a stressor is apparent, it's a good idea to employ a regular stress-management routine which protects you from the effects of daily stressors. Several practical stress-reducing suggestions and elaborations follow. The challenge is to put them into regular practice.

- Whenever possible, reduce or wisely schedule major life events. For example, don't begin college, start a job, move, get married, quit college, and get divorced in the same year!

- Prioritize hassles in your life. Take action to eliminate or reduce the most annoying ones. If a messy desk is bothering you, take the time to clean it. Carry extra keys in case you lock one inside the car or house.

- Challenge worrisome or anxiety-provoking thoughts. Don't be afraid to seek information. When faced with physical pain or other symptoms, don't ignore it if you have the slightest worry. Ask questions so that you feel in control. Act when you feel concerned rather than succumb to worrying.

- Change stress-producing thoughts. Much unnecessary stress is manufactured by the ideas we have. Try asking, "What's the worst thing that can happen here?" Many times the worst isn't so awful. Or, if you think that saying "no" isn't a nice thing to do, change your thinking to, "Nice has nothing to do with this."

- Develop a decision-making process and use your thinking preference. Don't be hasty, yet remember that "staying on the fence too long" is stressful.

- If you feel frustrated or worried, ask yourself what you can do about it, then either act or let go of the feeling. Be realistic about what is possible.

- Say "no" and stick with it if you truly don't want to do something. Pent-up resentment is stressful.

- Learn to manage your time constructively and to schedule well enough so you aren't rushing through life. Make time for relaxing, pleasurable activities. If you are a person who is always in a hurry or a workaholic, attempt to change. Add variety to your daily routine. Slow down and "smell some roses."

- Escape from stressors periodically. Physical and mental changes of scene offer temporary respite.

- Express your feelings and begin to communicate and share more with others. Find a reliable support system. Write in a journal or diary. Studies confirm the value of expressing stressful thoughts to others or getting them down on paper (Pennebaker, 1991). Have a good relieving cry. Find someone to hug and a pet to love.

- Develop a healthy degree of self-efficacy and an internal locus of control.

- Schedule pleasurable activities and engage in them often. Laugh and enjoy life. Engage in an enjoyable hobby or diversion. Don't take most things so seriously.

- Breathe deeply and frequently into the diaphragm. Slow, regular, and deep breaths, characteristic of abdominal breathing, are associated with physical calm (Eliot and Breo, 1984). See instructions in KEY STEPS (page 308).

- Keep your body well rested, nourished with nutritious food and water, and in the best possible health.

- Raise your self-esteem level. Low self-esteem affects reactions to stress.

- Engage in a type of regular exercise. Select something you enjoy and stick with it or try something new.

- Use a deep-relaxation technique and learn biofeedback.

- Develop or utilize more often a sense of humor. If you try, you can find something humorous in most situations.

Along with deep breathing, the last three are among my favorite methods. Exercise has become a popular antidote for stress. Exercise offers other stress-reducing benefits such as relief of depression; reduction in the risk of heart disease and infection; an increase in the level of high-density lipoprotein (HDL), or "good" cholesterol; possible prevention of cancer; improvement in quality of sleep; and slowing of the aging process (Koontz, 1988). Another is a more pleasing appearance. When asked to identify the everyday hassles in life, middle-aged people listed weight as their main concern (Lazarus, 1981). Doesn't it seem likely that exercise would do much to alleviate this problem, thus reducing stress?

Even if you don't engage in a full-scale aerobic exercise program, try walking, an activity that has earned much praise for its stress-reducing benefits. A longitudinal study of nearly 17,000 Harvard University alumni showed that stress symptoms decreased among subjects who were physically active. In addition, risk of death among male participants who walked nine or more miles a week was 21 percent lower than for those who walked less than three miles (Elmer-DeWitt, 1986). Enthusiastic walkers talk as much about the relaxation benefits as they do the physical benefits. Nothing keeps most people from becoming more physically active except their own thoughts. You have the power to change yours. Take those extra 10 minutes over a lunch period and *WALK*. A medical examination before you begin any strenuous program is suggested. If reduction in stress and other listed benefits are not motivational enough, consider that you can feel better, have more energy, and save money on medical bills. The time spent exercising could be the wisest investment you'll ever make.

"Give me an hour of your time because what I want to show you could make all the difference in the world," said Andrea Sime, a biofeedback and stress-management specialist and a friend. She suggested this after learning that I was facing surgery for removal of what would, in all probability, be a cancerous eye tumor. I gave her the hour, and I am tremendously grateful to her for introducing me to biofeedback and deep-relaxation techniques and teaching me that I can change my physiological reactions to stress.

Progressive relaxation is one method of **deep relaxation**, a profoundly restful condition in which one feels physically relaxed, somewhat detached from the immediate environment, and usually to some extent even from body sensations. Deep relaxation allows the body to become balanced, or homeostatic, and, thus, work as it is intended to. This may explain why relaxation is the most powerful proven behavioral therapy to reduce high blood pressure without drugs (Eliot and Breo, 1984).

In addition to progressive relaxation and meditation, methods that produce similar results are self-hypnosis, yoga, guided imagery, and autogenic training. Patience is beneficial. Relaxation and meditation are especially difficult for Americans. The typical diet of advertising, noise, media stimulation, and haste makes it hard to endure even a few minutes of inactivity and quiet (Siegel, 1986). Using a relaxation technique for only about 15 to 20 minutes on a regular basis can produce astonishing results. Most people report feeling more energetic, exuberant, optimistic, cheerful, and congenial. The effects of stress on the body are remarkably diminished.

A sense of humor can change a potentially stress-damaging experience into a funny incident. Bob Dinkel, a business owner, told of driving on a highway behind Ken, one of his employees, frantically trying to get his attention to retrieve another employee's car keys left in Ken's truck. "I'm sure the other drivers on the road wondered about me while Ken remained totally oblivious to my honking and light flashing," he said as he demonstrated his actions. Bob's sense of humor helped him through a stressful experience. A study showed that people who express more positive humor at work have higher levels of mental health, job satisfaction and involvement, and are less likely to want to quit. They are also less anxious and less depressed (Abramis, 1992). In almost every stressful situation, you can find a measure of humor if you try. Perceiving events in a more humorous light and then laughing about yourself in the situation can significantly alleviate the harmful effects of stress.

Stress will be present in your life. What you do with it is up to you. Several earlier recommendations in this book—having a positive attitude, taking responsibility for self, developing an internal locus of control, expressing emotions constructively, building self-esteem and self-efficacy, and changing irrational, negative thoughts—will lead to stress reduction. Additionally, learning all you can about stress and practicing the active coping techniques that have been outlined will have a major impact on your career success. Use KEY STEPS (page 308).

No matter what challenge you face during your career, you can either take action or find coping strategies. Within many companies is an Employee Assistance Program (EAP) that can help you with any type of problem. Designed to help employees with life's "rough spots" whether they occur on or off the job, experienced clinical professionals are available. Having the courage to face a challenge and, when necessary, to seek help are characteristics of a well-adjusted person.

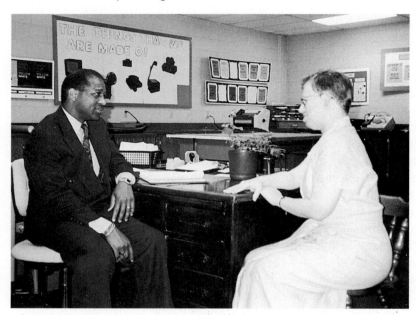

▲ An empathetic supervisor is open to concerns about stress.

KEY POINTS

- Discrimination in the work place still exists. Recognizing its sources and learning how to handle any actual instances provide protection from its negative effects.

- A challenge for many is sexual harassment. Because of public awareness, guidelines are in place to help any victim.

- Balancing work and family continues to be a problem. Employers need to be encouraged to do all that is possible to help employees balance professional and family lives.

- Rather than have a personal life, some people are addicted to work. Recently identified as a challenge, a work addict is wise to assume more balance in life.

- Time management is a matter of understanding the reality of time, finding time, identifying time wasters, and defeating chronic procrastination. Understanding the costs and causes of procrastination helps to overcome the habit.

- Making use of self-knowledge, moving faster, and planning and scheduling efficiently are key elements of controlling your time and accomplishing your goals.

- Burnout, a state of emotional, mental, social, and physical exhaustion, is quite likely at some time. You can overcome it by recognizing the symptoms, possible causes and effects, and by employing effective techniques to combat it.

- Stress is present in everyone's life. Even though a certain amount and type of stress, known as eustress, is beneficial, a major challenge is too much stress.

- Because too much stress can take its toll on physical and mental health, everyone can benefit from knowing how to cope with it. Several strategies are effective.

- An Employee Assistance Program, offered by many employers, can help employees face personal and professional problems.

RECOMMENDED READING

Benson, H. (1975). *The relaxation response.* New York: Avon.

Bravo, E. and Cassedy, E. (1992). *The 9 to 5 guide to combating sexual harassment* New York: John Wiley.

Burka, J. B. and Yuen, L. M. (1983). *Procrastination: Why you do it, what to do about it.* Reading, MA: Addison-Wesley.

Goulding, M. M. and Goulding, R. L. (1989). *Not to worry.* New York: William Morrow.

Handly, J. and Handly, R. W. (with Neff, P.) (1990). *Why women worry and how to stop.* New York: Fawcett Crest.

Lakein, A. (1989). *How to get control of your time and your life*. New York: NAL/Dutton.

Leatz, C. A. and Stollar, M. W. (1993). *Career success/personal success: How to stay healthy in a high-stress environment*. New York: McGraw-Hill.

NiCarthy, G., Gottlieb, N., and Coffman, S. (1993). *You don't have to take it! A woman's guide to confronting emotional abuse at work*. Seattle: Seal Press.

Potter, B. (1993). *Beating job burnout: How to transform work pressure into productivity*. Berkeley, CA: Ronin Publishing.

References

Abramis, D. J. (1992, August). Humor in healthy organizations. *HR Magazine*, 72–74.

Barlow, L. E. (1994). *The job-seekers bible*. Lakeside, CA: Vocational and Career Asessment Publishing Division.

Baron, J. K. (1996). Life/career transitions...networking for success. *America Online Career Center*.

Beatty, R. H. (1995). *The résumé kit*. New York: John Wiley.

Benson, H. (1987). *Your maximum mind*. New York: Random House.

Bittel, L. R. (1984). *Leadership: The key to management success*. New York: Franklin Watts.

Bloomfield, H. H. (with Felder, L.) (1985). *Making peace with yourself*. New York: Ballantine Books.

Bolles, R. N. (1996). *What color is your parachute?* Berkeley, CA: Ten Speed Press.

Bortnick, S. M. and Ports, M. H. (1991, December). Job search methods and results: Tracking the unemployed. *Monthly Labor Review, 115*, 29–35.

Bramson, R. M. (1988). *Coping with difficult people*. Garden City, NY: Anchor Press/Doubleday.

Bramson, R. M. (1992). *Coping with difficult bosses*. New York: Carol Publishing Group.

Branden, N. (1983). *Honoring the self*. Los Angeles: Tarcher.

Branden, N. (1992). *The power of self-esteem*. Deerfield Beach, FL: Health Communications.

Braus, P. (1992, August). What workers want. *American Demographics*, 30–31, 34–37.

Bravo, E. and Cassedy, E. (1992). *The 9 to 5 guide to combating sexual harassment*. New York: John Wiley.

Brinkerhoff, J. R. (1994, March 15). The biggest obstacles to making things happen. *Bottom Line Personnel*, 9–10.

Buscaglia, L. (1992). *Born for love: Reflections on loving*. Thorofare, NJ: Slack, Inc.

Butler, P. E. (1992). *Self-assertion for women*. New York: HarperCollins.

Canfield, J. and Siccone, F. (1993). *101 ways to develop student self-esteem and responsibility*. Boston: Allyn and Bacon.

Capell, P. (1995, August). Nerds get best jobs—tough guys finish last. *American Demographics*, 13–14.

Career Opportunities News (1995, October). Jobs are tight: What should you do? Garrett Park, MD: Garrett Park Press.

Carl, H. (1980, December). Nonverbal communication during the employment interview. *ABCA Bulletin*, 14–18.

Carter, C. M. (1993, March 24–27). *Are you suited for the job?* Paper presented at the Annual Meeting of the Southeastern Psychological Association, Atlanta, GA.

Chapman, E. N. (1993). *Your attitude is showing*. Chicago: Science Research Associates.

Conroy, R. (1995, May). Addiction to work proves harmful. *The Menninger Letter*, 5,7.

Cormack R. W. (1992). The attitude factor in *Ready, aim, hire*. ed. Canning, M. B. Oak Brook, IL: PerSysCo Publishing.

Cousins, N. (1991). *The celebration of life*. New York: Bantam Books.

Covey, S. R. (1989). *The 7 habits of highly effective people*. New York: Simon & Schuster.

Derr, C. B. (1986). *Managing the new careerists: The diverse career success orientations of today's workers*. San Francisco: Jossey-Bass.

Diamond, D. and Golin, M. (1991, June). Dare to love your job. *Men's Health*, 6, 84–86.

Donaldson, L. and Scannell. E. E. (1986). *Human resource development: The new trainer's guide*. Reading, MA: Addison-Wesley.

The Economist. (1992, May 30). Ashes in their mouths. 323 (7761), 86–87.

Eliot, R. S. and Breo, D. L. (1984). *Is it worth dying for?* New York: Bantam Books.

Elmer-Dewitt, P. (1986, March 17). Extra years for extra effort. *Time*, 66.

Enright, R. D., Santos, M. J. D., and Al-Mabuk, R. (1989, March). The adolescent as forgiver. *Journal of Adolescence*, 12, 95–110.

Epes, B. (1994, September–October). How John Alden designed its employee-driven wellness program. *Compensation and Benefits Review*, 28–34.

Feagin, J. R. and Feagin, C. B. (1996). *Racial and ethnic relations*. Upper Saddle River, NJ: Prentice Hall.

Fisher, C. S., Jackson, R. M., Stueve, C. A., Gerson, K., Jones, L. M., and Baldassare, M. (1977). *Networks and places: Social relations in the urban setting*. New York: Free Press.

Fitzgerald, L. F. (1992). *Sexual harassment in higher education: Concepts and issues*. Washington, DC: National Education Association.

Foschi, M., Sigerson, K., and Lembesis, M. (1995). Assessing job applicants: The relative effects of gender, academic record, and decision type. *Small Group Research*, 26(3), 328–352.

Gallois, C., Callan, V. J., and McKenzie Palmer, J. (1992). The influence of applicant communication style and interviewer characteristics on hiring decisions. *Journal of Applied Social Psychology, 22*(13), 1041–1060.

Gardner, H. (1983). *Frames of mind: The theory of multiple intelligences*. New York: Basic Books.

Gest, E. (1995, August 20). The jobs of the past, the jobs of the future. *Los Angeles Times Magazine*, 26–27.

Gibbs, N. (1995, October 2). The EQ factor. *Time*, 61–68.

Gilbert, J. (1994, March). The best jobs in America. *Money*, 70–73.

Giobbe, D. (1995, August 5). Study: Classified ads remain most popular source for finding a job. *Editor & Publisher, the Fourth Estate*, 20.

Glasser, W. (1984). *Control theory: A new explanation of how we control our lives*. New York: Harper & Row.

Goffman, E. (1959). *Presentation of self in everyday life*. New York: Anchor Books.

Goleman, D. (1995). *Emotional intelligence*. New York: Bantam Books.

Gonyea, J. C. (1995). *The on-line job search companion*. New York: McGraw-Hill.

Gonyea, W. M. (1996). Keyword résumés—your new hi-tech way to get a job. *America Online Career Center*.

Goulding, M. M. and Goulding, R. L. (1989). *Not to worry!* New York: William Morrow.

Greene, S. D. and Martel, M. C. L. (1992). *The job hunter's guidebook*. Boston: Houghton Mifflin.

Greenwald, J. (1997, January 20). Where the jobs are. *Time*, 54–61.

Hall, E. T. (1969). *The hidden dimension*. New York: Anchor Press/Doubleday.

Hamburg, D. A. (1992). *Today's children: Creating a future for a generation in crisis*. New York: Time Books.

Handly, J. and Handly, R. W. (with Neff, P.) (1990). *Why women worry and how to stop*. New York: Fawcett Crest.

Hanna, S. L. (1995). *Person to person: Positive relationships don't just happen*. Englewood Cliffs, NJ: Prentice Hall.

Hatchett, D. (1994, October). Corporate America and affirmative action: The struggle continues. *Crisis*, 8–9.

Hill, L. A. (1994). Managing your career (Note 9-494-082). Boston: Harvard Business School Publishing.

Hirsch, S. and Kummerow, J. (1989). *Life types*. New York: Warner Communications.

Holland, J. L. (1985). *Making vocational choices*. Englewood Cliffs, NJ: Prentice Hall.

Holmes, T. H. and Rahe, R. H. (1967). The social readjustment rating scale. *Journal of Psychosomatic Research, 11*, 213–18.

Holton, E. (1996). The critical first year on the job. *Planning Job Choices: 1996*, 67–70.

Ianzito, C. (1995, July–August). Gut reaction (bias against overweight job applicants). *Psychology Today*, 20.

Jackson, T. (1981). *The perfect résumé*. New York: Doubleday.

Jackson, T. (1992). *Not just another job*. New York: Time Books.

Jackson, T. (1993). *Guerilla tactics in the job market*. Toronto: Bantam Books.

Jeffries, W. C. (1991). *True to type*. Norfolk, VA: Hampton Roads Publishing.

Jung, C. G. (1923). *Psychological types*. New York: Harcourt Brace.

Jung, C. G. (1968). *Analytical psychology: Its theory and practice*. New York: Vintage Books.

Kalb, L. and Hugick, L. (1990, September–October). The society: The American worker: How we feel about our jobs. *Public Perspective*, 21–22.

Keating, C. J. (1984). *Dealing with difficult people.* Ramsey, NJ: Paulist Press.

Keirsey, D. and Bates, M. (1984). *Please understand me.* Del Mar, CA: Prometheus Nemesis.

Kight, L. K. (1994). *Getting the lowdown on employers and a leg up on the job market.* Berkeley, CA: Ten Speed Press.

Kobasa, S. C. (1979). Stressful live events, personality, and health: An inquiry into hardiness. *Journal of Personality and Social Psychology, 37*(1), 1–11.

Koontz, K. (1988, July). Eight reasons why you should exercise. *McCall's,* 89.

Kovach, K. (1980, Spring). Why motivational theories don't work. *S.A.M. Advanced Management Journal,* 46.

Kroeger, O. and Thuesen, J. M. (1992). *Type talk at work.* New York: Delacorte Press.

Krokoff, L. J. (1991). Job distress is no laughing matter on marriage, or is it? *Journal of Social and Personal Relationships,* 5–25.

Kurtz, T. (1991, August). Dynamic listening: Unlocking your communication potential. *Public Management 73,* 26–28.

Latas, M. (1993). *Job search secrets.* St. Louis: Job Search Publishers.

Lazarus, R. S. (1981, June). Little hassles can be hazardous to your health. *Psychology Today,* 58–62.

Leatz, C. A. and Stolar, M. W. (1993). *Career success/personal stress: How to stay healthy in a high-stress environment.* New York: McGraw-Hill.

Lewis, R. (1996a, January). Jobs 2000. *AARP Bulletin,* 6–9.

Lewis, R. (1996b, June). Career changers find road to success marked by perils. *AARP Bulletin,* 8–11.

Lincoln Journal Star (1996, March 4). Conference to explore work, leisure, 1A.

Lindgren, A. (1996, July 14). Re-evaluate position before change. *Omaha World Herald,* 1G.

Lindsey, L. L. (1997). *Gender roles: A sociological perspective.* Upper Saddle River, NJ: Prentice Hall.

Lock, R. D. (1992). *Job search.* Pacific Grove, CA: Brooks/Cole.

Macionis, J. J. (1996). *Society: The basics.* Upper Saddle River, NJ: Prentice Hall.

Mackay, H. (1993). *Sharkproof.* New York: HarperCollins.

Madry, B. (1988, September–October). *Getting jobs,* 2(3). Bronx, NY: MPC Educational Publishers.

Manager's Legal Bulletin. (1993, June 2). Hands-on hiring tips for strong interviews. Ramsey, NJ: Alexander Hamilton Institute.

Marlowe, C. M., Schneider, S. L., and Nelson, C. E. (1996). Gender and attractiveness biases in hiring decisions: Are more experienced managers less biased? *Journal of Applied Psychology, 81*(1), 11–21.

Maslow, A. (1968). *Toward a psychology of being.* New York: D. Van Nostrand.

McKay, M. and Fanning, P. (1987). *Self-esteem.* Oakland, CA: New Harbinger.

Mehrabian, A. (1968, September). Communication without words. *Psychology Today,* 53–55.

Mehrabian, A. (1981). *Silent messages.* Belmont, CA: Wadsworth.

The Menninger Letter. (1994, July). Trust in supervisors fueled by communication, 1.

Messmer, M. (1996, March). Steer clear of the skills gap. *Personnel Journal,* 44–49.

Miller, K. I., Ellis, B. H., Zook, E. G., and Lyles, J. S. (1990, June). An integrated model of communication, stress, and burnout in the workplace. *Communication Research, 17,* 300-326.

Miller, S., Wackman, D. B., Nunnally, E. W., and Miller, P. A. (1988). *Connecting with self and others*. Littleton, CO: Interpersonal Communication Program.

Molloy, J. T. (1995, October 29). Camouflaging disabilities seems to help. *Omaha World Herald*, 11E.

Morris, C. G. (1993). *Understanding psychology*. Upper Saddle River, NJ: Prentice Hall.

Moyers, B. (1993). *Healing and the mind*. New York: Doubleday.

Murray, J. B. (1990, June). Review of research on the Myers-Briggs Type Indicator. *Perceptual and Motor Skills, 70*, 1187–1202.

Myers, D. (1992). *In pursuit of happiness*. Dresden, TN: Avon Books.

Myers, I. B. (1980a). *Introduction to type*. Palo Alto, CA: Consulting Psychologists Press.

Myers, I. B. (1980b). *Gifts differing*. Palo Alto, CA: Consulting Psychologists Press.

Nagy, S. and Nagy, C. M. (1992, October). Longitudinal examination of teachers' burnout in a school district. *Psychological Reports, 71*, 523–531.

Pennebaker, J. (1991). *Opening up: The healing power of confiding in others*. New York: Avon Books.

Perkins, K. (1992, November). Psychosocial implication of women and retirement. *Social Work, 37*, 526–532.

Ports, M. H. (1993, October). Trends in job search methods. *Monthly Labor Review*, 63–67.

Provenzano, S. (1995). *Slam dunk resumes...that score every time!* Lincolnwood, IL: VGM Career Horizons.

Reinemer, M. (1995, July). Work happy. *American Demographics*, 26–31.

Richardson, D. B. (1992, Spring). Getting an interviewer's attention. *Managing your career: The college edition of the National Business Employment Weekly*, 30–31.

Riordan, R. J. and Saltzer, S. K. (1992). Burnout prevention among health care providers working with the terminally ill: A literature review. *Omega, 25*(1), 17–24.

Robbins, A. (1991). *Awaken the giant within*. New York: Simon & Schuster.

Rodin, J. (1986). Aging and health: effects of the sense of control. *Science, 233*, 1271–1276.

Rodin, J., Schooler, C., and Schaie, K. W. (1990). *Self-directedness: Cause and effects throughout the life course*. Hillsdale, NJ: Lawrence Erlbaum.

Rowe, F. A. (1994). *Career connection for college education*. Indianapolis: JIST Works, Inc.

Schmidt, J. A. (1976). *Help yourself: A guide to self-change*. Champaign, IL: Research Press.

Seaward, B. L. (1995, January). Job stress takes a global toll. *Safety and Health, 151*, 64–66.

Seligman, M. E. P. (1990). *Learned optimism: How to change your mind and your life*. New York: Pocket Books.

Selye, H. (1974). *Stress without distress*. Philadelphia: Lippincott.

Selye, H. (1978, March). "On the real benefits of eustress" (as interviewed by Laurence Charry). *Psychology Today*, 60–63.

Shellenbarger, S. (1996, Jan. 28). Get a life: You may end up much more successful at work. *Lincoln Journal Star*, 3E.

Siegel, B. S. (1986). *Love, medicine, and miracles*. New York: Harper & Row.

Smolowe, J. (1996, May 6). The stalled revolution. *Time*, 6.

Spezzano, C. (1992). *What to do between birth and death: The art of growing up.* New York: William Morrow.

Stone, A. A., Cox, D. S., Valdimarsdottir, H., Jandorf, L., and Neale, J. M. (1987). Evidence that secretory IgA antibody is associated with daily mood. *Journal of Personality and Social Psychology, 52*(5), 988–993.

Strasser, S. and Sena, J. (1992). *Work is not a four letter word.* Homewood, IL: Business One.

Sundstrom, W. A. (1994, Spring). The poverty challenge. *Santa Clara Magazine,* 24.

Switzer, G. (1996, June 2). Plan now for your golden years in retirement. *Lincoln Journal Star,* 2J.

Szinovacz, M. and Washo, C. (1992, July). Gender differences in exposure to life events and adaptation to retirement. *Journals of Gerontology, 47,* 191–96.

Templeton, M. E. (1991). *Help! My job interview is tomorrow.* New York: Neal-Schuman Publishers.

Tieger, P. D. and Barron-Tieger, B. (1995). *Do what you are.* Boston: Little, Brown.

Time. (1993, August 30). Health report, 17.

Time. (1994, July 18). Health report, 14.

Tucker, I. F. (1991, October). Predicting scores on the Rathus Assertivenss Schedule from the Myers-Briggs Type Indicator categories. *Psychological Reports, 69,* 571–76.

Turban, D. B. and Keon, T. L. (1993). Organizational attractiveness: An interactionist perspective. *Journal of Applied Psychology, 78*(2), 184–93.

Turner, M., Fix, M., and Struyk, R. J. (1991). *Opportunities denied: Discrimination in hiring.* Washington, DC: Urban Institute.

Urban, W. H. (1992). Truthful interviews: Just the facts, ma'am in *Ready, aim, hire!* ed. M. B. Canning. Oak Brook, IL: PerSysCo Publishing.

Ury, W. (1993). *Getting past no: Negotiating your way from confrontation to cooperation.* New York: Bantam Books.

Van Oosting, J. (1992). *Practicing business communication in the workplace.* Boston: Houghton Mifflin.

Vasey, M. W. and Borkovec, T. D. (1992). A catastrophizing assessment of worrisome thoughts. *Cognitive Therapy and Research, 16*(5), 505–20.

Violette, G. R. and Violette, J. A. (1990, December). Employee wellness is good business. *The CPA Journal 60,* 90–92.

Washington, T. (1996). *Résumé power.* Bellevue, WA: Mount Vernon Press.

Weddle, P. D. (1994). *Career fitness.* New York: Cadell & Davies.

Wolfe, R. A. and Parker, D. F. (1994, May). Employee health management: Challenges and opportunities. *Academy of Management Executive,* 22–31.

Key Steps

The purpose of this section of the book is to get you actively involved in your own career design and development. By completing these activities, you can honestly assess yourself, make career and job search decisions, consider alternatives, and learn to deal with personal and interpersonal challenges. Several will help you immediately; others can be used for and in the future. We gain more by thinking and writing than just by reading. Be honest and thorough—and enjoy the process!

Self-Appraisal

Understanding yourself is necessary in designing a satisfying career. Before you read the book and complete the other activities in this section, honestly rate yourself using this scale. Then compute a score. Do this again after you've read the book.

5 = Perfect (couldn't improve)
4 = Very good (almost to the desired level)
3 = Average (could be improved)
2 = Below average (could be much better)
1 = Poor (needs a great deal of improvement)

_____ 1. How well do I really know and understand myself, including my personality, interests, and skills?

_____ 2. How much regard do I have for myself?

_____ 3. How would I rate my attitude about life?

_____ 4. How well do I handle my emotions and cope with stress?

_____ 5. How well do I know and understand my values?

_____ 6. How satisfied am I with my career choice?

_____ 7. How well have I researched career fields and job opportunities?

_____ 8. How would I rate my writing skills?

_____ 9. How prepared am I to participate in a job interview?

_____ 10. How well do I get along with people?

Total your scores and divide by 10 to get an average score. If you have less than a 5.0 average, this book will help you. If you scored a 5.0 (perfect), you can benefit from learning about perfectionism.

Honestly reflect on and write below what you hope to gain from this book as you design your career. Be specific. After reading the book and completing the KEY STEPS activities, check this page to see what you have gained.

CHAPTER 1

How Well Do I Really Know Myself?

> *Use the information in Chapter 1 to complete the first inventory about yourself (two pages), and have one other person fill out the second similar inventory about you. Do not work together. The object is to compare appraisals.*

DESCRIPTORS.   Describe yourself in the following four areas of self using at least four words, phrases, or sentences for each.

Physical (appearance, condition of body, health):

Mental (abilities, preferred ways of thinking and learning, interests, attitude):

Emotional (usual or general feelings or typical ones in certain situations, description of mood):

Social (behaviors around others, preferences of social activities):

If I were to achieve my ideal self, would these descriptors be different, and, if so, in what ways? Use other paper, if needed.

Physical:

Mental:

Emotional:

Social:

COMPLETE THE FOLLOWING SENTENCES.

The career field that interests me most is

Two of my skills or talents are

Three characteristics or behaviors I appreciate in myself are

One thing I would like to improve about myself is

I am proud of myself for

A goal I have for myself is

What do I value? Name at least five.

What would I do with one million tax-free dollars? Try to account specifically for all of it. Use other paper, if needed.

If I were told that I had only one to three months to live, what would I do during that time?

The X on the continuum below shows how I assess my attitude.

<u>Very negative   Negative   Average   Positive   Very positive</u>

How do I rate my current level of self-esteem?

1 = very low   2 = low   3 = average   4 = high   5 = very high

One belief I have about myself (self-fulfilling prophecy) is:

I have self-efficacy about (list three):

How Well Does Another Person Know Me?

Please answer the following questions about _____.

My relationship to this person is as a(an) _____.

DESCRIPTORS.   Describe this person in the following four areas of self using at least four words, phrases, or sentences for each.

Physical (appearance, condition of body, health):

Mental (abilities, preferred ways of thinking and learning, interests, attitude
    or mental outlook):

Emotional (usual or general feelings or typical ones in certain situations,
    description of mood):

Social (behaviors around others, preferences or social activities):

If this person were to achieve his or her ideal self, would these descriptors
be different, and, if so, in what ways?

Physical:

Mental:

Emotional:

Social:

COMPLETE THE FOLLOWING SENTENCES.

A career field that interests this person most is

Two of this person's skills or talents are

Three characteristics or behaviors this person appreciates about him or herself are

One thing about self this person would like to improve is

One thing about self this person is proud of is

One of this person's goals is

What does this person value? Name at least five.

What would this person do with a million tax-free dollars?

If this person had only one to three months to live, what would he or she do?

Thinking of attitude as a broad outlook on life, place an X on the continuum to describe this person.

Very negative	Negative	Average	Positive	Very positive

Thinking of self-esteem as a value placed on self or genuine regard for who one is, what is this person's current level of self-esteem?

1 = very low   2 = low   3 = average   4 = high   5 = very high

THANK YOU VERY MUCH FOR YOUR HELP!

Personality Awareness

> *Circle what you think (or know) your four MBTI preferences to be. For each, describe some behaviors that support the preference. If you have no supporting behaviors for one, explain why you think you tend to be the opposite preference. You may use other paper.*

Extraversion   Introversion

Sensing   Intuition

Thinking   Feeling

Judgment   Perception

◎ ◎ Identify a personality trait about yourself you especially like and one that is related to one of the preferences. Write the preference, how it helps you, and for what reason(s) you like it.

◎ ◎ Do the same with a personality trait about yourself you would like to change. Be sure to name the preference.

How Assertive Am I?

Answer the following as yes, no, *or* unknown *(i.e., neither yes nor no, or about half the time).*

_____ 1. I usually express my anger in constructive, nonthreatening ways.

_____ 2. My posture and manner reflect confidence.

_____ 3. I maintain steady eye contact.

_____ 4. I use "I" statements when expressing my opinion.

_____ 5. I am flexible and willing to compromise.

_____ 6. I tell people "no" when I don't want to do something, and I also say "yes."

_____ 7. I maintain my rights and don't let others take advantage of me.

_____ 8. I do what I think is best rather than follow others.

_____ 9. When someone is being offensive or annoying, I tell him or her.

_____ 10. I listen with an open mind.

The more yes *answers the more assertive you are. Select any behaviors that you lack and strive to develop them.*

Describe a past experience in which you were assertive or one where assertive behavior would have been advantageous.

Assets and Liabilities

Read in Chapter 1 about evaluating yourself by developing a balance sheet of assets and liabilities. Under each of the following categories, list your assets in the left column and your liabilities in the right. For example, under educational experiences: Diplomas, degrees, specialized training, certification, licensure, scholarships, a high grade point average, and the like would be assets. Lack of any of these and any evidence of weaknesses in education and training are liabilities. Be very complete and use other paper, if necessary. This activity can serve as the basic groundwork for designing your career and will help in all stages of a job search.

ASSETS   **LIABILITIES**

Interests

Skills

Educational Experiences

Work Experiences

Volunteer Work

ASSETS	LIABILITIES

Personality Characteristics

Work Habits

Personal and Professional Goals

> *Select what you consider to be your top two assets and your top liability (if any) in each category (16 assets; 8 liabilities) and write them below. Then considering all lists, select six major assets and three liabilities. Write these at the bottom. Practice discussing your assets so that you can use them to answer interview questions such as: "Why should we hire you?" and "What do you have to offer?" Think about the liabilities and decide how you could explain them in a positive way. If you have any liabilities that can be changed before your job search, set a goal to do so.*

ASSETS	LIABILITIES

FINAL LIST

ASSETS	LIABILITIES

CHAPTER 2

Characteristics of a Good Communicator

For each of the following, write about one recent behavior or situation in which you demonstrated the characteristic. If you draw a "blank," you will know what needs to be developed.

◎   Having a positive attitude about others

◎   Showing genuineness and authenticity (being my real self)

◎   Being open and willing to share about myself with others

◎   Expressing my emotions

◎   Showing an interest in others

◎   Being appropriate in how much I share and how much I ask

◎   Demonstrating flexibility (willingness to "give and take")

◎   Having a positive sense of humor

◎   Being understanding

◎   Making accurate interpretations of others' behavior

How Well Do You Listen?

Using the scale, answer the following questions.
5 = Almost always   4 = Usually   3 = About half the time
2 = Sometimes   1 = Hardly ever

_____ 1. I am interested in other people.

_____ 2. I ask questions about other people's interests.

_____ 3. The opinions of others are of interest to me.

_____ 4. I am able to focus my attention on what someone is saying.

_____ 5. I put aside my thoughts and feelings and concentrate on what is being said.

_____ 6. I try to create a positive listening environment by getting rid of distractions and other obstacles.

_____ 7. I realize I have a psychological filter and check it periodically so that it doesn't interfere with my listening.

_____ 8. I approach others with the idea that they have something of value to contribute to a conversation.

_____ 9. When listening, I face the person who is talking.

_____ 10. I keep an open body position.

_____ 11. When listening, my body is relaxed, yet attentive.

_____ 12. I maintain eye contact most of the time. When I look away, I quickly bring my eyes back to the speaker's face.

_____ 13. When listening, my facial expression registers what I am thinking and feeling.

_____ 14. My facial expression changes during a typical conversation.

_____ 15. When listening, I nod my head affirmatively an appropriate number of times.

_____ 16. During conversation, I am comfortable with appropriate touching.

_____ 17. When listening, I use brief verbal responses which show interest.

_____ 18. I ask encouraging questions of the speaker.

_____ 19. When listening, I try to find ways to clarify the speaker's point.

_____ 20. I avoid negative listening behaviors.

Total your score. Give yourself a grade as follows:

95–100 = A+	90–94 = A	85–89= B+	80-84 = B
75–79 = C+	70–74 = C	65–69 = D+	60–64 = D

59 OR BELOW = UNSATISFACTORY

Most importantly, what can you do to improve your listening?

Identifying Closed Communication

Use the following letters to identify closed types. If the statement has more than one type, use more than one letter.

D = Dogmatic   C = Commando   G = Grandiose

_____   Employers don't listen to their employees.

_____   He needs to work harder if he wants to get ahead.

_____   She never pays attention.

_____   I think you should be more cooperative.

_____   Her supervisor always finds something to criticize.

_____   All he does is complain.

Using Open Communication

Rewrite each of the statements above in the open style.

1. _____
   _____

2. _____
   _____

3. _____
   _____

4. _____
   _____

5. _____
   _____

6. _____
   _____

Listen for any example of closed communication in your everyday life. Write it, then reword in the open style.

Ask someone to listen to you for any uses of fillers. Identify the word or phrase.

Awareness of Content

> *Using the following, identify each statement.*
>
> S = Superficial   BD = Basic Data   P = Preference
>
>   I = Idea/Belief   F = Feeling

_____ I was disappointed when I didn't receive the promotion.

_____ I thought she expressed herself well in the interview.

_____ Isn't the weather great today?

_____ I have held three different jobs so far.

_____ I liked my last job best.

_____ I enjoyed her seminar.

_____ I am concerned about him.

_____ I don't think that was a wise choice.

_____ Good morning. How are you?

_____ I was quite proud after my employee review.

_____ I believe we have a good record of hiring well-qualified people.

_____ I want to eventually live in the Northeast.

_____ I am a nurse.

_____ As far as I'm concerned, she was treated unfairly.

_____ Have a nice day.

Using Dimensions of Awareness

Your supervisor has been watching you closely, even leaning over your shoulder, and then checking your work.

Sensation:

Thought:

Feeling:

Want:

Action:

Becoming More Aware of Paralanguage and Body Language

While listening to a conversation, be aware of examples of paralanguage and body language. Describe some of these below. As much as possible, disregard what is actually being said. Briefly write what could be interpreted just from the paralanguage and body language.

Carry on a conversation with someone and try not to vary your body language during the time (same posture, facial expression, etc.). Describe how it felt and what happened. This is not a recommended way to communicate!

CHAPTER 3

Achieving Satisfaction

Under the following columns, list as many as you possibly can. Stretch your thinking and consider all aspects of your life.

WHAT I LIKE TO DO   **WHAT I DO WELL**

Identify a career field, preferably, the one you have chosen.

_____

Now circle any entries from both columns that would be used as one pursues this particular career.

If you have a present job or before you take a job, do this same activity and compare it with the specific job duties.

The more you *do* of what you enjoy and are good at doing, the more satisfied you will be!

Matching Values to Career and Jobs

Go back to "How Well Do I Really Know Myself," the activity in KEY STEPS for Chapter 1, and write below the five values you listed. Then add any from the other person's inventory that are true for you. After reading the material in Chapter 3 about work orientations and other values, add to the list.

From the list above, check those that you think will be in harmony with your chosen career field. If you are considering a particular job, be sure to pay attention to how your responsibilities and duties will coincide with your values.

Setting and Achieving a Career Goal

> *Think of a short-term goal that will aid in your career development. Using the information from Chapter 3, complete this page. Give yourself credit for reaching a goal.*

My short-term career goal is:

Final date of completion:

1. Evaluate this goal by answering the questions in the section of the book "Assessing Goals." Write any potential problem.

2. If any of these obstacles exist, write what you can do.
   Pessimism:

   Optimism:

   Procrastination:

   Lack of money:

   Lack of time:

3. Below, draw a series of stair steps, then write a specific action and date by each. Use pinpointing to make them measurable.

Researching Potential Employers

Contact an employer in a chosen field of interest and arrange an informational interview. Develop questions in the following areas and add some of your own to the list. If possible, also take a tour of the business. Be sure to write a thank-you letter to the person you interview.

- History of this company or business
- Current business projects, activities, services
- Working conditions and benefits
- Organizational scheme ("chain of command")
- Decision-making procedures, use of teamwork
- Strengths and challenges
- Future outlook
- Interviewee's career path including the present position
- Interviewee's likes and dislikes about the job
- Typical workday
- Responsibilities of positions in this career field
- Requirements and desired characteristics for positions
- Salary ranges and benefits
- Advancement possibilities
- Expected changes for this career field
- Specific advice for you in this career field
- Names of others in the career field
- How one would go about seeking a job with this employer

Can you think of additional questions?

Contacts and Resources

> *Do yourself a favor and complete the following important steps.*

1. Begin to develop a list of potential employers. Consider making a file card on each, as described in the book. Then you can group the cards in whatever way is most useful (alphabetically, geographically, job-focused, etc.).

2. If you have not yet done so, visit a college career and placement center to see what is offered. Definitely register in your college or university placement office.

3. Spend five to ten minutes and write below every name that comes to mind to include in your network of contacts.

4. From the list, select at least five, if not more, who would provide impressive recommendations. Write their names below. Then, contact each one and ask if he or she would serve as a reference.

Making Direct Contact

> *Using the three-step method of direct contact by telephone, write what you would say in each of the following situations.*

⚙   You are interested in employment at Henderson and Associates and are calling for the first time. You do not know the name of the person who can hire you. A receptionist answers the telephone.

⚙   You are calling to talk with Margaret Henderson and Associates because you would like to work there and she is in charge of hiring. A receptionist answers the telephone.

⚙   You have talked with Margaret Henderson and have been told that there are no current openings.

⚙   You have talked with Margaret Henderson and have been told that there are no future prospects for hiring.

CHAPTER 4

Putting Your Writing Skills to Work

Your list of assets identified in a Chapter 1 KEY STEPS activity contains essential information you can use for résumés, cover letters, and applications. After reading the material about résumés, answer the following questions. Then, show that you can impress a potential employer in writing by filling out the basic job application that follows this section.

◉   What type of résumé will best serve me?

◉   Will I use an objective? If yes, write a few possibilities below.

◉   What experiences, skills, and achievements would I list in a summary? Write these below.

◉   Will my first category be education or employment?

◉   From Table 4–1 in Chapter 4, select or mark all the action words I can use in describing what I have done. Write ones I can use.

◉   What key words can I use in an electronic résumé?

◉   How will I head the education category?

    ◉   List what I will include in this category.

    ◉   How will I head the employment category?

    ◉   List what I will include in this category.

    ◉   List what I will include in the following areas.
         Memberships and affiliations:

         Volunteer work:

         Honors, activities:

         Certification, licensure:

    ◉   What else might I want to include?

Look at your list of assets from Chapter 1. How many have you emphasized?

> *Select a possible employer and draft a cover letter following the suggestions in Chapter 4. Ask someone to proofread it and give you honest feedback.*

APPLICATION FOR EMPLOYMENT
(Type or print in black ink)

Last Name   **First**   **Middle**

_____

Street Address

_____

City   **State**   **ZIP Code**

_____

Home Telephone Number   **Work Telephone Number**

(   )_____   (   )_____

Social Security Number   **Are you age 18 or over?**
(used for computer retrieval only)

_____   ___ Yes   ___ No

EDUCATION RECORD

Do you have a high school diploma or GED?
                                    ___ Yes   ___ No

Name and Location of Secondary School   **Highest grade completed____**

_____

Name of College   **Location**   **Dates Attended**

_____

Major Field of Study   **Degree**

_____

Name of College   **Location**   **Dates Attended**

_____

Major Field of Study   **Degree**

_____

Other

_____

EMPLOYMENT RECORD (Begin with current employer and list all employment for the past 10 years. Use other paper, if necessary.)

Present or Last Employer _____ Job Title _____

Address _____ Name of Supervisor _____

City _____ State _____ ZIP _____ Date Started _____ Date Left _____

Hours Worked per Week_____ Total Time Employed _____ Pay at Start _____ Pay at End _____

Describe duties: _____
_____
_____

Reason for leaving or wanting to leave: _____
May we contact? ___ Yes ___ No

****

Employer _____ Job Title _____

Address _____ Name of Supervisor _____

City _____ State _____ ZIP _____ Date Started _____ Date Left _____

Hours Worked per Week_____ Total Time Employed _____ Pay at Start _____ Pay at End _____

Describe duties: _____
_____
_____

Reason for leaving: _____
May we contact? ___ Yes ___ No

Employer _____   Job Title _____

Address _____   Name of Supervisor _____

City _____   State ____   ZIP ____   Date Started _____   Date Left _____

Hours Worked
per Week_____   Total Time
Employed _____   Pay at Start _____   Pay at End _____

Describe duties: _____

_____

_____

Reason for leaving: _____

May we contact?   ___ Yes   ___ No

MILITARY

Have you ever served on active duty in the U.S. Armed Forces?

___ Yes   ___ No   Branch _____

Primary Duties: _____

_____

_____

OTHER INFORMATION

Are you a United States citizen?   ___ Yes   ___ No

If no, do you have the legal right to work in the U.S.?   _____

Please explain: _____

Have you ever been convicted of any violation other than a minor traffic violation?
___ Yes   ___ No   If yes, please explain:

_____

_____

Type of employment desired (check all that apply):

___ Permanent   ___ Full-time   ___ Part-time   ___ Temporary

Date Available:_____

REFERENCES

Name

_____

Title

_____

Address

_____

City   **State**   **ZIP**

_____

Telephone Number(s)

_____

Name

_____

Title

_____

Address

_____

City   **State**   **ZIP**

_____

Telephone Number(s)

_____

Name

_____

Title

_____

Address

_____

City   **State**   **ZIP**

_____

Telephone Number(s)

_____

_____   _____

APPLICANT'S SIGNATURE   **DATE**

CHAPTER 5

Preparing for an Interview

Write an effective answer to each of the following questions.

⊚   Tell me about yourself.

⊚   Why did you choose this career field?

⊚   What are your career goals?

⊚   How well do you get along with other people?

⊚   What are your strengths?

⊚   **What are your weaknesses?**

⊚   **What would satisfy you in a job?**

⊚   **What motivates you?**

⊚   **Why should I hire you?**

Check in Chapter 5 and compare your responses against what's recommended. Are you emphasizing your assets? Now select any other question from Chapter 5 that might be troublesome and write a response. Verbally practice all responses.

Interview Checklist

Use this checklist to be thoroughly prepared for an interview.

_____ Do I know exactly where I am to go? Where to park?

_____ Have I made a "trial run" so I know how long it will take me to get there?

_____ Can I pronounce the name of the interviewer?

_____ Do I know exactly what I plan to say as a greeting?

_____ Have I rehearsed all the typical interview questions?

_____ Do I have at least five good questions to ask? Write these below.

_____ Do I have ready the items I want to take?

_____ Do I have in writing anything I might forget? (questions to ask, assets, etc.)

_____ Do I look clean? (check fingernails, hair, teeth, etc.)

_____ Do I look neat? (check hair, lint on clothes, etc.)

_____ Do I look professional?

_____ Am I dressed comfortably?

_____ Am I wearing any jewelry or cologne that could be distracting or bothersome?

_____ What could possibly go wrong, and am I prepared for what I can be prepared for? (extra pair of hosiery for women, etc.)

_____ Have I done all I can do to calm myself?

_____ Am I remembering that an interview is a "two-way street" and that my evaluation of the employer is equally important?

How Well Did I Do?

On the following scale, rate your interview.

5 = Perfect   *4 = Very good*   *3 = Average*
          2 = Not very good   *1 = Unsatisfactory*

_____ 1. Did I arrive at least five minutes ahead of time and feel little or no time pressure?

_____ 2. Was my appearance neat, clean, and professional?

_____ 3. Did I feel relatively calm?

_____ 4. How was my first impression including smile, greeting, and handshake?

_____ 5. Did I use the interviewer's name?

_____ 6. Was my body language open and positive?

_____ 7. Did I listen?

_____ 8. Did I appear to be listening?

_____ 9. How were my answers (content)?

_____ 10. How were my answers (verbalizing style including paralanguage)?

_____ 11. How were my questions?

_____ 12. Did I appear interested and enthusiastic?

_____ 13. Did I thank the interviewer for the opportunity?

_____ 14. Do I know the next step in the process?

_____ 15. Have I written a follow-up letter?

Total your points.

CHAPTER 6

Knowing What You Want

Before accepting a position, answer the following.

⚙ From your research and what you know about yourself, what is the minimum starting salary you will accept?

⚙ From the list of possible benefits, identify at least five that you consider most important and write them below.

⚙ How many hours of work are you willing to put in per week?

⚙ List any other factor that you consider necessary before you would accept a job. *Be sure that you find out about this before you accept a position.*

Positively Responding to Criticism

Learning to handle criticism will help you in performance reviews as well as in everyday experiences. Review positive responses.

Your employer has said to you, "Lately you don't seem to want to work here."

Following the suggestions in Chapter 6, write the two-step response if you understand the reason for the criticism.

1.

2.

Write the two-step response recommended in Chapter 6 if you do not understand the reason for the criticism.

1.

2.

Progressing in Your Career

Below write a number of possible ways you can continue to learn and update yourself after you accept a position. What you write can be useful during an interview as this is one of the typical questions.

If you would like to own a business, challenge yourself by conducting an informational interview with a business owner or contact a local SCORE group and find out what is involved. Below, write any concerns you have or personal drawbacks that might be obstacles.

Assess your leadership capabilities by honestly answering the following questions with yes, no, or unknown.

_____ 1. Am I reasonably intelligent?

_____ 2. Have I or will I achieve an adequate education?

_____ 3. Do I show good judgment?

_____ 4. Am I creative?

_____ 5. Do I demonstrate initiative?

_____ 6. Am I usually objective in dealing with situations?

_____ 7. Do I have a balance between personal and professional?

_____ 8. Am I enthusiastic?

_____ 9. Do I think optimistically?

_____ 10. Am I energetic?

_____ 11. Do I "stick with things?" Am I perseverant?

_____ 12. Am I self-confident?

_____ 13. Do I anticipate problems before they happen?

_____ 14. Am I continually seeking to improve myself?

_____ 15. Do I manage my time well?

_____ 16. Can I work well with others?

_____ 17. Am I an understanding person?

_____ 18. Do I approach conflict resolution as win-win?

_____ 19. Can I give clear directions?

_____ 20. Do I use the open style of verbalizing?

_____ 21. Am I an excellent listener?

_____ 22. Am I a good planner?

_____ 23. Am I well-organized?

_____ 24. Am I a visionary? Do I have vision?

_____ 25. Can I delegate?

_____ 26. Do others look to me for leadership?

_____ 27. Do I openly praise others?

_____ 28. Can I build teamwork?

_____ 29. Do I promote positive relationships?

_____ 30. Can I deliver criticism in a positive way?

Count the number of *yes* answers as they indicate leadership. If you marked #30 as *unknown* or *no*, complete the next activity.

Practice delivering criticism. Using the suggestions given in Chapter 6, pretend you are a supervisor and you are talking to an employee who has been repeatedly late to work. Write exactly what you would say.

CHAPTER 7

Improving Work Relationships

> *If you are employed, use your current work situation. If you are not employed, either use past employment or a personal situation to describe demonstrations of the following behaviors. Then start or continue to behave positively in these areas.*

Realistic expectations:

Positiveness and friendliness (attitude/actions):

Sensitivity and understanding:

Supportiveness:

Cooperation and collaboration:

Consideration and helpfulness:

Teamwork:

Recognition of another's contributions:

Praising:

Appreciation of diversity:

Managing conflict effectively:

Dealing with a difficult person:

Forgiving and moving on:

Unloading Your Gunnysack

Using "I" statements, describe three resentments you either have or have had, then express your feeling and want with "I" statements.

RESENTMENT (I resent it when you)	FEELING (When this happens, I feel)	WANT (I want you to)
1.		
2.		
3.		

Dealing with Difficulty and Conflict

⊚   Identify at least three behaviors that do or would irritate you in the work place.

⊚   In the past, what have you done that could have been irritating to someone at work or in your personal life?

⊚   Complete the following sentences.

To me, a person is being difficult when he or she

I usually deal with this by

An effective way to deal with it might be to

I probably am "difficult" to others when I

CHAPTER 8

How Do You Spend Your Time?

For one week, keep a detailed record of how you spend your time. Then, see if you can find at least an hour of time that you could put to better use.

	MON.	TUES.	WED.	THURS.	FRI.	SAT.	SUN.
1:00 A.M.							
2:00 A.M.							
3:00 A.M.							
4:00 A.M.							
5:00 A.M.							
6:00 A.M.							
7:00 A.M.							
8:00 A.M.							
9:00 A.M.							
10:00 A.M.							
11:00 A.M.							

	MON.	TUES.	WED.	THURS.	FRI.	SAT.	SUN.
12:00 P.M.							
1:00 P.M.							
2:00 P.M.							
3:00 P.M.							
4:00 P.M.							
5:00 P.M.							
6:00 P.M.							
7:00 P.M.							
8:00 P.M.							
9:00 P.M.							
10:00 P.M.							
11:00 P.M.							
12:00 A.M.							

Are You Burned Out?

Use this scale to check burnout now and in the future.

1. Do I dread going to work more times than not?

2. Am I more rigid than usual in my thinking?

3. Am I thinking unrealistically about my job?

4. Is it hard to make decisions that were once rather simple?

5. Is my attitude less positive than normal?

6. Do I doubt my work abilities and often feel defeated?

7. Do I feel pessimistic about my career?

8. Do I feel as if I am not in control of my life?

9. Am I more often depressed? helpless? hopeless? frustrated? annoyed?

10. Am I more irritable than I usually am?

11. Have I displayed more hostility than I usually do?

12. Is my sense of humor less evident?

13. Am I choosing to be alone more at work than usual?

14. Do I feel less energetic?

15. Am I tired more often than normal?

16. Recently, have I had any of the following?

    | headache | muscle tension and aches | gastric problems |
    | backache | insomnia | complexion problems |
    | colds | change in eating habits | nausea |

17. Have I been late to work more frequently?

18. Have I missed more work than usual?

19. Is my productivity at work lower than normal?

20. Do I feel less zest for life than I used to?

Even though these symptoms can be associated with other ailments, the more yes *answers you give, the more burnout is indicated.*

Coping with Stress

Use the following to deal with stress. Coping is of utmost importance.

⊚   Identify sources of stress in your life from these areas.

A major life change:

A common hassle or everyday irritant:

Internal or self-imposed:

⊚   What can you do about any of these?

⊚   Try deep breathing several times during the day.

Breathe in slowly and deeply through your nose, hold briefly, then exhale through your mouth. To check if you are breathing deeply enough, place your outstretched fingers (middle fingers lightly touching each other) over your diaphragm. Inhale. Did your middle fingers separate slightly? If not, you are not breathing deeply. Deeply inhaled air will expand the diaphragm area (like a balloon), and your fingers will spread slightly. A few of these deep breaths can relieve stress and anxiety in most situations, including before an interview. If you want to use a relaxation technique, get into a comfortable position and use several deep breaths to lower your body's state of arousal.

Take charge of your stress by putting into practice one of the stress-reducing suggestions in Chapter 8.

The one I've selected is:

When I will start is:

Index